Dr. Warren Wiersbe approached me one day with the idea that he and Harold Berry produce a daily devotional book, taking the material from the various books I have written. My first reaction was, "Oh no, not another book!"

I reconsidered, however, when it was explained that this devotional book would be unique. The idea was that the material would be selected from what I have written concerning Bible characters and studies of certain books of the Bible. This material would then be arranged so the reader would progressively work his or her way through the Bible from Genesis to Revelation.

God creates children with curious minds—they are always asking questions about this or that. In this sense, I have never outgrown the curiosity stage. Especially in the spiritual realm, I have always been motivated to see not only what God has said but also how it is to be applied to our lives. For instance, God has given many instructions about godly living, but I have always been curious about how these are to be implemented. This drove me to much research in the Bible to see how God worked out these truths in the various people He presents to us in His Word.

Harold Berry selected the devotional readings from some of my books based on the Old Testament. These studies were of Bible characters who reveal how God worked out His principles of godly living in their lives.

Warren Wiersbe selected the devotional readings from some of my books based on the New Testament. These studies were of the books of the Bible that especially emphasize both the doctrine and the practice involved in victorious Christian living.

Through this devotional book, it is my desire that God will stir your heart to further study His Word concerning the proper doctrine and practice of godly Christian living.

Theodore H. Epp
Founding Director
Back to the Bible Broadcast

FORWARD

Theodore Epp's Gift to Us—Back to the Bible's Promising Future

For 75 years the name Back to the Bible has stood for solid Bible teaching and the mission of leading people into a dynamic relationship with Jesus Christ

The vision began in 1939 when our founder, Theodore Epp, aired his first radio broadcast from Lincoln, Nebraska, with the goal of getting people back-to-the-Bible. This simple message struck a nerve in America's heartland, propelling the ministry first to a national stage … and ultimately a global one.

At his 75th birthday chapel just a few years before he died, Dr. Epp quoted these words from Revelations 3:8 "Behold I have set an open door before thee." He then emphatically stated that "setting an open door before us means we've got to go through it, we've got to do something about it. He's not going to push us. He may cause circumstances sometimes to be pushy, but nevertheless He says 'I have set. There it is now go through it an open door.'"

Dr. Epp went on to declare "we have the adversary, he's hard at work, we're possibly meeting up with some of the hardest times… And so we're having all types of troubles, but God says 'I have set an open door before thee and no man can shut it.' But we have to take God at His Word, we have to believe Him for it, we have to trust Him for it, we have to take the open door."

Strength for the Journey is a powerful devotional that captures the heart and passion of Dr. Epp's ministry and the legacy he built through the years. My name is Dr. Arnie Cole, the CEO of Back to the Bible, and I share Dr. Epp's passion that began 75 years ago of going through that door that God has opened to us.

Just as Dr. Epp tapped into the technology of his time—radio—we are continuing his innovative spirit utilizing cellular communication and wireless networking to accomplish even more ministry in ways and places we never envisioned possible. Using mobile apps and the web, our newest ministry, *goTandem*, reaches worldwide connecting people to God through His Word. This daily discipleship tool cultivates spiritual growth by encouraging users to receive, reflect on and respond to Scripture multiple times each day. *goTandem* is truly a means of discipleship—friends helping friends to know God intimately and to follow Him passionately.

Today our radio program with Dr. John Munro can be heard in over 65 countries and *goTandem* is reaching a new generation around the world. We have offices in twelve countries and exist to help people of all ages know Christ as Savior and then walk with them daily to help them grow spiritually. We are committed to teaching God's Word and delivering Truth into the hands, hearts and lives of people all over the world, and, God willing, look forward to many more years of serving Him.

As you study these pages, please celebrate with us God's goodness for 75 years of ministry. And more importantly, I encourage you to go through that door God has opened up specifically for you!

Dr. Arnie Cole
Lincoln, Nebraska

JANUARY

During January you will receive strength for the journey as you read about Abraham's obedient faith. Abraham was not perfect—he had his problems—but his life was characterized by an obedient and aggressive faith.

When we have an obedient faith, we will present our bodies to Jesus Christ and renew our minds, as we are instructed to do in Romans 12:1–2. The result will be our discovering, or proving, what is God's good, acceptable and perfect will. God will reveal His will to us when we are obedient to Him. From the life of Abraham, we see the importance of living by faith one step at a time. As we are obedient in one step, God will show us the next one. We can find ourselves and realize the true meaning of life only as we place our confidence in God and obey Him with unquestioning loyalty.

The readings for January are excerpted from *The God of Abraham, Isaac and Jacob.*

OBEYING GOD'S CALL
GENESIS 12:1–3

Abraham was chosen, or elected, on the basis of the sovereignty of God. He had no Bible, so he was not able to receive his call through God's written Word. God sought a man, and on the basis of His sovereign will and purpose, He chose Abraham.

As to calling or electing, we are reminded of Peter's words: "Elect according to the foreknowledge of God the Father" (1 Pet. 1:2). Abraham was not chosen because of any merits in his life. His was a supernatural call based on God's own purpose and will. When God calls according to His own purpose and will, it is always a call for the good. Abraham had no choice in the matter. God did not ask, "Abraham, would you like to be the man that I can use?" Instead, God said, in effect, "Abraham, I want you to come out of your country."

Abraham was called to begin a special, chosen nation through which salvation would eventually come to all mankind. There was much involved in this great call. God staked His whole plan of redemption on the possibility of a man's being willing, by his faith and obedience, to become the bridgehead for delivering an erring world.

Who hath saved us, and called us with an holy calling, not according to our works, but according to his own purpose and grace, which was given us in Christ Jesus before the world began (2 Tim. 1:9).

WANTED: FAITHFUL SERVANTS
HEBREWS 11:8–18

Have you ever thought about the fact that you and I have the Gospel today because Abraham and others who were chosen of God were faithful? God has chosen to work through men; therefore, the future of God's work rests on what He is able to motivate men to do. In Old Testament times, the work of God depended on men such as Abraham, Isaac and Jacob. In New Testament times, Jesus Christ made His future program dependent on the apostles. He spent time with these men and properly trained them for the work they had to do.

Not only was faithfulness required of the patriarchs and the disciples, but it is also required of us because God has committed to us the ministry of reconciliation. Paul wrote: "God was in Christ, reconciling the world unto himself, not imputing their trespasses unto them; and hath committed unto us the word of reconciliation. Now then we are ambassadors for Christ, as though God did beseech you by us: we pray you in Christ's stead, be ye reconciled to God" (2 Cor. 5:19–20). There is no choice in the matter. We are the sovereign appointees of God to represent Him to others. Abraham was faithful. The disciples were faithful. Are we faithful?

Without faith it is impossible to please him [God] (Heb. 11:6).

ALL OF GRACE
EPHESIANS 2:1–10

God dealt in judgment at Babel when He scattered the people and confused their language, but God dealt in mercy and grace as He called Abraham. Abraham did not receive God's call because he merited God's esteem. Rather, in God's foreknowledge He knew Abraham and chose him for a special purpose. God's election must always be traced to God's will and purpose. It is all of grace, for it is by God's sovereign choice.

It is the same with our salvation. If it were not for God's grace, we would be doomed to an eternity in hell. But notice what God has done because of His grace: "But God, who is rich in mercy, for his great love wherewith he loved us, even when we were dead in sins, hath quickened us together with Christ, (by grace ye are saved;) and hath raised us up together, and made us sit together in heavenly places in Christ Jesus" (Eph. 2:4–6). God did not do this for us because we merited it—it was while we were yet sinners that Christ died for us. It is important that we realize that our salvation is all of grace.

Abraham was not chosen because he was a special kind of person nor because he had a high IQ nor because he had great faith. It was totally of the grace of God that He called Abraham out of idolatry, and it is only of the grace of God that we have been called out to salvation.

But where sin abounded, grace did much more abound (Rom. 5:20).

REWARDS FOR OBEDIENCE
1 CORINTHIANS 3:10–15

A call to be a missionary is much like Abraham's call. It is necessary to leave home, possessions, relatives, worldly ambitions and to go to another country to which God has led. But one can never outgive God. Though Abraham was called to give up much, he was promised much more. God always promises blessings when we obey and follow Him.

Hebrews 13:5 says, "Let your conversation be without covetousness; and be content with such things as ye have: for he hath said, I will never leave thee, nor forsake thee." Much the same thing was said to the people of Israel: "Be strong and of a good courage, fear not, nor be afraid of them: for the LORD thy God, he it is that doth go with thee: he will not fail thee, nor forsake thee" (Deut. 31:6).

The psalmist said, "Trust in the LORD, and do good; so shalt thou dwell in the land, and verily thou shalt be fed" (Ps. 37:3). God promised to bless Israel, and He promises to bless us when we trust and obey. God's call for us today is that we might be separated unto Him.

No good thing will he withhold from them that walk uprightly (Ps. 84:11).

FRUITFULNESS REQUIRES SEPARATION
GENESIS 11:27–32

The trip from Ur of the Chaldees to Haran was not exceedingly hard because Terah and his family were able to travel northwest along the Euphrates River. Along the river there was grass for their livestock. However, from Haran to the land of Canaan was quite a different type of trip. They would have to leave the Euphrates River and strike out across the desert. This was a real test and was too much for Terah and his family. Besides, God was not going to take Abraham into the land until he separated from his father. The years Abraham spent at Haran were wasted years of waiting.

Many Christians today start off like Abraham. They launch out with great enthusiasm to follow the Lord, perhaps as a result of a crisis experience, but then later grind to a standstill in their Christian walk. Has this happened to you? Remember, the key issue for Abraham was separation. It is the same for us. This age of materialism has gripped even the Christians. We cannot expect God to lead us into fruitfulness unless we become separated from the things of the world. Each Christian must make the decision for himself, even as Abraham had to make the decision for himself. Once we break from the things of the world, we will see that the treasures of God far more than take the place of the things of this world.

Wherefore come out from among them, and be ye separate (2 Cor. 6:17).

NOT ALWAYS REASONS, BUT PROMISES

ROMANS 4:16–25

In the days of Abraham, to start out for a land one had never seen was as great a venture of faith as astronauts going to the moon today. It took a great deal of faith for Abraham to leave Ur of the Chaldees and go to a strange land. Like Abraham, we Christians are pilgrims on this earth, and by faith we are traveling to a land we have never seen.

Abraham only partially obeyed at first and did not go directly to the land God wanted to show him. There were the years of wasted time in Haran, which to Abraham meant lost time and lost rewards. As Abraham left Haran, he still had no clear directive about the land to which he was going. God had not even so much as described the land as "a land flowing with milk and honey," as He did later for the Israelites in Egypt. Abraham had nothing to rely on except God's clear command to go. By faith he was to walk a step at a time.

God seldom accompanies His commands with reasons or explanations, but He always accompanies them with wonderful promises. Do you trust God? When you know God wants you to do something, can you step out for Him and claim His promises, even though He hasn't given you reasons why He wants you to do it?

Commit thy way unto the LORD; trust also in him; and he shall bring it to pass (Ps. 37:5).

SEPARATION OFTEN PRODUCES CONFLICT

GENESIS 12:4–9

Abraham finally left Haran and forsook everything. Speaking of Abraham and those who were with him, Hebrews 11:15–16 says, "And truly, if they had been mindful of that country from whence they came out, they might have had opportunity to have returned. But now they desire a better country, that is, an heavenly: wherefore God is not ashamed to be called their God: for he hath prepared for them a city." Abraham's separation from Haran was complete.

Once Abraham was in the land, he did not stop to possess it but merely passed through it. He did not stop because God did not order him to stop. Genesis 12:6 says, "And Abram passed through the land unto the place of Sichem, unto the plain of Moreh. And the Canaanite was then in the land." As to Abraham's inheritance in the land, Acts 7:5 says that "he [God] gave him none inheritance in it, no, not so much as to set his foot on: yet he promised that he would give it to him for a possession, and to his seed after him, when as yet he had no child." At this time, therefore, Abraham was not occupying the land but merely passing through it. The Scriptures comment that "the Canaanite was then in the land" (Gen. 12:6). The Canaanites posed a problem and were the source of future conflict.

Our separation is similar. God calls for an all-out separation, which often results in conflict. There will be persecution and problems, but we must remember the words of Jesus: "In the world ye shall have tribulation: but be of good cheer; I have overcome the world" (John 16:33).

Yea, and all that will live godly in Christ Jesus shall suffer persecution (2 Tim. 3:12).

A TENT AND ALTAR LIFE

GENESIS 12:7–9

The tent symbolized Abraham's dependence on God. Hebrews 11:9–10 says of Abraham that "by faith he sojourned in the land of promise, as in a strange country, dwelling in tabernacles [tents] with Isaac and Jacob, the heirs with him of the same promise: for he looked for a city which hath foundations, whose builder and maker is God." Every child of God is a pilgrim in this world and is to have his eyes fixed on his home in heaven.

The altar that Abraham built indicated his dependence on God and his worship of God. Note the order. First, the believer is to take his place as a stranger and pilgrim on earth; then comes true acceptance and worship. This is not referring to an acceptance as far as salvation is concerned, which comes by faith in Christ Jesus. This is acceptance in the realm of being a child true to God.

In what we commonly call "The Lord's Prayer," we say, "Hallowed be thy name. Thy kingdom come" (Matt. 6:9–10). This has to do with the altar—not a literal altar such as Abraham built but our relationship to, and worship of, God. We want His name to be holy, which means that we are not seeking a holy place for ourselves. We want His kingdom to come; that is, we want Him to rule supreme. To sincerely pray this means that we are not trying to build a little kingdom for ourselves. The phrase "Thy will be done" (v. 10) shows that we want God's will, not ours, to be done. This is worship. This is a vital relationship with God.

Call unto me, and I will answer thee, and show thee great and mighty things, which thou knowest not (Jer. 33:3).

ALTAR NEGLECT BRINGS FAILURE
GENESIS 12:9–13

After Abraham pitched his tent, built an altar and called upon the name of the Lord, the Scriptures say that "Abram journeyed, going on still toward the south" (Gen. 12:9). Instead of staying where he had his altar—his contact with God—Abraham went farther south. He went away from the altar and made "provision for the flesh" (Rom. 13:14).

Have you not also found that failures arise when you neglect the altar? The altar is representative of our communion and fellowship with God. Do you have an altar? It is common to refer to the "family altar." This means having a time when the family reads the Word of God and prays together. But do you also have an individual alta—a time alone with God for Bible reading and prayer? You desperately need this time with God; to omit it is to invite all kinds of trials and failures into your life. I do not think I am exaggerating when I say that 85 percent of the failures and trials that Christians have can be traced to the fact that their altar relationship with God is not right. They have moved away from the time of fellowship with Him.

Thy word is a lamp unto my feet, and a light unto my path (Ps. 119:105).

FRIEND OF THE WORLD OR OF GOD?

GENESIS 12:14–20

Abraham's downward steps away from God eventually led to open rebuke. The Bible says, "Pharaoh called Abram and said, What is this that thou hast done unto me? why didst thou not tell me that she was thy wife? Why saidst thou, She is my sister? so I might have taken her to me to wife: now therefore behold thy wife, take her, and go thy way" (Gen. 12:18–19). It is sad when a child of God has to be corrected by the world. All of this came about because of Abraham's lack of faith, which resulted in his going to Egypt—a symbol of the world of unbelief.

We, too, need to be careful about our friendship with the world. The Word of God says, "Know ye not that the friendship of the world is enmity with God? whosoever therefore will be a friend of the world is the enemy of God" (James 4:4). Check your life. Are you a friend of the world? According to this verse, if you are a friend of the world, you are an enemy of God.

The time that the Christian spends in a backslidden state is wasted time. Abraham's time in Egypt was wasted as far as his spiritual progress was concerned. While trying to be a friend of the world, the believer is only building with wood, hay and stubble—which someday will be consumed by the fire of judgment. The believer will receive no reward for this kind of work (see 1 Cor. 3:12–15).

Whosoever therefore will be a friend of the world is the enemy of God (James 4:4).

RESULTS OF BACKSLIDING
GENESIS 13:1–4

Even though Abraham returned to fellowship with God, irreparable damage had been done. When a believer backslides, he does things he will never be able to undo. Abraham's testimony had been weakened, and damage beyond repair had been done to worldly Lot, Abraham's nephew. Lot had gone with Abraham to Egypt. The backslider never backslides alone; he always takes others with him.

Even though Abraham had backslidden and had brought about much damage, Genesis 13:3–4 tells us that he went back "to Bethel, unto the place where his tent had been at the beginning, between Bethel and Hai; unto the place of the altar, which he had made there at the first: and there Abram called on the name of the LORD."

God has made provision for every backslider. Just as Abraham returned to fellowship with the Lord, you, too, can come back into fellowship with Him if you have backslidden. First John 2:1 says, "My little children, these things write I unto you, that ye sin not. And if any man sin, we have an advocate with the Father, Jesus Christ the righteous." In the first chapter of 1 John, every believer is assured, "If we confess our sins, he is faithful and just to forgive us our sins, and to cleanse us from all unrighteousness" (v. 9). Do not stay in the miserable place of disobedience. Come back to God and confess your sin.

There is a way which seemeth right unto a man, but the end thereof are the ways of death (Prov. 14:12).

SPIRIT-CONTROLLED OR CARNAL?

GENESIS 13:5–13

In considering the lives of Abraham and Lot, we see that Abraham's life was symbolic of the Spirit-controlled Christian, whereas Lot's life was symbolic of the carnal Christian. Unconsecrated Christians who are living according to the flesh are referred to as "carnal" in the Scriptures (see 1 Cor. 3:1,3).

It is never recorded that Lot built an altar. He was not known for his communion with God. As a result, he got into trouble, just as any believer gets into trouble when he does not take time for daily fellowship with God. I am not referring to a time when the entire family reads the Bible and prays together. This, too, is extremely important, but I am referring particularly to your personal time alone with God. Perhaps you say you do not have enough time because you are too busy with life's activities. Anything that takes you away from this time of fellowship with God is sin. Regardless of how much work you have to do, you can find some time to spend with God alone. As a believer, this is your number one prerogative.

The devil will always see to it that we have little or no time to fellowship with God. But we can—and we must—make time for such fellowship. We must put first things first.

Walk in the Spirit, and ye shall not fulfil the lust of the flesh (Gal. 5:16).

RESTORING A BROTHER
GENESIS 14:10–16

What should be our attitude when a brother is taken captive by the things of this world? Some have a distorted concept of separation. When they see a brother fall into sin, they shout it from the housetops and publish it in their magazines. This is not what Christ instructed.

Galatians 6 tells us what our attitude should be toward a fallen Christian brother. The apostle Paul exhorted, "Brethren, if any person is overtaken in misconduct or sin of any sort, you who are spiritual [who are responsive to and controlled by the Spirit] should set him right and restore and reinstate him, without any sense of superiority and with all gentleness, keeping an attentive eye on yourself, lest you should be tempted also" (v. 1, Amplified).

When Abraham realized what had happened to Lot, he became very bold. "When Abram heard that his brother was taken captive, he armed his trained servants, born in his own house, three hundred and eighteen, and pursued them unto Dan. And he divided himself against them, he and his servants, by night, and smote them, and pursued them unto Hobah, which is on the left hand of Damascus" (Gen. 14:14–15). God rewarded his courage because Abraham "brought back all the goods, and also brought again his brother Lot, and his goods, and the women also, and the people" (v. 16).

If a man be overtaken in a fault, ye which are spiritual, restore such an one (Gal. 6:1).

REFUSING THE WORLD'S OFFERS

GENESIS 14:17–24

When the king of Sodom tempted Abraham by urging him to take the earthly goods, Abraham's attitude was the same as the apostle Paul's. In 2 Corinthians 4:18, Paul said, "We look not at the things which are seen, but at the things which are not seen: for the things which are seen are temporal; but the things which are not seen are eternal."

Because Abraham had been spiritually fortified beforehand, he was ready when the king of Sodom offered him earthly riches. There was no problem because he had already made his choice between that which is temporal and that which is eternal. Joshua told the people of his day, "Choose you this day whom ye will serve" (Josh. 24:15). The greatest need among present-day believers is to realize there is a choice that has to be made.

Abraham was ready, and his answer was quick, concise and final. Abraham declared God to be his God and that he was confident and determined that God alone would provide his portion. Abraham declared unashamedly that he would trust God for his every need. He did not want to give either Satan or man the opportunity to say that he had made him rich. What a challenge to us!

A little that a righteous man hath is better than the riches of many wicked (Ps. 37:16).

THE BELIEVER'S REWARD
GENESIS 15:1–6

God assured Abraham that He was Abraham's "exceeding great reward" (Gen. 15:1). The king of Sodom had offered Abraham all the riches that Abraham and his servants had brought back, but he turned them down. Notice that the tense is not past or future, but present. Not "I was" or "I will be" but "I am"—"I am thy shield, and thy exceeding great reward" (v. 1).

We see from God's promise to be Abraham's reward that God never permits His children to lose when they honor Him and seek His glory. God never leaves His child without spiritual blessings after His child has taken a stand for the glory of God.

Although Abraham had no children at this time, his faith in the Lord is recorded in verse 6: "He believed in the LORD; and he counted it to him for righteousness." Because of Abraham's faith in God, he was able to look into the future and trust God for everything.

Ephesians 1:3 tells us that present-day believers have been blessed with "all spiritual blessings in heavenly places in Christ." But we, too, must set our eyes on the future. We must be those who look to their reward for glorifying God, rather than looking at the temporal satisfactions of the present.

The judgments of the LORD are true and righteous altogether.... And in keeping of them there is great reward (Ps. 19:9,11).

TESTING FOLLOWS TRIUMPH

GENESIS 16:1–6

Ten years had passed since God had first promised Abraham descendants, and now three years had gone by since God had reassured Abraham of this same thing. Whereas in Genesis 15 Abraham is seen as a man of faith, in chapter 16 we see him as a man of unbelief. He could wait no longer for God to fulfill His promise. A lack of patience tends to foster unbelief. In chapter 15 Abraham believed the Lord; in chapter 16 he hearkened unto the voice of his wife. In chapter 15 Abraham walked after the Spirit; in chapter 16 he walked after the energy of the flesh. What a sad inconsistency in the life of this man of God. Only Jesus Christ could say, "I do always those things that please him" (John 8:29).

Abraham was tested by the suggestion of a well-meaning wife. Would he take matters out of the hand of God and act in the energy of the flesh? This test was the trying of the patience of his faith. Would he wait on God to fulfill His word in His own time and way, or would Abraham's patience give out and the flesh take over? God wanted him to have a mature faith. What would you have done in his situation?

Cast not away therefore your confidence, which hath great recompence of reward. For ye have need of patience, that, after ye have done the will of God, ye might receive the promise (Heb. 10:35–36).

RESULTS OF THE LACK OF FAITH
GENESIS 16:6–16

After Hagar fled from Sarah's presence, before Ishmael was born, the angel of the Lord said to her, "Behold, thou art with child, and shalt bear a son, and shalt call his name Ishmael; because the LORD hath heard thy affliction. And he will be a wild man; his hand will be against every man, and every man's hand against him; and he shall dwell in the presence of all his brethren" (Gen. 16:11–12). The Arabs are the descendants of Ishmael, and this prophecy of international trouble is being fulfilled today. The centuries-old conflict between the Arabs and the Jews had its beginning when Abraham tried to use the means of the flesh to produce a spiritual result.

Not only did Abraham's sin produce family and international trouble, but it also produced spiritual trouble. In the New Testament, the apostle Paul wrote of this trouble in Galatians 4:22–26.

When churches or believers leave the simplicity and liberty that is in Christ and return to the works of the flesh, there is nothing but bondage. When religious ceremonies or other activities are substituted for the work of the Holy Spirit, bondage results. From this incident in Genesis we see the sad results of relying on the flesh to bring about spiritual results.

And he did not many mighty works there because of their unbelief (Matt. 13:58).

GOD'S PERFECT TIMING
GENESIS 17:1–2

In Genesis 17:1 we are told, "And when Abram was ninety years old and nine, the Lord appeared to Abram, and said unto him, I am the Almighty God; walk before me, and be thou perfect." Thirteen years had gone by since Abraham had hearkened unto Sarah, and during this time there was no mention of God's appearing to Abraham. In the Scriptures, these 13 years are passed over as a period of spiritual barrenness. For Abraham it was what is known spiritually as a time of wood, hay and stubble.

But why all of this waiting? God had promised Abraham a son, and by this time only Ishmael had been born into his home—by a means that was not pleasing to the Lord. The reason for God's delay was so God could bring Abraham to the end of himself. Later it was said of Abraham, "And being not weak in faith, he considered not his own body now dead, when he was about an hundred years old, neither yet the deadness of Sarah's womb" (Rom. 4:19). Before divine power is put forth, man must learn his own impotency. Not until Abraham's body was as good as dead would God fulfill His word. Man's extremity is God's opportunity. Though to Abraham this seemed like a long delay, God was right on time. God has a perfect time for everything.

As for God, his way is perfect (Ps. 18:30).

THE ALMIGHTY GOD
EPHESIANS 3:14–21

By the time of the 17th chapter of Genesis, it had been 24 years since God's first promise to Abraham that he would have a seed and that the land would be given to his seed. When God now appears to Abraham, He appears to him as "the Almighty God" (v. 1). The Hebrew name for God here is actually *El Shaddai. El* means "God" or "the Strong One." *Shaddai* means "nourisher" or "strength-giver." As *El Shaddai,* God is "the all-sufficient One."

Thus, when Abraham was 99 years old, God appeared to him and gave him a promise that was greater than ever: "I am the Almighty God ... [I] will multiply thee exceedingly" (vv. 1–2). Whereas Abraham longed for physical seed so that God's promises could be fulfilled, do we long for spiritual seed—for others to come to know Christ under our ministry?

Perhaps in your life you have found times when spiritual fruit does not come. This frequently happens to pastors and evangelists. The tendency then is to resort to unworthy methods to produce results, maintaining that the end justifies the means. How patiently God bore with Abraham! After the first promise 24 years earlier, God now reveals Himself to Abraham as "the Almighty God." No one but the all-powerful, all-sufficient God could meet Abraham's need at this time.

He that dwelleth in the secret place of the most High shall abide under the shadow of the Almighty (Ps. 91:1).

ABRAHAM'S GOD IS OUR GOD
GENESIS 17:3–8

In Genesis 17 when God changed Abram's name to Abraham, the reason is given: "For a father of many nations have I made thee" (v. 5). Notice the expression "have I made thee." At this time no child has been born to Abraham and Sarah, yet God says He has made Abraham "a father of many nations." What God has promised, He is able to perform. What He has begun, He is able to finish. When God says it, it is as good as done.

This same principle is seen in Romans 8:30: "Moreover whom he did predestinate, them he also called: and whom he called, them he also justified: and whom he justified, them he also glorified." We have not yet been glorified, but God speaks of it as a finished work. Why? Because what He begins, He finishes. When it is His undertaking, He sees it through. The time element is in His hands.

We need to realize that Abraham's God is our God. The promises made to Abraham were promises that almighty grace alone could utter and that almighty power alone could fulfill. When the almighty, all-sufficient God displays Himself, man's self must be excluded. Abraham is set aside in the account at this point. He only listens. Sarah is not mentioned. The bondwoman and her son are, for the moment, not in view. Nothing is seen but the Almighty God in the fullness of His grace and sovereign power.

Jesus Christ the same yesterday, and to day, and for ever (Heb. 13:8).

FLESH AND SPIRIT IN CONFLICT
GENESIS 17:9–21

God did not refuse to bless Ishmael, but He caused Abraham to clearly understand that the covenant would be established with Isaac, who was not yet born. Ishmael was not to be an heir with Isaac. The Scriptures build on this principle in showing that the flesh (Ishmael) cannot be heir with the Spirit (Isaac).

In the New Testament, the apostle Paul referred to Ishmael and Isaac and drew a parallel to Christians. Paul was emphasizing that the Christian is made mature through the freedom of the Spirit and not through the bondage of the Law. He wrote: "Nevertheless what saith the scripture? Cast out the bondwoman and her son: for the son of the bondwoman shall not be heir with the son of the freewoman. So then, brethren, we are not children of the bondwoman, but of the free" (Gal. 4:30–31).

Paul continued the parallel in Galatians 5 when he said, "This I say then, Walk in the Spirit, and ye shall not fulfil the lust of the flesh. For the flesh lusteth against the Spirit, and the Spirit against the flesh: and these are contrary the one to the other: so that ye cannot do the things that ye would" (vv. 16–17). In this same chapter, Paul also wrote: "They that are Christ's have crucified the flesh with the affections and lusts. If we live in the Spirit, let us also walk in the Spirit" (vv. 24–25).

For I know that in me (that is, in my flesh, dwelleth no good thing: for to will is present with me; but how to perform that which is good I find not (Rom. 7:18).

GOD HONORS HIS OWN

GENESIS 18:1–5

Genesis 18 records how God greatly honored Abraham: "He lift up his eyes and looked, and, lo, three men stood by him: and when he saw them, he ran to meet them from the tent door, and bowed himself toward the ground, and said, My LORD, if now I have found favour in thy sight, pass not away, I pray thee, from thy servant" (vv. 2–3). The Lord Himself, together with two angels, appeared to Abraham. Think of it! The Lord did not honor the sumptuous halls and princely palaces of Egypt with His presence, but He accepted hospitality in the tent of a pilgrim and stranger. Nor did God go to Lot, who was a believer with many worldly possessions, although later He sent two angels to him. Think of the high privilege of Abraham, the stranger and pilgrim, to host the Lord and two angels!

We, too, are privileged because of our union with Christ. After Christ's resurrection, before He ascended to heaven, He told the believers, "I will not leave you comfortless: I will come to you. Yet a little while, and the world seeth me no more; but ye see me: because I live, ye shall live also. At that day ye shall know that I am in my Father, and ye in me, and I in you" (John 14:18–20). The believer has God Himself dwelling in him! No higher privilege can be known by those in this life.

He shall call upon me, and I will answer him: I will be with him in trouble; I will deliver him, and honour him (Ps. 91:15).

NOTHING IS IMPOSSIBLE
GENESIS 18:6–15

Sarah had overheard the Lord saying she would have a son; "therefore Sarah laughed within herself, saying, After I am waxed old shall I have pleasure, my lord being old also?" (Gen. 18:12).

Sarah was surprised the Lord had detected her laugh, and she "denied, saying, I laughed not; for she was afraid. And he said, Nay; but thou didst laugh" (v. 15).

Even though Sarah found it difficult to believe, God had given His final announcement that she and Abraham would have a son. They had waited nearly 25 years, but now was God's time. Abraham was as good as dead, and Sarah was past the age of childbearing, but what God had promised, He was able to perform.

Even though God was going to work the impossible, He was going to use human means. God also wants to work the impossible through us if we will allow Him to do so. Christ said, "If ye abide in me, and my words abide in you, ye shall ask what ye will, and it shall be done unto you" (John 15:7). God wants to perform the impossible by using believers as His human instruments.

God asked Abraham and Sarah, "Is any thing too hard for the Lord?" (Gen. 18:14). We, too, must respond to this question. As we face seeming impossibilities, do we think God is unable to perform what He has promised?

For with God nothing shall be impossible (Luke 1:37).

LIVING BY FAITH

ROMANS 4:9–16

Romans 4:16 refers to Abraham as "the father of us all." It is logical to ask, "How can this be?" Inasmuch as Abraham separated himself unto God, he is the father of all those who are separated.

There are two aspects of separation indicated by the words "from" and "unto." The believer is to be separated from the world unto God. The command for present-day believers to have such separation is recorded in 2 Corinthians 6:14: "Be ye not unequally yoked together with unbelievers: for what fellowship hath righteousness with unrighteousness? and what communion hath light with darkness?" The two aspects of separation are seen in verse 17 of this passage: "Wherefore come out from among them, and be ye separate, saith the Lord, and touch not the unclean thing; and I will receive you." What a wonderful promise!

Because Abraham was such a spiritual giant in the walk of faith, he is also called "the father of all them that believe" (Rom. 4:11). We are not his physical descendants, but we are his spiritual descendants. We are the children of Abraham in the sense that we walk by faith even as he walked. Galatians 3:29 says, "And if ye be Christ's, then are ye Abraham's seed, and heirs according to the promise." We are the children of Abraham in the sense that we live by faith in the promises of God even as Abraham lived.

But without faith it is impossible to please him: for he that cometh to God must believe that he is, and that he is a rewarder of them that diligently seek him (Heb. 11:6).

CONSTANT GRACE
GALATIANS 5:16–26

There are also many contrasts in the life of Abraham. By faith he left his country; in unbelief he stopped short at Haran. By faith he entered the land; in unbelief he forsook it for Egypt. By faith he returned to the land to sojourn; in unbelief he took Hagar to bear a child rather than waiting on God. By faith he rescued Lot; in unbelief he lied to Abimelech.

In Abraham we see the conflict of the two natures. The sin nature was constantly in conflict with the nature he had received from God. This conflict of present-day believers is described in Galatians 5:16–17: "This I say then, Walk in the Spirit, and ye shall not fulfil the lust of the flesh. For the flesh lusteth against the Spirit, and the Spirit against the flesh: and these are contrary the one to the other: so that ye cannot do the things that ye would." Verses 24–25 of this same chapter tell us, "And they that are Christ's have crucified the flesh with the affections and lusts. If we live in the Spirit, let us also walk in the Spirit."

Like Abraham, we are frequently inconsistent. But God is calling so He might lead us through to triumph. The Lord referred to Himself as the God of Abraham, not because Abraham was always consistent, but because he allowed God to bring him through to victory. God did not abandon His man, and in His mercy He will not abandon us. Grace is always at hand.

God is able to make all grace abound toward you; that ye, always having all sufficiency in all things, may abound to every good work (2 Cor. 9:8).

WITNESSING TO UNBELIEVERS

GENESIS 23:1–16

Abraham had daily contact with his unbelieving neighbors, but he was always careful that they knew where he stood with God. Especially was this true at the time of Sarah's death. Sarah lived 37 years after Isaac was born and died at the age of 127. Abraham mourned for her and sought for a place to bury her. He said to the sons of Heth, "I am a stranger and a sojourner with you: give me a possession of a buryingplace with you, that I may bury my dead out of my sight" (Gen. 23:4). Abraham referred to himself as a "stranger" and a "sojourner," even though he was a man of much wealth. He owned several wells, and that alone made him wealthy. In addition, he had many cattle. But even with all of this, Abraham had not allowed himself to become attached to worldly possessions. He unashamedly confessed by his words and actions where he stood with God.

These people recognized Abraham's greatness because of the way he lived before them. Although they were not concerned about Abraham's God, he had made such an impact on them by the way he lived that they were willing to give him any land he wanted for a burying place for Sarah. Abraham refused to be chargeable to his ungodly neighbors. He let it be known that he was a separated man and was going to stay in this separated position. May the same be true of us.

Let your light so shine before men, that they may see your good works, and glorify your Father which is in heaven (Matt. 5:16).

OUR HIGHEST GOAL
GENESIS 25:1–8

Genesis 25 records the closing events in Abraham's life. In his last days, he made provision that Isaac would receive all of his inheritance.

In addition to Isaac, Abraham had a son by Hagar and six others by Keturah. Abraham had married Keturah after Sarah's death. Abraham wanted to make it clear to his other sons that Isaac was the chosen son of promise. By giving gifts to the other sons and sending them away, Abraham took the necessary steps to make Isaac's position free from as many difficulties as possible.

After Abraham had given all that he had unto Isaac, we are told, "Then Abraham gave up the ghost, and died in a good old age, an old man, and full of years; and was gathered to his people. And his sons Isaac and Ishmael buried him in the cave of Machpelah" (vv. 8–9). This was the cave that Abraham had purchased to bury Sarah in. God's ways of working are seen in the last statement concerning Abraham: "And it came to pass after the death of Abraham, that God blessed his son Isaac" (v. 11).

From Abraham's life recorded in the Old Testament and from verses recorded in the New Testament, we see that God's purpose in placing man on earth is so that man might do His will. Our highest goal is to glorify God by doing His will.

Even every one that is called by my name: for I have created him for my glory, I have formed him; yea, I have made him (Isa. 43:7).

FEBRUARY

Whereas Abraham (as seen from the January readings) had an obedient faith, Isaac (the subject for February) had a passive faith. As seen from the Scriptures, Isaac led a quiet life that one might characterize as unassuming and uneventful.

Isaac's life was not one of magnificent action or great, daring triumphs. God never caused Isaac to experience the thick darkness of trial that Abraham passed through or the alarming struggle at Peniel that Jacob endured.

It is important to remember that we are all needed in God's great plan. It is not necessary for everyone to be a trailblazer or pioneer of faith as Abraham was. Let us not forget that the God of Isaac is also our God. God loves ordinary people, and they can have as vital a relationship with God as the pioneers of faith.

The readings for February are excerpted from *The God of Abraham, Isaac and Jacob.*

GOD LOVES ORDINARY PEOPLE
GENESIS 21:1–7

The birth of Isaac was the second great step toward the fulfillment of God's purpose. The first was the selection of Abraham to be the father of the chosen nation. Isaac's birth marked a crisis in connection with the history of the chosen line of Christ.

Even though Ishmael had been born 13 years earlier, God made it clear to Abraham that "in Isaac shall thy seed be called" (Gen. 21:12). This was the crisis concerning the line of Christ. God had promised Abraham a son, but none had been given. Abraham had gone in to Hagar, Sarah's handmaid, and a son had resulted from their union—but not the son of God's choice. But at this time in Genesis, God provided the son He had promised.

Isaac led a quiet, peaceful life. He was the ordinary son of a great father, and he was the ordinary father of a great son. Thus, God calls Himself the God of Isaac. The God of Isaac is the God of ordinary people—those involved in the routine of daily living.

Isaac's life was not filled with glory and spectacular events. Yet he had a very meaningful life. He filled his place in life with complete contentment, not looking for the spectacular. Therefore, a study of Isaac's life will greatly benefit us because most of us are ordinary people desiring to please God in the routine of daily living.

For the LORD seeth not as man seeth; for man looketh on the outward appearance, but the LORD looketh on the heart (1 Sam. 16:7).

LESSONS FROM ISAAC'S BIRTH
ROMANS 8:31–39

From the account of Isaac's birth there are many important lessons we should learn. Five are extremely significant. First, God is in no hurry to work out His plans. He is never too late; He is always on time. Man frets and worries and is always in a hurry to work out his plans.

Second, God is almighty. Nothing can hinder or thwart the outworking of God's purpose. Abraham was old and Sarah was barren, but these obstacles presented no difficulty to God.

Third, God is faithful. He promised Sarah a son. From the standpoint of human reasoning, it seemed like a foolish promise. However, the promise of God was sure because He is always faithful in keeping His promises. Because God's word is absolutely sure, in times of doubt and discouragement we need to come to the Word of God to check our spiritual lives and to remind ourselves of His faithfulness. Although we may not be able to understand how God can fulfill His promises to us, our attitude should be: If God says it, that settles it.

Fourth, faith is tested so it might be proven to be genuine. A faith that cannot endure trial is really no faith at all.

Fifth, God has a set time for everything. It is important that we learn this lesson well. God has an appointed time for accomplishing His will. Nothing is left to chance.

To every thing there is a season, and a time to every purpose under heaven: a time to be born (Eccles. 3:1–2).

GOD KEEPS HIS PROMISES
LUKE 1:26–38

Isaac was the child of promise. There were progressive promises made to Abraham, and at first there was some doubting on his part. But in the New Testament, when God recounted Abraham's life, He completely passed over the fact that Abraham doubted at first (see Heb. 11:11). So also our sins are blotted out once they have come under the blood of Jesus Christ.

Isaac was a child of miracle because Sarah's womb was "dead." In describing Abraham, the apostle Paul said, "Being not weak in faith, he considered not his own body now dead, when he was about an hundred years old, neither the deadness of Sarah's womb" (Rom. 4:19). At first Sarah did not think there was any possibility she could bear a child, but God asked, "Is any thing too hard for the LORD?" (Gen. 18:14).

This reminds us of the virgin birth of Christ. When the angel Gabriel appeared to Mary and told her she would have a son and that she should call His name Jesus, Mary asked, "How shall this be, seeing I know not a man?" (Luke 1:34). Gabriel assured Mary, "With God nothing shall be impossible" (v. 37). Then Mary responded, "Behold the handmaid of the Lord; be it unto me according to thy word" (v. 38). Let us also count on the fact that God is able to do what He has promised.

Blessed be the LORD, that hath given rest unto his people Israel, according to all that he promised: there hath not failed one word of all his good promise, which he promised by the hand of Moses his servant (1 Kings 8:56).

GOING ON TO MATURITY
GENESIS 21:8; 1 SAMUEL 1:22–28

The Scriptures say that after Isaac was born, he "grew, and was weaned: and Abraham made a great feast the same day that Isaac was weaned" (Gen. 21:8). During Old Testament times, weaning referred to the time in a child's life when he was old enough to be entrusted to strangers. This took place between three and five years of age—and sometimes older. Samuel is a biblical example. The Scriptures say that when Hannah "had weaned him, she took him up with her, with three bullocks, and one ephah of flour, and a bottle of wine, and brought him unto the house of the LORD in Shiloh: and the child was young" (1 Sam. 1:24).

Growth is also important to the Christian. The Bible instructs believers: "As newborn babes, desire the sincere milk of the word, that ye may grow thereby" (1 Pet. 2:2). While the milk of the Word is needed for young Christians, older Christians should be feeding on the meat of the Word.

When Isaac had matured enough to be weaned, Abraham made a great feast "the same day that Isaac was weaned" (Gen. 21:8). This significant time in a child's life was celebrated with a feast. So also it is a time of much rejoicing when a believer passes from the "milk stage" into the "meat stage" in his walk with the Lord. It is at this time that the believer leaves his dependence on others and depends on the leadership of the Holy Spirit.

I have more understanding than all my teachers: for thy testimonies are my meditation (Ps. 119:99).

CONFLICT IS INEVITABLE
GENESIS 21:9–21

After the birth of Isaac, the true nature of Ishmael was revealed. Nothing of his life is known before Isaac's birth. Even this points out a significant truth for the believer. It is not until a person receives the new nature, through receiving Christ as Saviour, that he discovers the real character of his old nature. The discovery is a painful one and even causes some to doubt their salvation as they see the struggle taking place in their lives. However, the very fact that there is conflict is proof of salvation. There is no conflict when there is only the old nature. But when the new nature comes in to control the life, the old nature sets up an intense conflict.

Paul referred to this conflict when he said, "For the flesh lusteth against the Spirit, and the Spirit against the flesh: and these are contrary the one to the other: so that ye cannot do the things that ye would" (Gal. 5:17). This is the condition that results when a person receives Christ as Saviour. He receives a new nature, which is in opposition to the old nature. There is conflict between the spirit of liberty and the spirit of bondage. Even as in the case of Ishmael and Isaac, where one had to be expelled, the believer cannot yield to both natures but must choose the one he will obey.

For whatsoever is born of God overcometh the world: and this is the victory that overcometh the world, even our faith (John 5:4).

THE BASIS OF UNITY
GENESIS 21:11; EPHESIANS 2:11–16

The Scriptures say that when Sarah demanded that Ishmael be expelled from the household, "the thing was very grievous in Abraham's sight because of his son" (Gen. 21:11). The word "grievous" means "bad" or "evil." Abraham viewed the conflict between his two sons as something evil. No doubt he was also grieved over the necessity of having to send Ishmael away. Perhaps Abraham thought that Ishmael and Isaac would someday be able to live together in harmony. This is the way many believers view the conflict between their old and new natures. They mistakenly think that the old nature will improve with time and they will have less conflict.

There are also those who think that believers and unbelievers can dwell in harmony and even cooperate in promoting the same organization. This is what the proponents of the ecumenical movement are trying to tell us today. They stress organizational unity and peace, but they do not emphasize salvation by faith in Christ, which is the only thing that can bring about spiritual unity and lasting peace.

He that is not with me is against me; and he that gathereth not with me scattereth abroad (Matt. 12:30).

PARTING WITH THE DESIRES OF THE FLESH
GENESIS 21:12; ROMANS 6:6–14

Although having to send Ishmael away was grievous to Abraham, God said to him, "Let it not be grievous in thy sight because of the lad, and because of thy bondwoman; in all that Sarah hath said unto thee, hearken unto her voice; for in Isaac shall thy seed be called" (Gen. 21:12). Abraham was to depend on what God had done for him and had given him in the person of Isaac. This had to do primarily with Isaac's being the covenant heir and being in the lineage of Christ. Abraham was grieved about having to part with Ishmael, so God emphasized to him again that "in Isaac shall thy seed be called."

Present-day believers also find it exceedingly difficult to part with the desires of the flesh. The struggle is intense, but to cling to the flesh only results in bondage. God has provided a way for the believer to be free from bondage to the flesh. Paul explained it when he said, "Knowing this, that our old man is [was] crucified with him, that the body of sin might be destroyed, that henceforth we should not serve sin" (Rom. 6:6). Verse 11 of this same chapter says, "Likewise reckon ye also yourselves to be dead indeed unto sin, but alive unto God through Jesus Christ our Lord." We need to recognize what has been done for us, count it as a fact, appropriate its benefits and continually live for God.

Submit yourselves therefore to God. Resist the devil, and he will flee from you (James 4:7).

THE NECESSITY OF TESTING
GENESIS 22:1–8

The offering of Isaac is recorded in Genesis 22. This chapter sees father and son together in this great test. That they were "together" is one of the keys to this chapter. Verse 6 says, "And they went both of them together." Verse 8 also emphasizes: "So they went both of them together." It is significant that the first record of Isaac's active participation in life had to do with his being willing to offer his life. He willingly surrendered to the will of his father and to the will of Almighty God.

Testing and discipline are necessary for the believer because they prove whether or not his spiritual experiences have really become a part of his life and character. The tests that Abraham had successfully passed prepared him for the greatest test of his life— the offering of Isaac.

God's testing of an individual is evidence that He has confidence in that individual. God never tests a person who hasn't the capacity to pass the test. God never tested Lot to the degree He tested Abraham, because Lot never reached a spiritual plane that was high enough to warrant God's testing in his life. Sodom tempted Lot, but it was no temptation to Abraham. By his life Abraham proved he loved God more than the things of Sodom.

There hath no temptation taken you but such as is common to man: but God is faithful, who will not suffer you to be tempted above that ye are able; but will with the temptation also make a way to escape, that ye may be able to bear it (1 Cor. 10:13).

TESTING HAS A PURPOSE
GENESIS 22:1–2; 1 PETER 1:3–7

God wanted Abraham to prove that he loved Him more than the things of this life and more than any other person. For this test God chose the person who was the dearest object of Abraham's life—Isaac. God may sometimes test you this way also. Although the test may be severe and may involve the dearest person or thing in your life, you will be a better person for God as a result of the test.

The offering of human sacrifices was a common practice of the heathen in Abraham's time. However, there is no other incident where God tested a believer in this particular way. Human sacrifices were strongly condemned by God in the Old Testament. His people, Israel, were to totally abstain from this heathen practice. But with Abraham, God chose this test to prove whom Abraham loved most. God knew what he would do.

When God promised him a son, Abraham believed God, and it was counted to him for righteousness. But having received the promised son, there was the danger that Abraham would give more of his attention to the gift than to the Giver. He knew that out of Isaac would come the descendants God had promised. Abraham was in danger of concentrating on the fulfillment of God's promise to the exclusion of God Himself, who had made the promise.

Christ also suffered for us, leaving us an example, that ye should follow his steps (1 Pet. 2:21).

THE RESPONSE OF FAITH
GENESIS 22:3; GALATIANS 1:11–17

Even though Abraham could not understand why God would command him to offer his son, he was not slow in responding. Genesis 22:3 says, "And Abraham rose up early in the morning, and saddled his ass, and took two of his young men with him, and Isaac his son, and clave the wood for the burnt offering, and rose up, and went unto the place of which God had told him." In Abraham's response there was no reluctance, no hesitation, no doubt, no staggering, no unbelief. Abraham did not delay. He did not endeavor to reason things out or spend time consulting with other people about the matter.

So also when the apostle Paul was called to preach the Gospel, he said, "Immediately I conferred not with flesh and blood" (Gal. 1:16). This is important. There are occasions when no time should be taken to counsel with men.

God found ready faith in Abraham. Faith triumphed over natural affections, over reason, over self-will. God's grace found a ready outlet through which it could manifest itself.

Might our faith be as Abraham's faith. As we yield our lives to the Lord, He will work in us "both to will and to do of his good pleasure" (Phil. 2:13). Then we will be able to say with the apostle Paul, "I can do all things through Christ which strengtheneth me" (4:13).

For we walk by faith, not by sight (2 Cor. 5:7).

TRUSTING IN SPITE OF CIRCUMSTANCES

GENESIS 22:4–5; HEBREWS 11:17–19

Genesis 22:4–5 says, "Then on the third day Abraham lifted up his eyes, and saw the place afar off. And Abraham said unto his young men, Abide ye here with the ass; and I and the lad will go yonder and worship, and come again to you." In these verses there are three things in particular that reveal the tremendous faith of Abraham. First, he told the young men who were with him, "Abide ye here." Once Abraham saw the mountain that God was going to send him to, he wanted to be sure that nothing or no one would hinder what he had undertaken.

Second, Abraham told the young men, "I and the lad will go yonder and worship." Thus Abraham gave up all of his desires and ascribed everything to God. It was a true act of worship when Abraham was willing to give up everything for God.

Third, Abraham told the young men, "I and the lad will ... come again to you." His faith was in the God of the resurrection. He believed that God would bring his son back to life.

Can we trust God when we are totally unable to see how He is going to work out His will? Abraham demonstrated that he could.

Though he slay me, yet will I trust in him (Job 13:15).

A SUBMISSIVE FAITH

GENESIS 22:7–9; COLOSSIANS 2:6–7

Isaac probably knew that he was the sacrifice. He could have resisted because he was no longer a child. He was probably between 17 and 25 years of age. Physically, all the advantages were his. His father was old; he was young.

Here the Word of God introduces us to the submissive trait that seems to have been the strong factor in Isaac's life. He was characterized more by submissiveness than by aggressiveness. Abraham was the one with an aggressive faith, but Isaac had a submissive faith, willing to be what God wanted him to be. Even when he was offered as a sacrifice, Isaac submitted himself to his father because God had so willed it.

Isaac's submission was a picture of Christ's submission to the Father. Jesus Christ was the sacrifice for the sins of the world so that the holy standards of the Heavenly Father might be satisfied. Concerning Christ, 1 John 2:2 tells us that "he is the propitiation [satisfaction] for our sins: and not for ours only, but also for the sins of the whole world." Jesus was submissive to the Heavenly Father's will. The purpose of the Father and the Son was one. God the Father willed the sacrifice to be made, and the Son willed to be the sacrifice. The life of the Lord Jesus Christ is summed up in the statement "I come ... to do thy will, O God" (Heb. 10:7). What a wonderful God we have!

Yield yourselves unto God, as those that are alive from the dead, and your members as instruments of righteousness unto God (Rom. 6:13).

ACTION PROVES FAITH
GENESIS 22:9–12

This was the triumph of both Abraham and Isaac. Faith was now a proven fact. God said, "Now I know that thou fearest God" (Gen. 22:12). Abraham had passed the supreme test, and God's voice broke into the awful silence and said, "Now I know."

Faith is always proven by action. In his epistle James said, "Was not Abraham our father justified by works, when he had offered Isaac his son upon the altar? Seest thou how faith wrought with his works, and by works was faith made perfect?" (2:21–22). Along with these statements, Romans 4:2–3 needs to be taken into consideration: "For if Abraham were justified by works, he hath whereof to glory; but not before God. For what saith the scripture? Abraham believed God, and it was counted unto him for righteousness." It is common to hear people say, "You must have faith." But faith itself is as rare as a true gem. The kind of faith that causes a man to launch out into the deep from the shore of present circumstances is practically missing. Where is our faith today? Perhaps you ask, What is faith? When taken in its most basic meaning, faith is believing what God says and then acting upon it. If we do not act upon what God says, this is an evidence that we really do not believe.

Even so faith, if it hath not works, is dead, being alone (James 2:17).

PASSING THE TEST
GENESIS 22:13–19

Abraham had proven he was willing to sacrifice everything—even his son of promise. He evidenced that his greatest need was to know God. This reminds us of the apostle Paul's statement: "That I may know him, and the power of his resurrection, and the fellowship of his sufferings, being made conformable unto his death" (Phil. 3:10).

Genesis 22:16 records God's words: "By myself have I sworn." Because there is no one greater, God can swear by no one greater than Himself. God told Abraham that He would bless him and multiply his seed as the stars of heaven (spiritual seed) and as the sand on the seashore (earthly seed) and that his seed would possess the gate of his enemies. The time is coming when the nation of Israel will possess the gate of her enemies—both her religious and earthly enemies. Abraham experienced the truth of the principle stated in Romans 8:31–32: "What shall we then say to these things? If God be for us, who can be against us? He that spared not his own Son, but delivered him up for us all, how shall he not with him also freely give us all things?" Abraham had graduated. His days of probation and testing were over. His diploma was inscribed with the words "Abraham, the friend of God and the father of the faithful."

Yet if any man suffer as a Christian, let him not be ashamed; but let him glorify God on this behalf (1 Pet. 4:16).

GOD HONORS QUIET DEDICATION
GENESIS 24:63; PSALM 119:9–16

Have you ever considered yourself so small in the sight of God that you thought He would never do for you what He has done for men like Abraham, Isaac or Jacob? I am sure you have. In our study of the life of Isaac, we find a man who was very common like most of us. Yet God chose to call Himself "the God of Isaac."

In contrasting Isaac's character with that of his father and that of his son, we see that Isaac experienced fewer of Abraham's triumphs of faith and fewer of Jacob's failures.

Of the three patriarchs—Abraham, Isaac and Jacob—the only one who never left the land of Canaan was Isaac. He was born in the land of Canaan, and he died there without ever going outside the boundaries of the land. This was quite different from Abraham and Jacob. Perhaps this was because God realized Isaac had a weakness so great that if he had left the land, he might not have returned.

Genesis 24:63 helps us to understand the kind of man Isaac was: "Isaac went out to meditate in the field at the eventide." Thus, we see that Isaac was a quiet and retiring man. He did not have the active, aggressive disposition of his eminent father, but he was deeply concerned about his relationship with God. He was gentle, retiring and unresisting in his relationship with God. Are we, too, concerned about our relationship with God?

But let it be the hidden man of the heart, in that which is not corruptible, even the ornament of a meek and quiet spirit, which is in the sight of God of great price (1 Pet. 3:4).

DON'T RELY ON THE FLESH

GENESIS 26:1–6

Genesis 26 tells us of an important test that Isaac experienced: "There was a famine in the land, beside the first famine that was in the days of Abraham. And Isaac went unto Abimelech king of the Philistines unto Gerar" (v. 1). Isaac forsook the place where he was living—the place of his fellowship with God. He went to Gerar and left behind the place of the altar. Isaac was headed toward Egypt—and possibly that is where he would have gone—but he stopped enroute at a place called Gerar. This city was in the land of Canaan, although it was well on the way toward Egypt. Because those who went to Egypt usually did so as a reliance on the flesh, Egypt became a symbol of the world. Those who live independently of God and rely on natural resources are spiritually in Egypt.

God was not going to allow Isaac to go into Egypt. His position on the outer fringes of the land certainly evidenced an advanced position of backsliding within the range of very dangerous influences. This was a test for Isaac, and he failed it utterly. However, God remained true to His time-honored principle of not testing a believer beyond what he is able to bear but making a way of escape (1 Cor. 10:13). God knew how much Isaac could stand, and He knows how much we can stand.

And the world passeth away, and the lust thereof: but he that doeth the will of God abideth for ever (1 John 2:17).

LIKE FATHER, LIKE SON
GENESIS 26:7–11

Had Isaac not gone to Abimelech, he would not have had to lie about his wife. He lied about his wife just as his father, Abraham, had lied about his wife, Sarah. Isaac left his communion with God and ended up by sinning against the Lord.

There are two important lessons we need to learn from Isaac's imitating his father's example. First, it is much easier for children to imitate the weaknesses or vices of their parents than to excel in their virtues. It is easier because it is natural. Second, while Abraham and Isaac were men of vastly different temperaments, each succumbed to the same temptation. When famine arose, they fled for help. While they were in the land of the enemy, they both became afraid and lied about their wives.

This proves that natural man is under the control of the same adamic nature in which there is no good thing. The apostle Paul recognized this and said, "For I know that in me (that is, in my flesh,) dwelleth no good thing: for to will is present with me; but how to perform that which is good I find not" (Rom. 7:18). Abraham and Isaac both had the adamic nature, even as we do, and they yielded to temptation in similar situations. They had to realize that unless they applied the grace of God, they would inevitably fall into sin. This should also serve as a warning to us.

Train up a child in the way he should go: and when he is old, he will not depart from it (Prov. 22:6).

BACKSLIDDEN BUT BLESSED
GENESIS 26:12–14

How is it possible for God to bless a person who is out of fellowship with Him? God had permitted Isaac to go to Gerar to be tested. Isaac was yet too weak in the faith to be severely tested. God told Isaac, "Sojourn in this land, and I will be with thee, and will bless thee; for unto thee, and unto thy seed, I will give all these countries, and I will perform the oath which I sware unto Abraham thy father" (Gen. 26:3).

God's blessing was upon Isaac even though Isaac was out of the center of His will. God often brings His children back to Himself by showering unexcelled goodness upon them. Romans 2:4 emphasizes this as a principle of God's working when it says, "Or despisest thou the riches of his goodness and forbearance and longsuffering; not knowing that the goodness of God leadeth thee to repentance?"

God allows these things to happen for a purpose. Since Isaac was not able to endure ultimate testing, God permitted him to go as far as Gerar where He was able to teach him some valuable lessons. Isaac was blessed of God and prospered, but this does not mean that every person who prospers is blessed of God. There are many in our day who are prosperous, yet they believe and live contrary to the teaching of the Word of God. Many leaders of false cults have been prosperous, but this is no indication they have been blessed of God. In Isaac's case, however, his prosperity did result from the blessing of God.

But unto every one of us is given grace according to the measure of the gift of Christ (Eph. 4:7).

BLESSING AND PRESENCE
GENESIS 26:14–16

Many people confuse the blessing of the Lord with the presence of the Lord. How often we measure a person or his work by the outward appearance, rather than seeking to understand the inner essence of the person himself. "The LORD seeth not as man seeth; for man looketh on the outward appearance, but the LORD looketh on the heart" (1 Sam. 16:7). John 7:24 reminds us: "Judge not according to the appearance, but judge righteous judgment."

It is possible for a man to become very great and have many possessions and yet not have the full joy of the Lord's presence. Isaac was such a man.

In Genesis 26:3, when God told Isaac, "I will be with thee, and will bless thee," this was the same as saying, "I will never leave thee, nor forsake thee" (Heb. 13:5). This was the presence of God. Many times we are more concerned about the blessings of God than we are about the presence of God.

Where do you stand in your relationship with the Lord? People often say, "God is good to me," by which they mean that they have experienced good health or prosperity. What a person possesses is not always a safe measure of his dedication to the Lord.

My presence shall go with thee, and I will give thee rest (Ex. 33:14).

HEADING HOME
GENESIS 26:17–20

After Abimelech's command, the Bible says that "Isaac departed thence, and pitched his tent in the valley of Gerar, and dwelt there" (Gen. 26:17). Isaac left Abimelech, but he did not go very far. The Bible again refers to Isaac's digging wells when it says, "Isaac digged again the wells of water, which they had digged in the days of Abraham his father; for the Philistines had stopped them after the death of Abraham: and he called their names after the names by which his father had called them" (v. 18).

Isaac had to redig the wells his father had dug, but even this was used of God because the trouble that came to Isaac kept forcing him to move closer to his home and to the place of the altar. At Gerar, he was only partway home and had pitched his tent where he should not have done so.

Isaac was a weakling in this respect, but probably no weaker than most of us. Perhaps God has been speaking to you and you wonder why you have troubles. Maybe you have suffered a financial loss and you find it very difficult to understand. Is God speaking to you in an effort to bring you back to Himself? You need to face these matters squarely and be honest with God as He deals with you.

Before I was afflicted I went astray: but now have I kept thy word (Ps. 119:67).

NOT INSISTING ON RIGHTS
GENESIS 26:21–22

Isaac sought for satisfaction without a complete return, so he dug wells. However, there could be no real spiritual satisfaction until he completely returned to the Lord. God was forcing Isaac back to his homeland by permitting the Philistines to close up the wells he reopened. However, even in this, Isaac showed a very lovely trait in his life. He did not insist on his own rights. He simply moved to another place. First Peter 2:19–20 says, "For this is thankworthy, if a man for conscience toward God endure grief, suffering wrongfully. For what glory is it, if, when ye be buffeted for your faults, ye shall take it patiently? but if, when ye do well, and suffer for it, ye take it patiently, this is acceptable with God." The Philistines were treating Isaac wrongfully, but he did not insist on his own rights.

God rewarded Isaac for not insisting on his own rights. God patiently worked with Isaac until He had him in the place He desired him to be.

In 1 Peter 3:8–9 believers are exhorted: "Be ye all of one mind, having compassion one of another, love as brethren, be pitiful, be courteous: not rendering evil for evil, or railing for railing: but contrariwise blessing." That is, we are to do good toward those who do us evil. God richly blesses the Christian who does this.

Humble yourselves in the sight of the Lord, and he shall lift you up (James 4:10).

RESTORED FELLOWSHIP

GENESIS 26:23–24

After Isaac dug the well at Rehoboth, the Bible says that "he went up from thence to Beersheba" (Gen. 26:23). The name "Beersheba" means "the well of the oath [covenant]." Isaac's father, Abraham, had earlier made a covenant with Abimelech and gave him seven ewe lambs as a witness that he had dug the well (21:28–31). Isaac made things right with the Lord at this well of the covenant—he had had enough of the wrangling of the world. Isaac went back to his life of the altar.

How long does it take us to get back to the altar after we have backslidden? When we have left the place of fellowship with God, we need to return to the first works as Christ told the Church of Ephesus: "Remember therefore from whence thou art fallen, and repent, and do the first works; or else I will come unto thee quickly, and will remove thy candlestick out of his place, except thou repent" (Rev. 2:5). Let us not fool ourselves when we are out of fellowship with God. Our need is to return to fellowship with God, and the way back is Calvary itself. The Word of God promises that "if we confess our sins, he is faithful and just to forgive us our sins, and to cleanse us from all unrighteousness" (1 John 1:9).

If we confess our sins, he is faithful and just to forgive us our sins, and to cleanse us from all unrighteousness (1 John 1:9).

THREE ABSOLUTES
GENESIS 26:25; ROMANS 12:1–2

If we want the power of God in our lives, we must observe the absolutes of God. There are three absolutes in particular that we must heed in order to have spiritual power. First, we must recognize that all power belongs to God. In this age, it is God the Holy Spirit who is responsible to direct the work of God. Thus, we must recognize the sovereignty of the Holy Spirit to direct all spiritual work.

Second, we must recognize the sovereignty of the Holy Spirit in delegating this power to anyone He chooses. It is the Holy Spirit's responsibility to give spiritual gifts to people as He desires so the work of God will be carried out.

The third absolute we must recognize in order to have spiritual power in our lives is that of absolute commitment to the Holy Spirit.

Just as Isaac had to go back to the place God intended him to be, present-day believers must live according to the absolutes of God and be in the place He wants them to be if they are to have spiritual power. Notice particularly that when Isaac returned to the place where God wanted him, he built an altar and called on the name of the Lord. He experienced the joy of God's presence and immediate progress took place in his spiritual life. He dug a well, and no one bothered him as they had earlier.

But the manifestation of the Spirit is given to every man to profit withal (1 Cor. 12:7).

IN THE WORLD BUT NOT OF IT
GENESIS 26:26–29; 2 CORINTHIANS 6:14–18

As long as Isaac lived in Gerar, there was nothing but strife and contention. He was mixing with the people even though he was not one of them. In witnessing there is no greater mistake than to imagine we can be one with the world and still be an influence for Christ. This cannot be done. For any who doubt, they need only to study the life of Lot. He learned the hard way that he could not be one with the world and also have a spiritual impact on the world.

The believer is to be in the world, but he is not to be of the world. When Jesus prayed to the Heavenly Father concerning His followers, He said, "I pray not that thou shouldest take them out of the world, but that thou shouldest keep them from the evil [one]" (John 17:15). Then He said, "As thou hast sent me into the world, even so have I also sent them into the world" (v. 18). We are in the world, but we are not of the world.

The moment Isaac took his stand in separation from unbelievers, they immediately saw God's blessing on him and they sought him out to make a covenant with him. In order for believers to affect the stubborn hearts of the unsaved, the believers must first be right with God.

Love not the world, neither the things that are in the world. If any man love the world, the love of the Father is not in him (1 John 2:15).

GOD EXALTS THE TOTALLY COMMITTED

GENESIS 26:30–33

When we are abused by the unbelieving world, we need to remember the words of Psalm 37:5–6: "Commit thy way unto the LORD; trust also in him; and he shall bring it to pass. And he shall bring forth thy righteousness as the light, and thy judgment as the noonday." God will vindicate us if we are totally committed to Him and trust Him for everything. Our need is to entrust ourselves completely to Him by committing all of our ways to Him.

Because Isaac dared to live the separated life, God poured out His blessing on him. Isaac was not offensive to the unbelievers, but he did that which was right in the sight of God. As a result, God blessed Isaac, and the well his servants had dug produced water.

I urge you to seriously consider the benefits of not insisting on your own rights. As a believer, you have friends and neighbors who are closely watching you. Are you the quarrelsome type who is driving them farther from the Lord? Even if they are saying things about you that are not true, why not suffer for the Lord's sake? Do not try to reach them by compromising your standards, but rather live a life that is separated unto God, and He will mightily use you in reaching others for Christ.

Humble yourselves therefore under the mighty hand of God, that he may exalt you in due time (1 Pet. 5:6).

THE EFFECTS OF SELFISHNESS
GENESIS 27:30–37

Isaac is suddenly awakened to his failure to heed God's plan. When Isaac learned that the last son to appear to him was actually Esau, he "trembled very exceedingly, and said, Who? where is he that hath taken venison, and brought it me, and I have eaten of all before thou camest, and have blessed him? yea, and he shall be blessed" (Gen. 27:33).

The key to Isaac's faith is that after he realized what he had done, he emphasized that the blessing would remain Jacob's—"and he shall be blessed." Although we can never thwart God's plan, we can reap bitter results by sowing to the flesh. God's Word says that "he that soweth to his flesh shall of the flesh reap corruption" (Gal. 6:8).

Although Isaac did not upset the plan of God, he reaped serious results from what he had sown. Jacob had to flee from home as a result of his conniving. Rebekah never saw Jacob again because she died before he returned. Even though Isaac lived another 43 years after the incident of the blessing, nothing else is recorded about him except his death. After sending Jacob away, Isaac disappeared from the biblical scene. About 30 years later Jacob saw his father again, but his mother had already died. The entire family was affected because they had sown to the flesh. They had sought their selfish desires rather than seeking to please God.

In the last days perilous times shall come. For men shall be lovers of their own selves (2 Tim. 3:1–2).

THE BLESSING OF DIFFICULTIES
GENESIS 35:28,29

In review of Isaac's life of 180 years, there are some special lessons we should learn. It was not easy for Isaac to follow in the footsteps of his great father. In a sense, Isaac's life was made too easy because he occupied his father's position without having had his father's experiences. He passed into his inheritance without having passed through the various means of discipline that Abraham experienced.

There is the expression "practice makes perfect." In an even more real sense it can be said "experience makes perfect." The suffering we experience in our lives brings about personal discipline. Jeremiah wrote: "It is good for a man that he bear the yoke in his youth" (Lam. 3:27).

Our youth today are experiencing what Isaac experienced. They find themselves living in an advanced age with advanced positions in life without having passed through the experiences of those who made these things possible. Although the younger generation does not need to experience everything we did, some extremely difficult experiences are essential for the kind of maturity God wants to produce. This is the blessing of difficulties!

But we glory in tribulations also: knowing that tribulation worketh patience (Rom. 5:3).

WHEN GOD FORGIVES, HE FORGETS

EXODUS 3:6; PSALM 51:5–10

Even though Isaac lacked the experience for occupying his father's position, God chose to refer to Himself as "the God of Isaac." The common, everyday life of a person is precious to God. Because Isaac had faith in God and walked humbly before Him, God blotted out Isaac's mistakes and weaknesses. Those who walk humbly before God and confess their sins to Him are promised: "I will be merciful to their unrighteousness, and their sins and their iniquities will I remember no more" (Heb. 8:12).

When God forgives, He forgets. This was seen in Isaac's case, for when God referred to him in the New Testament, He did not mention his weaknesses—only his faith. Isaac's great mistake of seeking to pass the blessing on to Esau rather than to Jacob is completely passed by in the New Testament. That sin had been covered over and removed through Christ's shed blood for the sins of the world.

God will also do the same for you. His Word promises: "If we confess our sins, he is faithful and just to forgive us our sins, and to cleanse us from all unrighteousness" (1 John 1:9).

I, even I, am he that blotteth out thy transgressions for mine own sake, and will not remember thy sins (Isa. 43:25).

 **FEBRUARY 29**

MEEKNESS: STRENGTH UNDER CONTROL

NUMBERS 12:3; GALATIANS 5:22–23; COLOSSIANS 3:12

In reviewing Isaac's life, we should also take special note of his spirit of meekness. All through his life his temperament was of a passive nature rather than of an active or aggressive nature. In childhood he was subjected to the insults of Ishmael, but there is no record that he became angry about them. As a young man he was taken to Mount Moriah to be offered as a sacrifice, and in meekness he surrendered and made himself available. He did not even choose his own wife, as she was chosen for him through his father's arrangements and the leading of the Holy Spirit. Isaac also accepted the rebuke of Abimelech in meekness. There were no reprisals. He and his men yielded whenever they were wrongly driven away from the wells they had redug. Isaac's meek spirit brought forth praise from even his enemies. They testified concerning his great power and might and their realization that the Lord was with him.

The world thinks little of meekness, yet it is the fruit of the Holy Spirit (Gal. 5:23). The apostle Paul urged all Christians, "Let your moderation be known unto all men. The Lord is at hand" (Phil. 4:5).

Meekness involves the self-sacrifice of our own desires and interests. Because Isaac gladly gave up his own personal desires, it pleased God to refer to Himself as "the God of Isaac."

For thus saith the Lord GOD,... In quietness and in confidence shall be your strength (Isa. 30:15).

MARCH

Abraham had an obedient faith, Isaac had a passive faith, and Jacob (the subject for March) had a restless faith. Not every believer needs to be a pioneer of faith as Abraham was, but neither should everyone be like Jacob, a man with a restless spirit who was never securely anchored in God until he was crippled at Peniel. God dealt with Jacob in an entirely different manner than with Abraham and Isaac because Jacob was an entirely different kind of person. The greatest aspect of Jacob's life is that he was a man who believed God. Nevertheless, he was a man of restless activity because he had a restless faith.

When God finds obedient faith (as in Abraham's life), He leads forward quickly. Where there is passive faith (as in Isaac's life), God comforts and strengthens. But where there is restless faith (as in Jacob's life), God checks and corrects toward the ultimate realization of His goal.

The readings for March are excerpted from *The God of Jacob*.

FLESH AND SPIRIT IN CONFLICT
GALATIANS 6:16–23

Jacob and Esau were the sons of Isaac and Rebekah. These two sons represent the conflict of the flesh and the Spirit.

Esau represents that which is natural, whereas Jacob represents that which is spiritual. The conflict between the natural and the spiritual is present in every believer's heart. It is the conflict of the two natures. The Scriptures say, "The flesh lusteth against the Spirit, and the Spirit against the flesh: and these are contrary the one to the other: so that ye cannot do the things that ye would" (Gal. 5:17). However, believers are encouraged to realize that, because of the greatness of God, the Spirit will ultimately triumph and the flesh will be brought into subjection.

In Esau we see the profane nature that despises the riches and promises of God. In Jacob we see the desire for that which is godly, even though he used fleshly (carnal) methods to attain the benefit of the promises.

Jacob's life was one of conflict. In him we see the conflict between the flesh and the Spirit. This is the key to understanding his life. Jacob's life strikingly exhibits the power of the old nature, but it also exhibits the power of God's love and grace. In Jacob we see the utter worthlessness and depravity of the human nature, but we also see the deepest instruction as to God's purpose and infinite grace.

If we live in the Spirit, let us also walk in the Spirit (Gal. 5:25).

TWO CHILDREN BECOME TWO NATIONS

GENESIS 25:21–26

Jacob was a miracle child. Abraham and Sarah had waited 25 years for Isaac to be born, and Isaac and Rebekah waited 20 years for the birth of Jacob. Genesis 25:21–22 says, "Isaac intreated the LORD for his wife, because she was barren: and the LORD was intreated of him, and Rebekah his wife conceived. And the children struggled together within her; and she said, If it be so, why am I thus? And she went to enquire of the LORD." Rebekah did not know she was going to give birth to twins, and she could not understand what the trouble was. God allowed this to happen to her so He could reveal His plan for the children she would bear.

God explained to Rebekah, "Two nations are in thy womb, and two manner of people shall be separated from thy bowels; and the one people shall be stronger than the other people; and the elder shall serve the younger" (v. 23).

Those nations would be in conflict, just as the two babies were in conflict in her womb. Because the firstborn was hairy, he was called "Esau," which means "hairy." The second son was named "Jacob," which means "supplanter." When Jacob came out of the womb, he took hold of Esau's heel. This was symbolic of his life, for Jacob went through life taking advantage of others—tripping them up so he could get ahead.

If a man say, I love God, and hateth his brother, he is a liar: for he that loveth not his brother whom he hath seen, how can he love God whom he hath not seen? (1 John 4:20).

RUNNING AHEAD OF GOD
GENESIS 25:27–34

Jacob had been waiting for an opportunity to get the birthright from Esau. Jacob could have rightfully expected the birthright since God had promised that the elder would serve the younger, but Jacob's methods of obtaining it were entirely wrong. Jacob sought the right thing in the wrong way. Using carnal methods to attain spiritual goals is never acceptable to God. Jacob felt that the end justified the means.

In this incident we see the value of waiting for God. The birthright was Jacob's by God's determinate will, and, in due time, He would have given it to Jacob. Although Jacob connived to get the birthright, it was 30 years later before he actually benefited from it. Jacob knew the importance of believing God, but he did not know the importance of waiting on God.

We also need to learn the discipline of patiently waiting on God to fulfill His will in His own time. God's Word says, "Cast not away therefore your confidence, which hath great recompence of reward. For ye have need of patience, that, after ye have done the will of God, ye might receive the promise" (Heb. 10:35–36).

And he gave them their request; but sent leanness into their soul (Ps. 106:15).

DESPISING GOD'S PROVISIONS
GENESIS 25:34; HEBREWS 12:14–17

After Esau had sold the birthright to Jacob and had finished eating and drinking, he "rose up, and went his way: thus Esau despised his birthright" (Gen. 25:34). The word "despise" means "to look down on with contempt or aversion." It also means "to regard as negligible, worthless or distasteful."

The Scriptures refer to others besides Esau who despised God's provisions for them. The Israelites were promised the land of Canaan, but God's Word says, "Yea, they despised the pleasant land, they believed not his word: but murmured in their tents, and hearkened not unto the voice of the LORD. Therefore he lifted up his hand against them, to overthrow them in the wilderness" (Ps. 106:24–26). The Israelites were more concerned about the things of the flesh than about the things of the Spirit.

What are you doing with the privileges you have as a result of being united with Christ? Do you regard as nothing and treat with contempt the blessings you have because you are a joint-heir with Christ? Part of the responsibility of this birthright is our ministry—taking the Gospel to all the world. It is our responsibility because we are in Christ—it is not an optional ministry.

Or despisest thou the riches of his goodness and forbearance and longsuffering; not knowing that the goodness of God leadeth thee to repentance? (Rom. 2:4).

IMPATIENT TO WAIT ON GOD
GENESIS 27:1–17

One faithless act leads to another. Having schemed to secure the birthright, Jacob deceived his father in order to secure the blessing, which was a vital part of the birthright. Jacob needed not only the birthright from Esau but also the blessing from his father. One was of no value without the other.

Although Esau was the favorite son of his father, Jacob was the favorite son of his mother. Isaac was making plans to pass the blessing on to his favorite son, but Rebekah was not about to have Jacob left out—especially since God had indicated the blessing was to be Jacob's. Rebekah devised a counterplot.

Rebekah's sin was that she lacked faith in God's ability. She felt she had to help God accomplish His will. While the intended goal was legitimate, the means she used to accomplish it were not honoring to God. She thought God must be frustrated concerning His plan and, therefore, needed her help.

Some people say, "The Lord helps those who help themselves." This is not true. The truth is that God helps those who come to the end of themselves. What we need is patience to wait on God. He is able to do everything He has said He will do, and He will always do it on time.

Wait on the LORD, and keep his way, and he shall exalt thee to inherit the land (Ps. 37:34).

DECEIVED BY A KISS

GENESIS 27:18–29

One lie always leads to another lie. Jacob kept adding sins to his previous ones. First, he impersonated his brother. Second, he lied to his father when he said, "I am Esau." Finally, he even went so far as to bring the name of the Lord into his deceit, for he said, "Because the LORD thy God brought it to me" (Gen. 27:20). Jacob most probably did not anticipate all of his father's questions; therefore, he had to have quick answers, which caused him to get into deeper and deeper trouble with his lies.

Jacob must have thought the scheme had worked. No doubt Rebekah was carefully listening to what was going on and also thought the plan had worked! The flesh prides itself on its achievements. But there were to be many sad results from the works of the flesh.

A kiss was part of Jacob's deception of Isaac, even as a kiss was part of Judas's betrayal of Christ. Isaac was deceived, and he pronounced the blessing on Jacob, but it was a long time before the blessing was fulfilled in Jacob's life. Because he had to reap what he had sown before he was ready to receive the benefits, 30 years passed before Jacob realized the benefits of the blessing.

How much we blame the Lord for things that are nothing but acts of the flesh—the reaping of what we have sown. How tragic it is when we blame the Lord for the works of the flesh.

He that worketh deceit shall not dwell within my house: he that telleth lies shall not tarry in my sight (Ps. 101:7).

BAD ATTITUDE BRINGS SPIRITUAL LOSS
GENESIS 27:30–40

Esau was bitter toward his brother because he had taken advantage of him twice. Desperate to have something, Esau asked his father, "Hast thou not reserved a blessing for me?" (Gen. 27:36). Isaac answered, "Behold, I have made him thy lord, and all his brethren have I given to him for servants; and with corn and wine have I sustained him: and what shall I do now unto thee, my son?" (v. 37).

Esau became more desperate and said to his father, "Hast thou but one blessing, my father? bless me, even me also, O my father. And Esau lifted up his voice, and wept" (v. 38). Esau did not weep because he was concerned about spiritual values, but because he could not change his father's mind. Hebrews 12:17 says of Esau, "For ye know how that afterward, when he would have inherited the blessing, he was rejected: for he found no place of repentance, though he sought it [the blessing] carefully with tears." Esau was not repenting of his sin. He was trying to get his father to repent, or change his mind, of having given the blessing to Jacob.

Esau was as much to blame for the loss of the birthright as Jacob was in securing it through deceit and cleverness. Had it not been for Esau's attitude toward his birthright, it would not have been as easy for Jacob to take it from him. Let us be careful about our attitude toward spiritual truths.

Looking diligently lest any man fail of the grace of God; lest any root of bitterness springing up trouble you, and thereby many be defiled (Heb. 12:15).

SOWING AND REAPING
GENESIS 27:41–46

Rebekah urged Jacob to flee to her brother and stay there until Esau forgot about the stolen blessing. Notice that Rebekah said to Jacob, "That which thou hast done to him" (Gen. 27:45). Jacob was guilty of stealing the blessing from Esau, but Rebekah had devised the plan. Rebekah schemed again and decided it would be best for Jacob to go to her brother's home to live until Esau forgot about his plot against Jacob.

Rebekah did not expect that Jacob would have to stay long with Laban, for she instructed Jacob, "Tarry with him a few days, until thy brother's fury turn away" (v. 44). Esau was apparently very temperamental, and Rebekah assumed that, even though he was so angry at the time, he would soon forget about the entire matter. Assuming that Esau would soon forget, Rebekah told Jacob, "Then I will send, and fetch thee from thence" (v. 45).

Rebekah did not realize all the sorrow that was to be reaped because of what she and Jacob had sown. After she sent Jacob away, she never saw him again. She died before he was able to return. Rebekah did not realize all the calamity that would come on her because of her disobedience to God. Like Rebekah, we sometimes think we can escape reaping what we have sown—but we may be sure that our sins will find us out.

Be not deceived; God is not mocked: for whatsoever a man soweth, that shall he also reap (Gal. 6:7).

BRINGING OUT THE BEST
GENESIS 28:1–5

After Rebekah's plea to Isaac that Jacob not be allowed to marry a Hittite woman, Jacob was sent away with Isaac's blessing. Isaac probably did not know that Esau had sworn to kill Jacob after Isaac's death. However, Isaac lived several years after this time, and nothing ever came of Esau's treacherous plot.

Rebekah and Isaac had one plan for Jacob, but God had quite another. God's ways are higher than our ways. While people are prone to point out another person's failures, God is concerned about bringing out what is best in him. God is able to discern the true yearning of the heart and to bring about its realization. Basically, Jacob's desires were for the things of God—he wanted spiritual blessing. God knew this, and He worked to bring out the best in Jacob, even though Jacob often ran ahead and used carnal methods to attain spiritual blessing.

Having blessed him, "Isaac sent away Jacob: and he went to Padanaram unto Laban, son of Bethuel the Syrian, the brother of Rebekah, Jacob's and Esau's mother" (Gen. 28:5). Jacob had some great surprises in store for him. While he believed God and had a deep-seated faith, he knew little about the ways of God for his life. Jacob had a restless faith, and it was very difficult for him to wait on God to work out His will.

Delight thyself also in the LORD: and he shall give thee the desires of thine heart (Ps. 37:4).

GOD KNOWS US THOROUGHLY
GENESIS 28:10–17

As Jacob lay under the stars while away from home that first night, he was alone with his own thoughts. No doubt he reflected on all that had happened. Perhaps he asked himself, *Was it really worthwhile? Will I ever return to claim the birthright and blessing for which I schemed and that I successfully obtained?*

This seems to be when Jacob experienced true conversion. One can know truth about God, as Jacob knew the truth, but not be identified with it. I, too, was reared in a godly home and knew much truth about God. I had learned the catechism and had been baptized, but it was not until five years later that I understood the truth of regeneration and received Christ as my Saviour.

Jacob suddenly realized that God knew all about him. God knew about his meanness, crookedness and scheming. But God also knew that deep within his heart he was longing for spiritual realities; therefore, He undertook to mold Jacob's life to the praise of His glory.

God knew every detail about Jacob's life, and He knows every detail about your life. He knows the good things, and He knows the ugly things. He knows when you are putting on a front—acting like you are something that you are really not. He knows whether or not you are genuine—how much of what you say is really the truth.

Neither is there any creature that is not manifest in his sight: but all things are naked and opened unto the eyes of him with whom we have to do (Heb. 4:13).

NOTHING BY CHANCE
GENESIS 29:1–12

His experiences at Bethel began a new life for Jacob. After he had established a memorial to God, "Jacob went on his journey, and came into the land of the people of the east" (Gen. 29:1). The phrase "Jacob went on his journey" is literally "Jacob lifted up his feet." Jacob probably traveled quickly—as if walking on clouds.

Remember the day you received Christ as Saviour? Or the day when you met God in a special way? Perhaps you made a great decision or had a great victory. Didn't it seem as if you were walking on a cloud? No doubt that is how Jacob felt with his new outlook. The revelation of God's presence and the assurance of blessing brought light and encouragement to his heart.

Jacob came to a well where some men were watering sheep. When he asked if they knew Laban, they replied that they did. They assured him that Laban was well and said, "Behold, Rachel his daughter cometh with the sheep" (v. 6). What a unique meeting! God had promised Jacob He would be with him, and this meeting with Rachel was not by chance or accident. This is the way God also works in our lives. We may go a certain direction, but we never get out of God's sight. All that happened to Jacob was by divine appointment—there is no such thing as chance as far as God is concerned.

Being predestinated according to the purpose of him who worketh all things after the counsel of his own will (Eph. 1:11).

GOD TEACHES US THROUGH OTHERS
GENESIS 29:13–15

Laban invited Jacob to stay with him, and thus began 20 years of grueling discipline that eventually led to Jacob's complete transformation. Jacob had experienced an inner spiritual change, but his outward life also needed to be transformed. During the 20 years, God subjected Jacob to hard discipline so that He could make him a worthy instrument. His life reminds us of Proverbs 13:15: "The way of transgressors is hard." In Jacob's life we also see the truth of Galatians 6:7: "Be not deceived; God is not mocked: for whatsoever a man soweth, that shall he also reap."

God purposed to train Jacob by having him live with Laban. These men were similar in many ways, but there was also a great difference between them. Jacob believed in God, whereas Laban apparently did not, as evidenced by the fact that we are later told of his idols. However, God did not allow Laban to bring harm to Jacob. Laban would have sent Jacob away with nothing, but God was in control of the situation, and He saw to it that Jacob received proper payment for his diligent work. Jacob must have been a hard worker, and God even blessed Laban because of Jacob. God wanted Jacob to have plenty, and He allowed Laban to have plenty also. When God undertakes for us, He always does the right thing.

Iron sharpeneth iron; so a man sharpeneth the countenance of his friend (Prov. 27:17).

THE COST OF REFUSING TO WAIT
GENESIS 29:16–28

Earlier, Jacob had not respected the rights of the firstborn, for he had schemed to get the birthright and the blessing away from Esau. Now, because of Laban's deceit, Jacob had to submit to the rights of the firstborn. By being required to marry Leah, the firstborn, before he could marry Rachel, Jacob learned his lesson the hard way.

Jacob also learned the lesson about waiting on God. He had refused to wait on God's fulfillment of His promise that "the elder shall serve the younger" (Gen. 25:23). Because he refused to wait for God to fulfill this promise in His own time, Jacob had to leave home to save his life. Because Jacob had such difficulty waiting on God, He taught him, through the incident with Leah and Rachel, the importance of waiting. He had to wait seven years for Rachel, and this in itself taught him many lessons in waiting. Although he most likely married Rachel a week after he married Leah, he still had to work another seven years for Rachel before he could receive any wages for himself—14 years of waiting before he began to accumulate possessions for himself. God has ways of teaching people how to wait.

They that wait upon the LORD shall renew their strength; they shall mount up with wings as eagles; they shall run, and not be weary; and they shall walk, and not faint (Isa. 40:31).

GOD FORGIVES THE ONE WHO REPENTS

GENESIS 30:25–33

When Laban told Jacob to name his wages, this gave Jacob another opportunity to scheme and gain more blessings by deceit. Although Jacob schemed and plotted, God did not let him out of His sight—and even continued to bless him. How marvelous was God's patience with His unworthy servant! God must have seen much in Jacob because of all the years He spent in disciplining him, leading him, overruling his mistakes and forgiving his sins.

When God was finally through with Jacob and had forgiven all of his sins, it is said of God, "He hath not beheld iniquity in Jacob, neither hath he seen perverseness in Israel: the LORD his God is with him, and the shout of a king is among them" (Num. 23:21). Consider the grace of God that is revealed in this statement: "He hath not beheld iniquity in Jacob." The verse does not say that Jacob did not sin, but God had forgiven it all and had blotted it from His mind.

What a marvelous God we have! Take time to examine your heart before God and confess any sin that is in your life. God has promised to forgive our sins when we confess them to Him (1 John 1:9). Clear the record with God so that there is no unconfessed sin in your life. Because Christ shed His blood to pay the penalty for sin, it is possible for God to blot out your sin.

He that covereth his sins shall not prosper: but whoso confesseth and forsaketh them shall have mercy (Prov. 28:13).

GOD KNOWS THE HEART
GENESIS 31:1–7

After God had made it clear to Jacob that He wanted him to leave Haran for Canaan, Jacob talked with his family. The Word of God says that "Jacob sent and called Rachel and Leah to the field unto his flock" (Gen. 31:4). He called them to a place where he could talk to them without being overheard. He had a scheme.

Having been cheated by Laban, Jacob learned by experience the kind of person he himself was and how his behavior had affected others. God uses this kind of lesson to teach us also. Perhaps we have been guilty of speaking against someone and have not realized how it may have hurt them. Then when someone speaks against us, we suddenly realize how deeply such words hurt, and we become sensitive to what we have done.

If you have been mistreated, cheated or deceived and if your heart has been right all along, be assured that God knows this. God will eventually vindicate you, but in the meantime you should be confidently aware that God knows the truth concerning what has happened to you. He knows if your heart has been right.

Search me, O God, and know my heart: try me, and know my thoughts (Ps. 139:23).

A COVENANT OF SEPARATION
GENESIS 31:43–49

This passage of Scripture is often used as a covenant of fellowship or a benediction. However, the context clearly indicates that it was not a covenant of fellowship but a covenant of separation. Laban said to Jacob, "This heap be witness, and this pillar be witness, that I will not pass over this heap to thee, and that thou shalt not pass over this heap and this pillar unto me, for harm" (Gen. 31:52).

This was the end result when two powerful schemers clashed with each other. They could not trust each other, so they had to make a covenant and set up a pillar of stones to mark the spot over which neither of them would cross for the purpose of harming the other. Each was really saying, "I cannot trust you out of my sight. The Lord must watch between us if we and our goods are to be safe from each other." Visiting between the families was not prohibited, but Jacob and Laban agreed never to cross the line for the purpose of harming the other.

How sad it is when there is deep-seated conflict between two individuals. May we live Christlike lives so we will not need to take such measures against our fellowman.

If it be possible, as much as lieth in you, live peaceably with all men (Rom. 12:18).

AT THE END OF SELF

GENESIS 32:1–8

As Jacob prepared to meet Esau, it was evident that he still had not grasped what it meant to really live by faith in God. Jacob still projected his own plans—he sent messengers to Esau and told them what to say: "Thus shall ye speak unto my lord Esau" (Gen. 32:4). How interesting that Jacob used the word "lord" in referring to Esau. After 20 years with Laban, Jacob had a different language. Before he had fled from his home, Jacob had lorded it over Esau and had taken away his birthright and blessing. But he now recognized Esau as lord.

Jacob told his messengers to tell Esau, "I have sent to tell my lord, that I may find grace in thy sight" (v. 5). They reported, "We came to thy brother Esau, and also he cometh to meet thee, and four hundred men with him" (v. 6). Time had only intensified the hatred. Esau must have strutted with pride when he went to show his great power to Jacob. He had been beaten by Jacob's cunning, but he would let Jacob know that he now had the power to humble him. Esau's attitude was "I'll show him who's the better of us."

Jacob was in real trouble. What was he going to do? How often God has to bring us up against a wall of calamity before He can truly deal with our souls.

I have heard of thee by the hearing of the ear: but now mine eye seeth thee. Wherefore I abhor myself, and repent in dust and ashes (Job 42:5–6).

PRAYING WITH PROPER MOTIVES
GENESIS 32:9–12

Because of Jacob's imperfect faith, he offered a prayer of panic and then resorted to his carnal planning. In fact, Jacob began to plan even before he prayed. He took time out of his planning to pray, then immediately returned to his own schemes. He didn't seem to really trust God but only asked God to sanctify his plans.

As Jacob prayed, he said, "Deliver me, I pray thee, from the hand of my brother, from the hand of Esau: for I fear him, lest he will come and smite me, and the mother with the children" (Gen. 32:11). What was the motive for Jacob's petition? At first, it might seem selfish, but verse 12 indicates that Jacob was seeking the glory of God. Jacob was claiming God's promises when he said, "And thou saidst, I will surely do thee good, and make thy seed as the sand of the sea, which cannot be numbered for multitude."

We also need to check our motives when we are praying for the salvation of our loved ones. Are we praying for them only because they are loved ones, or are we truly concerned about the glory of God? Our chief concern should always be the glory of God. Whatever we do, we should "do all to the glory of God" (1 Cor. 10:31).

Jacob still had fear, but it was an unnecessary fear. God had promised to bring him back to the land and to make his descendants as the sand of the sea.

You ask and do not receive, because you ask with wrong motives, so that you may spend it on your pleasures (James 4:3, NASB).

GOD'S PLAN OR OURS?
GENESIS 32:13–21

Genesis 32:13 tells how Jacob returned to his scheming immediately after praying: "And he lodged there that same night; and took of that which came to his hand a present for Esau his brother." Instead of trusting in God alone, Jacob plotted how he could appease Esau by giving of his possessions. Jacob substituted appeasement for deception. This perhaps shows some improvement, but his motives were still fleshly and debased in view of all the promises God had given him.

Because Jacob did not trust the Lord as he should have, he continued to carry the burden himself. Jacob leaned on his own plan more than on God's sure word of promise. This is a vivid illustration of the works of the flesh. The flesh is always in conflict with the Spirit. Galatians 5:17 says, "For the flesh lusteth against the Spirit, and the Spirit against the flesh: and these are contrary the one to the other: so that ye cannot do the things that ye would."

When we are in the habit of thinking that we provide for ourselves, it is hard to trust God completely. We feel that somehow we have to help God if our needs are to be met. Instead of fitting into God's plan, we expect Him to bless our plans.

For thou art my rock and my fortress; therefore for thy name's sake lead me, and guide me (Ps. 31:3).

ALONE WITH GOD
GENESIS 32:22–26

Some battles must be fought alone. There are times when no one can help us. This was just such a time in Jacob's life. Jacob's trouble was himself—his self-will, self-purpose, self-defense, self-desire and self-righteousness. Jacob's self-life had to be dealt with, and God chose to do so while Jacob was alone.

Jacob needed to learn that even though he was weak physically, he could be strong spiritually. It took more than spiritual wrestling to convince Jacob of his need. God had been dealing with him spiritually for more than 20 years, but Jacob had failed to learn. God now struggled with Jacob physically because it was something Jacob could comprehend. Jacob's spiritual level of discernment was not mature enough for God to deal with him on a spiritual basis alone.

Sometimes God also has to deal with us on a physical level because this is the only thing that some of us really understand. It may involve the loss of wealth, health or family, but whatever it is, the loss is intended to draw us closer to the Lord. If we cannot be led spiritually, the Lord will communicate with us in a language we can understand. Let us become so sensitive to the Lord's leading that He will be able to deal with us purely on a spiritual basis.

But thou, when thou prayest, enter into thy closet, and when thou hast shut thy door, pray to thy Father which is in secret; and thy Father which seeth in secret shall reward thee openly (Matt. 6:6).

IS ALL ON THE ALTAR?

GENESIS 32:27–32

The first key to God's victory in Jacob's life is that Jacob was left alone with God. The second key is that Jacob had to be brought to the end of himself. His own strength had to be broken. He had come to the end of his own resources. All confidence in his flesh had to be brought to an end, and this was done when his opponent crippled him. Then he realized his utter weakness.

Jacob could no longer fight his brother, Esau, in his own strength, for his thigh was dislocated. Four hundred men were coming with Esau, and Jacob was completely powerless to do anything. Previously, he had resisted relying completely on the Lord, but now he had to because of his helplessness. He had to depend on God.

What all must God do to us to bring us to the end of ourselves? What must He do to us individually, organizationally, nationally and internationally to bring us to the end of ourselves? We struggle, strive, fight and resist, but we must realize that surrender to God is the only answer.

I beseech you therefore, brethren, by the mercies of God, that ye present your bodies a living sacrifice, holy, acceptable unto God, which is your reasonable service (Rom. 12:1)

FEAR FOLLOWS GREAT EXPERIENCE
GENESIS 33:1–11

Jacob had just experienced a wonderful night with God that resulted in his becoming the new man, Israel. But when he saw the danger—Esau and his 400 men—fear gripped his heart.

Great experiences do not guarantee constant faithfulness. Jacob's experience at Peniel was a stepping stone to greater living, but it did not guarantee faithfulness on his part. He had made significant progress during his 20 years with Laban, but he was not yet all that God intended him to be. Even Paul wrote: "Brethren, I count not myself to have apprehended: but this one thing I do, forgetting those things which are behind, and reaching forth unto those things which are before, I press toward the mark for the prize of the high calling of God in Christ Jesus" (Phil. 3:13–14).

Experiences that result from crises are like open doors that make it possible for us to enter a new aspect of our Christian walk. Thus, Jesus said, "If any man will come after me, let him deny himself, and take up his cross daily, and follow me" (Luke 9:23). We are to daily take our position in Christ and follow Him. Galatians 5:16 assures us that when we walk in the Spirit, we will not fulfill the lust of the flesh. When we commit ourselves to following Him, the Holy Spirit controls our lives, and God lives His life through us.

Wherefore let him that thinketh he standeth take heed lest he fall (1 Cor. 10:12).

TOO TIMID TO TESTIFY
GENESIS 33:12–20

When Jacob and Esau met, Esau said, "Let us take our journey, and let us go, and I will go before thee" (Gen. 33:12). Esau offered to protect Jacob and those with him. Esau could easily have done this because 400 men were with him.

God had clearly instructed Jacob that he was to return to his father and to Bethel. Jacob knew this, but he failed to tell Esau he was following God's plan. Instead, Jacob led Esau to believe that he would follow him slowly and meet him in Seir. This was Jacob's second major step in backsliding after Peniel. Because of weakness and fear he lied to Esau. Jacob was afraid of what Esau might do, so he resorted to deceit. He feared Esau's temper more than God's disfavor.

Consider what Esau must have thought later when Jacob did not come as he had said he would. This supposedly spiritual leader lied to his brother because he did not have the courage to tell him he was following God. Words that are not supported by actions turn many people away from the Gospel. This is one reason the present-day church has lost rapport with the world. We are not direct in making our position with God known, and because of half-truths and timidity we are not winning people to the Lord as we should.

For God hath not given us the spirit of fear; but of power, and of love, and of a sound mind (2 Tim. 1:7).

A STEP AT A TIME
GENESIS 34:1–7

After Shechem had defiled Dinah, "his soul clave unto Dinah the daughter of Jacob, and he loved the damsel, and spake kindly unto the damsel. And Shechem spake unto his father Hamor, saying, Get me this damsel to wife" (Gen. 34:3–4). Shechem tried to remedy the situation by offering marriage. Observe that Satan, who brought about the fall of man, suggested a remedy of mixed marriage—a believer with an unbeliever. Verses 8–12 of this chapter tell how Hamor presented the case for further coexistence with Jacob and his people. Hamor said, "Make ye marriages with us, and give your daughters unto us, and take our daughters unto you" (v. 9).

Jacob had not come to this serious situation in one great fall. By a series of steps he had come to this despicable situation. First, he compromised. God had told him to go to Bethel, which involved a separation from the world. Second, he obeyed only partially. Jacob had gone only as far as Shechem—there was not total separation. Third, this situation caused their only daughter to be tempted to investigate the world around her. Fourth, she was defiled by Shechem, the son of Hamor. Fifth, the Hivites offered to intermarry and coexist with Jacob's family. Sixth, all of this led to further sin within Jacob's own family. Which way are our steps leading us?

But every man is tempted, when he is drawn away of his own lust, and enticed. Then when lust hath conceived, it bringeth forth sin: and sin, when it is finished, bringeth forth death (James 1:14–15).

IN SPITE OF SIN, GRACE
GENESIS 34:27–36:3

God allowed Jacob to go to the depths of sin. Worldliness completely overwhelmed him. He could not have gone any lower, and his family could not have gone any lower. Their reputation among the people around them was destroyed. They were guilty of murder because of their desire to right a wrong against their family. Even though Jacob had fallen to the depths of sin, God never stopped working with him. God did not leave Jacob alone until he was back in the center of His will. God commanded him, "Arise, go up to Bethel, and dwell there: and make there an altar unto God, that appeared unto thee when thou fleddest from the face of Esau thy brother" (Gen. 35:1). Even though Jacob often turned his back on God, God was never unfaithful to Jacob.

It is wonderful to know that the God of Jacob is our God also. How long-suffering and merciful God is to His own! With Jeremiah, every believer can say, "It is of the LORD's mercies that we are not consumed, because his compassions fail not. They are new every morning: great is thy faithfulness" (Lam. 3:22–23).

But where sin abounded, grace did much more abound (Rom. 5:20).

BETHEL AT LAST!
GENESIS 35:4–12

God protected Jacob, and he arrived safely at his destination. Bethel at last!

The princeliness of Jacob was restored. God called him Israel instead of Jacob. Ten years earlier, God had changed Jacob's name to Israel, but Jacob had not appropriated his position. From this time forward Jacob did not backslide to his old life of scheming and deception. He applied faith and appropriated the provisions of God. As a result, in Hebrews 11 his name is mentioned in the gallery of people of faith, along with Abraham and Isaac (vv. 17–21).

When Jacob returned to Bethel, his communion and prayer life were reestablished. Genesis 35:13 says, "And God went up from him in the place where he talked with him." After Jacob had made things right in his life, he was able to commune freely with God.

Have you also experienced the spiritual dryness that comes from a lack of communion with God? Are there things in your life that need to be confessed to God? If so, apply 1 John 1:9, and as you appropriate His forgiveness and cleansing, you will again know the sweetness and blessing that comes from talking and communing with God. How wonderful it is to be on good speaking terms with our God!

Now set your heart and your soul to seek the LORD your God (1 Chron. 22:19).

A MARRIAGE PARTNER DIES
GENESIS 35:16–20

Rachel named the child "Benoni," which means "son of my sorrow." However, Jacob named the child "Benjamin," which means "son of the right hand." Rachel's death was one of Jacob's deepest sorrows. She died sorrowing, but he triumphed in faith and called the child "son of the right hand."

Jacob took a victorious stand for God in spite of the fact that the most precious person in his life had been taken. Rachel's death and burial broke Jacob's main link with his past carnal life at Haran. He had gone there to get a wife and had been guilty of many carnal actions. "Jacob set a pillar upon her grave: that is the pillar of Rachel's grave unto this day" (Gen. 35:20). Jacob established a pillar in remembrance of the one who had been so very precious to him.

Because Jacob had returned to Bethel and had been fully restored to fellowship with God, he was now able to fulfill the second part of God's command: "Return ... to thy kindred" (31:3). Thus, Jacob was on his way to his father, Isaac, who lived in Mamre. That is where Jacob was going when Rachel died in childbirth along the way.

Blessed be God,... who comforteth us in all our tribulation, that we may be able to comfort them which are in any trouble, by the comfort wherewith we ourselves are comforted of God (2 Cor. 1:3–4).

A FATHER DIES

GENESIS 35:27–29

Finally, Jacob arrived at his father's home in Mamre: "Jacob came unto Isaac his father unto Marnre, unto the city of Arbah, which is Hebron, where Abraham and Isaac sojourned" (Gen. 35:27). Jacob had not seen his father for at least 30 years. What a reunion they must have had! During the next 13 years Jacob cared for his father. Then we are told, "The days of Isaac were an hundred and fourscore years. And Isaac gave up the ghost, and died, and was gathered unto his people, being old and full of days: and his sons Esau and Jacob buried him" (vv. 28–29). The death of Isaac meant Jacob's separation from the past generation. The responsibility of the family was now entirely his. He had deceived Esau out of the birthright and had stolen the blessing many years earlier, but now the birthright was his by divine appointment—and so was the responsibility.

In the account of Isaac's death, it is precious to see that Esau and Jacob had apparently been reconciled: "His sons Esau and Jacob buried him" (v. 29). Death is often a great reconciler. Esau had said years earlier, "The days of mourning for my father are at hand; then will I slay my brother Jacob" (27:41). But Isaac did not die as soon as was expected, and by the time he did, Esau and Jacob were seemingly reconciled.

May we who are Christians be sure we use the occasion of a death of a loved one as a time of reconciliation with family members rather than a time of division.

He will swallow up death in victory; and the Lord GOD will wipe away tears from off all faces (Isa. 25:8).

97

DEATH TO THE SELF-LIFE
GENESIS 43:1–10

Jacob did not know that Joseph was the ruler in Egypt who had demanded to see his beloved brother Benjamin. When Jacob agreed to let Benjamin go, the Bible refers to Jacob as Israel (Gen. 43:11). The Spirit had won, and death to the self-life had finally conquered.

God never leaves believers unrewarded when they totally commit themselves to the Holy Spirit. The reaping is always beyond our highest expectations. This is emphasized in Romans 6: "For if we have been planted together in the likeness of his [Christ's] death, we shall be also in the likeness of his resurrection.... Now if we be dead with Christ, we believe that we shall also live with him" (vv.5, 8).

We must die to self in order to really live. It is necessary to lose one's life in order to really find it. Jesus said, "Except a corn of wheat fall into the ground and die, it abideth alone: but if it die, it bringeth forth much fruit. He that loveth his life shall lose it, and he that hateth his life in this world shall keep it unto life eternal" (John 12:24–25). No matter how difficult circumstances may seem, nothing can separate us from the love of God, but rather "in all these things we are more than conquerors through him that loved us" (Rom. 8:37).

Neither yield ye your members as instruments of unrighteousness unto sin: but yield yourselves unto God, as those that are alive from the dead, and your members as instruments of righteousness unto God (Rom. 6:13).

TESTIFYING TO A KING
GENESIS 47:1–12

Pharaoh did as Joseph had hoped. He told Joseph, "The land of Egypt is before thee; in the best of the land make thy father and brethren to dwell: in the land of Goshen let them dwell: and if thou knowest any men of activity among them, then make them rulers over my cattle" (Gen. 47:6). The Israelites needed a place to grow as a people and, at the same time, remain separate from the Egyptians. The attitude of the Egyptians toward shepherds was used of God to make both of these things possible.

Jacob was both bold and spiritually courageous before Pharaoh. Although Pharaoh probably considered Jacob an outcast because he was a shepherd, Jacob conducted himself as a child of God before Pharaoh. After all, Jacob was a son of the King of kings and an ambassador of the Most High.

Jacob acknowledged his pilgrim status when he referred to the "years of my pilgrimage" (v. 9). Jacob viewed his entire life on earth as a pilgrimage. In this regard, he identified himself with Abraham and Isaac. Hebrews 11:9–10 says of Abraham, "By faith he sojourned in the land of promise, as in a strange country, dwelling in tabernacles [tents] with Isaac and Jacob, the heirs with him of the same promise: for he looked for a city which hath foundations, whose builder and maker is God."

As we recognize we are also but pilgrims in this life, we will have more spiritual courage as we have opportunity to testify to those highly honored by the world.

I will speak of thy testimonies also before kings, and will not be ashamed (Ps. 119:46).

A BELIEVER DIES
GENESIS 49:28–33

"When Jacob had made an end of commanding his sons, he gathered up his feet into the bed, and yielded up the ghost, and was gathered unto his people" (Gen. 49:33). This was the final scene for this man who had become great in the sight of God and in the sight of the world. Everything was now accomplished. The last counsel and the last blessing had been given. The last charge had been delivered to his sons. Then he "yielded up the ghost, and was gathered unto his people." Jacob's death was the death of a believer. He yielded his spirit to God and was reunited with his own people in the grave.

The Christian is inspired by the hope of the resurrection; the grave is not his goal. First Thessalonians 4:16–18 says, "For the Lord himself shall descend from heaven with a shout, with the voice of the archangel, and with the trump of God: and the dead in Christ shall rise first: then we which are alive and remain shall be caught up together with them in the clouds, to meet the Lord in the air: and so shall we ever be with the Lord. Wherefore comfort one another with these words."

Then we which are alive and remain shall be caught up together with them in the clouds, to meet the Lord in the air: and so shall we ever be with the Lord (1 Thess. 4:17).

APRIL

It is a timeless principle that "all things work together for good to them that love God, to them who are the called according to his purpose" (Rom. 8:28). Joseph's life (the subject for April) is an Old Testament demonstration of Romans 8:28.

Even though all things work together for good for the believer, what God is trying to accomplish is not always evident. Never has this been more true than in the case of Joseph. In fact, God kept His overall plan from Joseph so He could teach him needed lessons. God wanted Joseph to have explicit faith in Him in any kind of circumstance. The process God used was a series of tests in different areas of Joseph's life.

God's ultimate purpose in working everything together for our good is so that we might "be conformed to the image of his Son" (v. 29). When you grasp the reality of the sovereignty of God in your daily circumstances, you will be able to say as Joseph did, "God planned it for good" (Gen. 50:20, Berkeley).

The readings for April are excerpted from *Joseph: "God Planned It for Good"*.

INFLUENCE DURING FORMATIVE YEARS
GENESIS 37:1–4

After the record of Joseph's birth in Genesis 30:23–24, very little is said of him until he was 17 years of age. Genesis 37 begins the detailed record of his life.

In addition to the children of Bilhah and Zilpah, the children of Leah were also Joseph's early companions. The half brothers of Joseph were unfit companions for spiritual encouragement. They had naturally been affected by the life they had witnessed in Haran and the conflict they had seen between their father, Jacob, and Laban. They were also affected by the jealousies they saw in their homes among their mothers. These children were older than Joseph and had received their early impressions from the old Jacob—the Jacob before Peniel. These impressions came before their father was mellowed in spiritual things. Perhaps you say, "Yes, but couldn't they have learned differently after Jacob became Israel and had his experience with God and began to really walk with God?" This might seem logical, but indelible impressions had already been made on their lives.

Regrettably, we cannot go back and change the past, but this shows us the importance of training children in their formative years. Those who know Christ as Saviour and have children in this stage of life should be sure that they are doing their best for the Lord and their children.

Train up a child in the way he should go: and when he is old, he will not depart from it (Prov. 22:6).

GOD'S MYSTERIOUS WAYS
GENESIS 37:5–11

The Scriptures record that there was a twofold response to Joseph's dreams: His brothers "envied him; but his father observed the saying" (Gen. 37:11). His brothers were jealous of him, but his father pondered and heeded what Joseph said. He began to reflect on how all this might fit into God's program, although at first he had rebuked Joseph.

These prophetic dreams were God-given, and we are not told what Joseph's attitude was as he told his father and brothers about them. Whether it was wise or unwise for Joseph to have told them, God permitted him to do so and even used the brothers' reaction as a means toward fulfilling the prophetic aspect revealed in the dreams.

Many times in the years to follow, Joseph must have wondered about his dreams and their fulfillment. The next 13 years of his life were filled with many tests and trials. Humanly speaking, they all seemed to stem from the time when he incited his brothers' hatred by sharing his dreams with them.

Had Joseph been looking at only the circumstances, he would have despaired of all hope, but his trust was in God. God's ways are mysterious; they are beyond man's comprehension. As God sovereignly works, man is often unable to understand why he is being led down a certain path.

Man's goings are of the LORD, how can a man then understand his own way? (Prov. 20:24).

FACING DEATH PREPARES FOR LIFE
GENESIS 37:18–24

We do not know how many hopeless and hungry hours Joseph spent in the pit—possibly it was for an entire night. Although Reuben intended to deliver Joseph back to his father, no doubt the intent of the rest of the brothers was to let Joseph starve in the pit. They had cast him into a place of death.

Even in this there is a spiritual lesson for us. Resurrection comes only out of death. We must recognize ourselves as dead with Christ before we can experience the victorious life. Galatians 2:20 says, "I am [literally, "I have been"] crucified with Christ: nevertheless I live; yet not I, but Christ liveth in me: and the life which I now live in the flesh I live by the faith of the Son of God, who loved me, and gave himself for me." The believer has gone through death with Christ and also through the resurrection with Christ. The believer has Christ within him, and he is to live his life by the faith of the Son of God. All of these benefits must be appropriated by faith.

Joseph's night alone with God in the pit was really what he needed. Although Joseph lived a righteous life, he was not yet ready for what God purposed to do with him. So God brought him to this place of death to prepare him to live. We, too, must pass through the place of death to self before we become useful to God.

So teach us to number our days, that we may apply our hearts unto wisdom (Ps. 90:12).

FAITH FOR LIFE'S UNCERTAINTIES

GENESIS 37:25–36

The brothers sold Joseph into Egypt, "but God was with him" (Acts 7:9). In spite of what the unrighteous may do to the child of God, they can proceed no further than God permits. In the midst of such trials, the believer needs to put into practice what is stated in Psalm 37.

Notice that there are no limits to the cruelty of Satan. The brothers evidenced no shame for their sin and even tried to comfort their father. Imagine their trying to comfort him when they were the ones who were responsible for his grief. Although the brothers had apparently gotten rid of Joseph, they had not gotten rid of their responsibility.

From this account, we should realize the uncertainty of life itself. Joseph went on a mission, but he never returned—he never saw his homeland again. He was mightily used of God in the path in which God led him, but the opportunity to be a blessing in his own land was never his again. Let us take advantage of every opportunity to be a blessing to others.

Life itself is uncertain. Tomorrow we may be in eternity. Are you ready to meet God? You cannot be sure of tomorrow, so take advantage of the opportunity to receive Christ today.

Behold, now is the accepted time; behold, now is the day of salvation (2 Cor. 6:2).

A LIFE OF FAITHFULNESS
GENESIS 39:1–6

One of the great lessons that Joseph learned in Egypt was the lesson of obedience through suffering. He did not understand the mysterious circumstances, but he allowed God to be his circumstances. Because of this, God also became his basic environment—Joseph lived in the sphere of the spiritual even though he was a slave in the house of Potiphar. There was idolatry and corruption all around him, but Joseph was able to remain sensitive to sin and to grow even stronger in his confidence in God because his attention was fixed on God.

Joseph was only 17 years of age, but because of his simple trust in God, he performed his duties as a slave to the utmost of his power. He was indwelt by the Spirit; therefore, it was God's power that gave him the ability he needed. Instead of complaining, Joseph faithfully served as a slave. This was because he was serving not just a Gentile master—he was serving God.

Joseph's life of faithfulness was obvious to Potiphar. God's Word says that Joseph's "master saw that the LORD was with him, and that the LORD made all that he did to prosper in his hand" (Gen. 39:3). Even unbelievers are able to discern the Spirit-filled laborer. Do those who work closely with you see your faithfulness and observe that God is spiritually prospering your life?

He that is faithful in that which is least is faithful also in much (Luke 16:10).

RESISTING TEMPTATION

GENESIS 39:7–13

It is important to remember that Joseph was Potiphar's property. For this reason, Potiphar's wife perhaps thought she could do with this chattel as she liked. Humanly speaking, Joseph could have been very flattered that he was being tempted by his master's wife. What a feeling of importance Joseph might have had!

But Joseph loved God and did not want to do anything that would dishonor Him. This incident shows us, however, that even a believer is not able to build a wall around him high enough to keep out temptation. It is not sin to be tempted; it only becomes sin when one yields to the temptation. Joseph was at the time of life when his reaction to temptation would have lasting effects. If he had yielded to the temptation of Potiphar's wife, who can imagine the different course that history might have taken.

What a person accepts or rejects, particularly in the realm of sexual temptation, will affect the rest of his life. This is why God's Word says, "Keep thy heart with all diligence; for out of it are the issues of life" (Prov. 4:23). The apostle Paul solemnly charged young Timothy: "Flee also youthful lusts: but follow righteousness, faith, charity [love], peace, with them that call on the Lord out of a pure heart" (2 Tim. 2:22).

For if ye live after the flesh, ye shall die: but if ye through the Spirit do mortify the deeds of the body, ye shall live (Rom. 8:13).

 **APRIL 7**

GOD NEVER DESERTS HIS OWN

GENESIS 39:13–23

What a lie Potiphar's wife told about Joseph! He had refused her invitation to sin because he did not want to dishonor God, and now through her lie God was seemingly being dishonored anyhow.

When Potiphar heard his wife's report, he became very angry. He took Joseph and "put him into the prison, a place where the king's prisoners were bound: and he was there in prison" (Gen. 39:20). Could this be the reward Joseph received for his faithfulness to God?

Although everything seemed to be going against him, the Bible emphasizes that "the LORD was with Joseph, and showed him mercy, and gave him favour in the sight of the keeper of the prison" (v. 21). Even though Joseph's situation seemed hopeless, God never left him for one moment.

We, too, have the assurance of God's Word: "I will never leave thee, nor forsake thee" (Heb. 13:5). In the original language, this phrase is very emphatic: "I will by no means leave you nor will I by any means forsake you." God will never leave us helpless nor abandoned. Therefore, "we may boldly say, The Lord is my helper, and I will not fear what man shall do unto me" (v. 6). Do you have this confidence? Regardless of how adverse your circumstances are, as a Christian do you know that God will never desert you?

And I give unto them eternal life; and they shall never perish, neither shall any man pluck them out of my hand (John 10:28).

SERVING WILLINGLY AND FAITHFULLY

GENESIS 40:1–8

Service was one of the main links in the remarkable chain of events that God brought about in Joseph's life. Now he was made responsible for the king's butler and baker, for "he served them" (Gen. 40:4). Joseph was made responsible for them because his godly character had won him favor with those in authority. And Joseph was willing to serve in any way he could.

As Joseph faithfully served God by serving others, little did he know how God would use his association with the butler and baker to bring about His will. Because God was in it, the relationship of the Hebrew slave with Pharaoh's two servants had far-reaching results.

We also need to realize that the smallest circumstance of life has meaning. Even though we may not understand how God can use a particular thing to work out His glory, we need to realize that He can use small things as well as big things to accomplish His will. The words, "all things," are very important words in Romans 8:28: "And we know that all things work together for good to them that love God, to them who are the called according to his purpose."

Note particularly that Joseph's religious convictions did not stand in the way of earthly promotion. Men of the world soon detect when a person has quality of character. Joseph did not compromise to obtain promotions; the promotions came because he had a character that would not compromise.

Only fear the LORD, and serve him in truth with all your heart: for consider how great things he hath done for you (1 Sam. 12:24).

GOD KNOWS OUR HEARTACHES

GENESIS 40:9–15

Having assured the chief butler that he would be restored to his former responsibility, Joseph urged him, "But think on me when it shall be well with thee, and shew kindness, I pray thee, unto me, and make mention of me unto Pharaoh, and bring me out of this house: for indeed I was stolen away out of the land of the Hebrews: and here also have I done nothing that they should put me into the dungeon" (Gen. 40:14–15). These verses reveal the heart and thoughts of Joseph. They show how human he really was. But his trials were inhuman; they were extremely hard to bear.

There was nothing wrong with Joseph's seeking release, but he found that waiting for God's time is often one of the hardest things to do. Joseph was not rebuked by God for seeking his release because God knew the heartache Joseph had.

Regardless of what you are going through, God understands your deepest emotions; He knows how you feel. Hebrews 4:14–16 tells us, "Seeing then that we have a great high priest, that is passed into the heavens, Jesus the Son of God, let us hold fast our profession. For we have not an high priest which cannot be touched with the feeling of our infirmities; but was in all points tempted like as we are, yet without sin. Let us therefore come boldly unto the throne of grace, that we may obtain mercy, and find grace to help in time of need."

Like as a father pitieth his children, so the LORD pitieth them that fear him. For he knoweth our frame; he remembereth that we are dust (Ps. 103:13,14).

SPECIAL FAVORS FORGOTTEN
GENESIS 40:16–23

Joseph's faithfulness is seen even in his interpretation of the baker's dream. As sad as it was to deliver such a message, Joseph would not swerve from the truth for one moment, even for his own advantage. He realized that it was his responsibility to pass on what God had revealed to him.

Faithfulness is the characteristic that is so greatly needed in our lives today. The Word of God says, "It is required in stewards, that a man be found faithful" (1 Cor. 4:2). Time proved that Joseph had given God's interpretation of the dreams.

As Joseph knew that the chief butler was now back in his position, no doubt the hope of getting out of prison grew brighter. Surely the butler would remember Joseph to Pharaoh as Joseph had asked. But whatever hopes Joseph had were dashed to pieces, for the Scriptures say, "Yet did not the chief butler remember Joseph, but forgat him" (Gen. 40:23). Joseph had been concerned about the butler when he was sad and had tried to do all he could to encourage him, but now the butler forgot him completely. What ungratefulness!

Does the ungratefulness of people distress you? Perhaps you have done something for someone and have had to put forth much extra effort, but then they either take it for granted or soon forget it altogether. More importantly, are you grateful when others do things for you?

In every thing give thanks: for this is the will of God in Christ Jesus concerning you (1 Thess. 5:18).

TRAINING THROUGH CHASTENING
HEBREWS 12:1–11

If you are now going through testing, there are three things you should especially remember. First, God's way is the wisest way. Training is always accompanied by some type of hardship. Even athletes realize they cannot properly train without giving up some of the pleasures of life and enduring the hardship of training. God trains us through chastening.

Second, God's time is the best time. God was working out His purpose through Joseph. It was impossible for Joseph to realize it at the time, but later he could look back and see that God's time had been exactly right—everything had worked out. But imagine the lonely years of waiting. God does not act too early nor too late. He is never in a hurry but accomplishes things in His own time. Too many of us either lag behind or run ahead of God's time. But we need to remember that the clock of divine providence keeps strict time. Because of our circumstances it may appear to be slow at times and fast at others, but the all-wise God knows precisely when to act.

Third, God's grace is sufficient. He will give us the grace we need to be patient. James 1:4 says, "But let patience have her perfect work, that ye may be perfect and entire, wanting nothing." The word "perfect" means "mature" or "complete." God is seeking to teach us valuable lessons so we will be mature believers.

Behold, happy is the man whom God correcteth: therefore despise not thou the chastening of the Almighty (Job 5:17).

FAILURE OF THE WORLD'S WISDOM

GENESIS 41:1–14

The inability of the wise men to interpret Pharaoh's dreams, emphasizes the truth later recorded in 1 Corinthians 3:18–19: "Let no person deceive himself. If anyone among you supposes that he is wise in this age [let him become a fool discard his worldly discernment and recognize himself as dull, stupid, and foolish, without true learning and scholarship] that he may become [really] wise. For this world's wisdom is foolishness (absurdity and stupidity) with God, for it is written, He lays hold of the wise in their [own] craftiness" (Amplified).

Egypt was a symbol of the world. During the time of Joseph, Egypt was the center of learning and culture—it was a proud leader among ancient civilizations. But the people were idol worshipers; they did not know Jehovah. But now Pharaoh was made to see that all human resources and wisdom are powerless and worthless and that true wisdom comes only from God. How wonderful it would be if leaders in today's world would also come to that realization! "The secret of the LORD is with them that fear him" (Ps. 25:14). If world leaders would turn to the Scriptures and seek God's face, they would learn what is shortly going to come to pass.

From the results of Joseph's time in prison, we see that patience had had her perfect work. God's man was now ready. All things had been working together for Joseph's good, although he had not always recognized it.

Thus saith the LORD, thy Redeemer, the Holy One of Israel; I am the LORD thy God which teacheth thee to profit, which leadeth thee by the way that thou shouldest go (Isa. 48:17).

ADVICE WITHOUT SELF-INTEREST

GENESIS 41:25–36

After Pharaoh told his dreams to Joseph, God revealed through Joseph that the dreams had to do with seven years of plenty, followed by seven years of great famine.

Joseph then advised Pharaoh that every precaution should be taken during the seven years of plenty so there would be food available during the seven years of famine. In all of this, Joseph did not say a word about himself nor speak in behalf of his own need. He had died to self; the previous 13 years had completely erased any desires for self. He had seen God working, and that was his supreme desire.

We who know Jesus Christ as Saviour have also died to self. Note, it is not that we should die to self but that we have died to self. God's Word makes this truth very clear. Romans 6:6 says, "Knowing this, that our old man is [was] crucified with him, that the body of sin might be destroyed [rendered inoperative], that henceforth we should not serve sin." Our crucifixion took place when Christ died on the cross for us. It is not that we ought to die but that we have died. Our need now is to apply this truth, by faith, to ourselves. The Lord Jesus Christ said, "If any man will come after me, let him deny himself, and take up his cross daily, and follow me. For whosoever will save his life shall lose it: but whosoever will lose his life for my sake, the same shall save it" (Luke 9:23–24).

But what things were gain to me, those I counted loss for Christ (Phil. 3:7).

THE TEST OF POSITION AND PROSPERITY

GENESIS 41:37–45

Joseph now came to the greatest test of his life thus far—exaltation and prosperity.

The hands that had known the hard toil of a slave were now adorned by the king's ring. Joseph's feet had been freed from the torment of the fetters, and now a gold chain was put around his neck. Joseph had lost his coat of many colors 13 years earlier when his brothers took it from him in anger and jealousy. Later, he had left his outer garment behind in the hands of Potiphar's wife when he had fled from her. But now he was given a royal wardrobe of fine linen. Once Joseph was treated as offscouring by the Egyptians, but now all Egypt was commanded to bow before him as he rode on the second chariot as the prime minister of Egypt.

All of this took place because Joseph sought to please God and resisted the temptation to sin. Rather than gratifying the flesh, Joseph sought to glorify God. Joseph found that godliness paid great dividends. He experienced the truth of the principle later stated in Matthew 6:33: "But seek ye first the kingdom of God, and his righteousness; and all these things shall be added unto you."

Charge them that are rich in this world, that they be not highminded, nor trust in uncertain riches, but in the living God, who giveth us richly all things to enjoy (1 Tim. 6:17).

FORGETTING PAST TRIALS
GENESIS 41:46–57

As time passed, "unto Joseph were born two sons before the years of famine came, which Asenath the daughter of Potipherah priest of On bare unto him. And Joseph called the name of the firstborn Manasseh [forgetting]: For God, said he, hath made me forget all my toil, and all my father's house" (Gen. 41:50–51). This does not mean that God had caused Joseph to forget about his family, but He caused him to forget about the trials of the past as related to his family. This is exactly what happens when a person walks with the Lord. The blessings are so many he forgets about the trials.

Joseph named his second son "Ephraim," which means "fruitful." Joseph said, "For God hath caused me to be fruitful in the land of my affliction" (v. 52). Joseph had forgotten the trials and now saw only the fruit that God had brought about in his life.

So it will be with us when we really grasp the significance of the truths stated in Romans 8:28–29. As we are conformed more and more to the image of Jesus Christ, we will be so thrilled with what God has accomplished in our lives that we will tend to forget the tests and sufferings that were used to cause us to be conformed to God's Son.

But the God of all grace, who hath called us unto his eternal glory by Christ Jesus, after that ye have suffered a while, make you perfect, stablish, strengthen, settle you (1 Pet. 5:10).

BROTHERS MEET AGAIN

GENESIS 42:1–17

Joseph accused his brothers of being spies. Think of the contrast! More than 20 years ago they had accused Joseph of spying on them and telling their father on them; now he was accusing them of being spies. When they accused Joseph, they cast him into a pit. Now that he accused them, "he put them all together into ward three days" (Gen. 42:17). Joseph's actions paralleled their actions many years before, but be did not do it for revenge.

Memory is one of the most marvelous faculties of our nature. Often when a person receives the kind of evil treatment that he has dealt to others, he remembers his sin and is convicted. A step God used in awakening the consciences of Joseph's brothers was having them imprisoned. There God could bring even stronger conviction. Their guilt was beginning to strike home.

Joseph's heart was bursting with the desire to disclose himself to his brothers, but he realized he dare not do this and spoil God's program. Joseph looked on his brothers with compassion and saw them as ones needing to be made right with God.

When you see those who are without Jesus Christ, is your heart moved with compassion? When you are in a crowd of people and realize that maybe 98 percent of them are not born again, how does it affect you? Does it mean anything to you, or are they just people?

Be ye all of one mind, having compassion one of another, love as brethren, be pitiful, be courteous: not rendering evil for evil.... but contrariwise blessing (1 Pet. 3:8–9).

NO GRUDGES HELD
GENESIS 42:18–28

All of this was too much for Joseph, and "he turned himself about from them, and wept" (Gen. 42:24). His heart was still tender toward them in spite of what they had done to him. Controlling himself, he "returned to them again, and communed with them, and took from them Simeon, and bound him before their eyes" (v. 24). It is possible that Simeon had been the leader in what the brothers had done to Joseph earlier, but now all the brothers were beginning to show true repentance. Verse 21 shows three aspects of this repentance: conscience—"we are verily guilty"; memory—"we saw the anguish of his soul"; and reason—"therefore is this distress come upon us." The brothers were being brought to an end of themselves.

Joseph responded in two ways, although his brothers noticed only one of his responses. First, he wept with a broken heart because of his love for his brothers—especially Benjamin—and for his father. Second, he bound Simeon in their presence. The brothers saw only the hardness that Joseph expressed; they did not know how tender his heart was underneath it all.

As Joseph's tenderness of heart indicated when he stood before his brothers, he had forgiven them long ago—even though they did not realize it. Have you forgiven those who have wronged you?

And be ye kind one to another, tenderhearted, forgiving one another, even as God for Christ's sake hath forgiven you (Eph. 4:32).

JUDGING BY THE CIRCUMSTANCES

GENESIS 42:29–38

When the brothers returned to Canaan, they rehearsed to their father all that had taken place in Egypt.

Realizing the trouble they were in, Jacob said to his sons, "Me have ye bereaved of my children: Joseph is not, and Simeon is not, and ye will take Benjamin away: all these things are against me" (Gen. 42:36). Jacob later realized that all these things were really for him in God's sovereign plan.

All he could see was the immediate circumstances and, as far as he was concerned, there was no hope whatever. The son passed the tests better than the father. Joseph responded to hopeless situations better than Jacob. Faith had conquered for Joseph, but Jacob was slow to see that God could bring good out of these circumstances.

Reuben tried to assure his father that Benjamin would be safe when they took him to Egypt. Reuben said, "Slay my two sons, if I bring him not to thee: deliver him into my hand, and I will bring him to thee again" (v. 37). But it was impossible for Jacob to see any possibility of allowing Benjamin to go to Egypt.

Jacob did not think he could stand any more grief, but his sons knew it was hopeless to return to Egypt without their youngest brother.

Be of good courage, and he shall strengthen your heart, all ye that hope in the LORD (Ps. 31:24).

GUILT PRODUCES FEAR
GENESIS 43:1–18

Jacob reluctantly let his sons take Benjamin to Egypt, and he gave them instructions as to what they should take along so they might be well received. The sons did as Jacob instructed. They "took that present, and they took double money in their hand and Benjamin; and rose up, and went down to Egypt, and stood before Joseph" (Gen. 43:15). When Joseph saw his brothers—and Benjamin with them—he commanded the ruler of his house, "Bring these men home, and slay, and make ready; for these men shall dine with me at noon" (v. 16). Then conscience did its work again. The brothers had such guilt concerning Joseph that anything caused them to greatly fear—especially in the strange land of Egypt.

The ruler of Joseph's house "did as Joseph bade; and the man brought the men into Joseph's house. And the men were afraid, because they were brought into Joseph's house; and they said, Because of the money that was returned in our sacks at the first time are we brought in; that he may seek occasion against us, and fall upon us, and take us for bondmen, and our asses" (vv. 17–18).

The brothers had been so brave before when they sold Joseph into slavery, but now even hospitality brought fear to them. When a person is guilty of sin, almost everything brings fear to him.

And herein do I exercise myself, to have always a conscience void to offence toward God, and toward men (Acts 24:16).

A BROTHER IS HONORED
GENESIS 43:19–34

Joseph was unable to restrain himself, and he "made haste; for his bowels [heart] did yearn upon his brother: and he sought where to weep; and he entered into his chamber, and wept there" (Gen. 43:30). What a moving account of the love of Joseph for Benjamin! Finally gaining control of himself, Joseph "washed his face, and went out, and refrained [controlled] himself, and said, Set on bread" (v. 31). Joseph still did not identify himself to his brothers. God's program was not yet completed. Joseph was well trained to wait for God's time, regardless of how difficult it was because of his own emotions.

It is highly significant to observe the way they were seated at the meal. Most likely, the reason they marveled was that they were astonished that this Egyptian ruler knew their ages and was able to seat them in the right order. This especially would bring fear to the brothers, for they would wonder what else he knew about them.

The brothers were tested at the meal regarding their attitude toward their younger brother. They had been envious of Joseph because of their father's special love for him. They might well have felt the same way toward Benjamin.

How do you respond when someone receives more honor than you?

And whether one member suffer, all the members suffer with it; or one member be honoured, all the members rejoice with it (1 Cor. 12:26).

NO EXCUSES; MERCY SOUGHT
GENESIS 44:1–16

Perhaps you say this was cruel for Joseph to test his brothers. Maybe it seems cruel, but sometimes God has to do severe things to get people to see their sinfulness. Joseph's brothers were being severely tested to see what their reaction would be toward Benjamin when it was discovered that the silver cup was in his sack. Would they sacrifice him for their own safety as they once had done to Joseph?

When they were brought in before Joseph, he said to them, "What deed is this that ye have done? wot [know] ye not that such a man as I can certainly divine?" (Gen. 44:15). Earlier, the brothers had said, "We shall see what will become of his dreams" (37:20). Now they were completely at the mercy of Joseph because his dreams had been fulfilled, even though they did not realize it was Joseph before whom they stood.

In defense, Judah said, "What shall we say unto my lord? what shall we speak? or how shall we clear ourselves? God hath found out the iniquity of thy servants: behold, we are my lord's servants, both we, and he also with whom the cup is found" (44:16). The brothers had nowhere to turn; they could only cast themselves upon Joseph's mercy.

When we who know Christ experience difficulties, we should cast ourselves on His mercy.

Wash me throughly [thoroughly] from mine iniquity, and cleanse me from my sin. For I acknowledge my transgressions: and my sin is ever before me (Ps. 51:2–3).

A RIGHT HEART ATTITUDE

GENESIS 44:17–34

Through Joseph the Lord's objective had now been reached. God had wanted to give perfect rest and peace to the brothers, but this was impossible as long as there was unconfessed sin in their lives. God used the avenues of conscience and fear to bring about this repentance. The brothers were being tested to see if they could forgive Benjamin, who had brought them all of this trouble. If they had treated him in the spirit of the former days, as they had treated Joseph, they would have abandoned Benjamin to his fate. Had they done this, they could not have been forgiven. But Judah expressed their change of heart when he said he would rather stay in Egypt as a slave than go back and see his father die of a broken heart because of the loss of Benjamin.

The brothers had a forgiving spirit toward Benjamin. This is extremely important, for the Lord Jesus Christ said, "If ye forgive not men their trespasses, neither will your father forgive your trespasses" (Matt. 6:15). The four conditions of reconciliation had been met: Conscience had been awakened, sin had been confessed, repentance had been made, and a new life had been evidenced. Joseph's brothers now had the right heart attitude. Because God's work had been accomplished in the lives of the brothers, Joseph was now free to reveal his identity. Might we also be sensitive to sin.

Keep thy heart with all diligence; for out of it are the issues of life (Prov. 4:23).

"NOT YOU ... BUT GOD"
GENESIS 45:1–15

"Joseph said unto his brethren, I am Joseph" (Gen. 45:3). Previously he had spoken to them through an interpreter, but now in their own language he said, "I am Joseph."

When Joseph disclosed his identity, "his brethren could not answer him; for they were troubled at his presence" (v. 3). They had reason to be troubled and terrified. Joseph was standing before them as one who had risen from the dead. They could not think of what to say, because any act of self-defense would surely only bring them into deeper trouble.

Joseph recognized their hesitation and said to them, "Come near to me, I pray you. And they came near. And he said, I am Joseph your brother, whom ye sold into Egypt. Now therefore be not grieved, nor angry with yourselves, that ye sold me hither: for God did send me before you to preserve life" (vv. 4–5).

Joseph told his brothers that the One responsible for his coming to Egypt was "not you ... but God" (v. 8). This is a truth we desperately need to see—that God moves behind the scenes to accomplish His purpose in our lives. For the Christian, things are not explained on a human basis—it is "not I, but Christ" (Gal. 2:20). It is only as we allow God to test, try and train us that He can accomplish His overall program and use us as He desires.

For our light affliction, which is but for a moment, worketh for us a far more exceeding and eternal weight of glory (2 Cor. 4:17).

A FATHER HEARS GOOD NEWS
GENESIS 45:16–28

When the brothers reached home, they told their father, "Joseph is yet alive, and he is governor over all the land of Egypt" (Gen. 45:26). Jacob was so surprised by the news that it was impossible for him to believe it. The Scriptures say, "Jacob's heart fainted, for he believed them not" (v. 26). Earlier, when it was demanded that Benjamin go to Egypt with the brothers so they would be able to see Joseph, Jacob had said, "All these things are against me" (42:36). He did not realize that just the opposite was true—all those things were really working together for good. God had patiently worked to accomplish His will. When God undertakes a program, He continues with it until it is finished. The apostle Paul wrote: "Being confident of this very thing, that he which hath begun a good work in you will perform it until the day of Jesus Christ" (Phil. 1:6).

When Jacob saw the wagons, he believed. Some say, "Seeing is believing." However, the Bible says quite the opposite is true. Jesus told Thomas, "Because thou hast seen me, thou hast believed: blessed are they that have not seen, and yet have believed" (John 20:29).

Believers are to walk by faith, not sight; let us take God at His word.

And let us not be weary in well doing: for in due season we shall reap, if we faint not (Gal. 6:9).

A FAMILY REUNION
GENESIS 46:1–7,28–34

When Jacob and his family arrived in Goshen, "Joseph made ready his chariot, and went up to meet Israel his father, to Goshen, and presented himself unto him; and he fell on his neck, and wept on his neck a good while" (Gen. 46:29). Again Joseph demonstrated that he was not ashamed to be associated with his family even though shepherds were an abomination to the Egyptians. What a tender scene it must have been when Joseph met his father and embraced him, weeping for joy. Jacob said to Joseph, "Now let me die, since I have seen thy face, because thou art yet alive" (v. 30).

It was at this time that we see Joseph's wise strategy as he prepared his family for their meeting with Pharaoh. Joseph's plan was to consult with Pharaoh at once. By bringing these matters before Pharaoh, Joseph was preventing the possibility that someone would accuse him of favoritism. Also, when Pharaoh gave the word, the chiefs of the people would not thwart Joseph's plan. Later, it was in God's plan to have another Pharaoh—who did not know Joseph—afflict the Israelites in order to cause them to want to leave Egypt.

How Joseph must have thanked God to be united with his family again. Let us be sure to praise God for the many good things He brings into our lives.

This is my commandment, That ye love one another, as I have loved you (John 15:12).

GOD'S PURPOSE FULFILLED
GENESIS 47:1–13, 27–31

God had promised Jacob that He would make a great nation of him in Egypt and that they would return to the land. Jacob's faith in God's promises was revealed in that he asked Joseph to bury him back in Canaan. His request must have had a great impact on Joseph because Joseph later requested the same thing for himself (Gen. 50:24–25).

God had fulfilled His purpose through Joseph. Joseph had been used to preserve the posterity of the Hebrews. They were now safe in the land of Goshen. Years later, when it was time to lead the Israelites out of Egypt, God used another man—Moses. God has limited Himself to working through people to accomplish His will.

Joseph had experienced the fulfillment of the truths stated in Psalm 37. He had delighted himself in the Lord, and the Lord had given him the desires of his heart (v. 4). He had waited upon the Lord and had inherited the earth (v. 9). Being meek, he had delighted himself in the abundance of peace (v. 11). Because he was a good man, his steps had been ordered by the Lord, and he had delighted in the Lord's way (v. 23). He had waited on the Lord and had kept His way; therefore, he had been exalted to inherit the land and had seen the wicked cut off (v. 34). He had been a perfect (mature) man; therefore, his end was peace (v. 37). We need to apply this psalm to ourselves.

Blessed be the LORD, that hath given rest unto his people Israel, according to all that he promised: there hath not failed one word of all his good promise (1 Kings 8:56).

 **APRIL 27**

NEW HEIRS APPOINTED
GENESIS 48:1–5,14–22

After the famine was over, Joseph lived about 66 more years. Jacob lived only about 10 or 11 more years. Little is said about either of them during these years. However, there was one highly significant thing that occurred before Jacob's death.

Jacob said that his grandsons, Ephraim and Manasseh, would be counted among his own sons, which was significant as far as the inheritance was concerned. Although Reuben was the firstborn of Leah, he had lost the birthright because of the gross sin of lying with his father's concubine. This birthright was then passed on to Joseph, the firstborn of Rachel. The birthright, having come to Joseph, was then given to his sons. This was later referred to in 1 Chronicles 5:1–2: "Now the sons of Reuben the firstborn of Israel, (for he was the firstborn; but, forasmuch as he defiled his father's bed, his birthright was given unto the sons of Joseph the son of Israel: and the genealogy is not to be reckoned after the birthright. For Judah prevailed above his brethren, and of him came the chief ruler; but the birthright was Joseph's)."

Joseph had received the double portion of inheritance, and his two sons were numbered among the 12 tribes of Israel as the recipients. God rewards those who honor Him.

If ye be willing and obedient, ye shall eat the good of the land (Isa. 1:19).

FEARING GOD
PSALM 34:9–22

The secret of Joseph's life was summed up in his own words when his brothers first came to Egypt. He told them, "This do, and live; for I fear God" (Gen. 42:18). The last three words of this statement were the key to his life—"I fear God."

There were four things that were particularly significant about Joseph's secret—"I fear God." First, he learned this secret early in his life while he was still at home. This shows us the importance of giving our children the spiritual training they need while they are yet young.

Second, the secret of Joseph's life was developed by his loyalty and obedience in the routine of daily duty. It did not matter whether things were small or large—he was faithful.

Third, the secret of Joseph's life was proved by the results. God honored His servant for his simple trust and confidence and justified his actions in his home life, slavery, prison and in Pharaoh's court.

Fourth, the secret of Joseph's life was made effectual in daily living by faith. Faith in God was evidenced throughout all his life, even when he faced death. The divine commentary is that "by faith Joseph, when he died, made mention of the departing of the children of Israel; and gave commandment concerning his bones" (Heb. 11:22). Faith is powerful and always brings results.

O that there were such an heart in them, that they would fear me, and keep all my commandments always, that it might be well with them, and with their children for ever! (Deut. 5:29).

FAILING TO ACCEPT FORGIVENESS
GENESIS 50:1–17

A lack of faith was demonstrated by Joseph's brothers after the death of their father. Joseph had assured the brothers that all had been forgiven (Gen. 45:8). The brothers had seemed to accept Joseph's statement, but after their father died, they began to wonder again if Joseph might retaliate.

The brothers pleaded that Joseph might take heed to their father's words and forgive them for what they had done. Notice Joseph's reaction when he heard these words from his brothers: "And Joseph wept when they spake unto him" (50:17). Joseph wept because his brothers refused to believe him. It was heartbreaking for him to realize that his brothers had so little faith in him.

This gives us a small picture of how God's heart is broken when we do not take Him at His word. God can be trusted; therefore, let us exercise faith and take Him at His word.

We see the emotions of God when we read of how Jesus sorrowed over Jerusalem. He grieved because they rejected Him—they refused to place their faith in Him. Jesus cried, "O Jerusalem, Jerusalem, thou that killest the prophets, and stonest them which are sent unto thee, how often would I have gathered thy children together, even as a hen gathereth her chickens under her wings, and ye would not!" (Matt. 23:37). Let us take God at His word.

Blessed are they that have not seen, and yet have believed (John 20:29).

CONFIDENCE IN GOD'S WORD

GENESIS 50:18–26

Joseph then said to his brothers, "But as for you, ye thought evil against me; but God meant it unto good, to bring to pass, as it is this day, to save much people alive" (Gen. 50:20). Joseph realized that even though his brothers had had evil in mind when they sold him into slavery, "God planned it for good" (v. 20, Berkeley). Oh, that we might grasp the sovereignty of God as Joseph did.

Just as his father, Jacob, was determined that Egypt was not to be the final resting place for his bones, so Joseph determined the same about his bones. It was this final and crowning statement of faith that won Joseph his place in God's hall of fame (Heb. 11).

It was not Joseph's striking victory at Potiphar's house nor his vast administrative achievements that won him this place. Rather, it was this last commandment of faith concerning his bones. God's Word says that "by faith Joseph, when he died, made mention of the departing of the children of Israel; and gave commandment concerning his bones" (v. 22).

God is pleased when we trust Him and demonstrate our confidence in Him by the way we live. It is by this faith principle that God works in our lives. If we want to please the Lord more and glorify Him more, then we must start believing Him more and trusting Him more. When we really believe Him, we will act upon our faith because we have taken God at His word.

Being fully persuaded that, what he had promised, he was able also to perform (Rom. 4:21).

MAY

From Adam to Christ, none was greater than Moses (the subject for May). Yet Moses was just like any other man. Although he had great qualities that needed to be developed, he had flaws and deficiencies that would have made him powerless apart from God's all-sufficient grace.

The Bible sketches the life of Moses from his infancy to his death. The Lord has not given this much information about every great Bible character. Moses experienced weakness and failure when he relied on himself, but he experienced strength and victory when he relied on God.

The key to Moses' life was the simplicity of his faith, his constant communion with God and his willingness to become a channel through which God's purpose was achieved.

The readings for May are excerpted from *Moses*, Vol. I: *God Prepares and Strengthens His Man,* and *Moses*, Vol. II: *Excellence in Leadership.*

MAY 1

TRAIN A CHILD; AFFECT THE WORLD
EXODUS 2:1–15

Although Moses belonged officially to Pharaoh's daughter, God allowed his own mother to have the privilege of giving him his early training. The exact number of years Moses was in the care of his own mother is unknown, but it was long enough for her to give him the basic training that would last throughout his lifetime. It was doubtlessly under his mother's care that Moses trusted God for his salvation. Also, it would have been only normal for his mother to have impressed on him the need for the Israelites to be delivered from Egypt. Perhaps his mother reminded him often that God promised to deliver the Israelites in the fourth generation and that he was a member of that generation.

The faith of Moses' parents caused them to risk the wrath of the king. Their love for God and for their child caused them to devise an ingenious way to evade the king's ruthless edict. God honored their faith and rewarded their love. As a result, Moses had the benefit of a godly home and the heritage of his Hebrew parents, which proved to be more than enough to counteract the later adverse education received from the Egyptians.

In a sense, Moses' parents influenced the course of history, although they were slaves to the Egyptians at the time. Think of what they personally accomplished by properly rearing Moses. One never knows how one person or group may affect large numbers of people—even the world.

For I know him, that he will command his children and his household after him, and they shall keep the way of the LORD, to do justice and judgment (Gen. 18:19).

FRAIL MAN CANNOT LIMIT GOD
EXODUS 3:1–14

At the burning bush, Moses was intensely aware of his previous failures. "Moses said unto God, Who am I, that I should go unto Pharaoh, and that I should bring forth the children of Israel out of Egypt?" (Ex. 3:11). Moses was aware that he had tried this once and it hadn't worked. He had so thoroughly mastered the lesson of human inadequacy that he was too timid, too reserved and too nonaggressive to respond to the call of God. Before, he had been confident of his own ability, but now he had absolutely no confidence. This is what God had taught him during his 40 years in the desert, but God wanted Moses to respond to Him and to His ability.

The verses following Exodus 3:11 record a deeply revealing dialogue between God and Moses. The once self-sufficient Egyptian prince pleaded total lack of qualification for the task God was calling him to do. Moses was negative, but God was now dealing with him to be positive.

Moses had yet to understand what God meant when He said, "Certainly I will be with thee" (v. 12) and "Thus shalt thou say unto the children of Israel, I AM hath sent me unto you" (v. 14). Before, Moses had been too quick and impetuous; now he was too slow and reluctant. But what a lesson God had for Moses and for us; His purpose will not be thwarted by the whims and moods of His servants.

For the eyes of the LORD run to and fro throughout the whole earth, to shew himself strong in the behalf of them whose heart is perfect toward him (2 Chron. 16:9).

GOD ENABLES WHOM HE CALLS
EXODUS 4:1–17

Moses gave seven reasons why he wasn't the man for God's task: lack of capability, lack of message, lack of authority, lack of eloquence, lack of fitness or adaptation, lack of previous success and lack of previous acceptance.

Instead of receiving God's approval, the excuses Moses gave only kindled God's anger. The Bible says, "The anger of the LORD was kindled against Moses" (Ex. 4:14). This does not mean that God had a fit of temper; rather, it means that God was not pleased with the excuses Moses offered. In effect, God was saying, "Moses, you have no right to make these excuses, and if your faith were in the right place and Person, you would not be making them."

Just as God became angry with Moses because of his excuses, so He becomes angry with any believer who limits Him by a lack of faith. Actually, the excuses Moses gave were the exact reasons why God had selected him for the task.

For each lack that Moses expressed, God had a satisfying and abundant provision. What Moses failed to understand at this time was that when God calls, He always guarantees and furnishes all that is needed to accomplish His will. This is also true of believers today. When God calls you to do something, He always guarantees and furnishes all you need to do what He asks.

Being confident of this very thing, that he which hath begun a good work in you will perform it until the day of Jesus Christ (Phil. 1:6).

REJECTED BY ONE'S OWN

EXODUS 5:10–23

As Moses was rejected by Pharaoh and then by his own people, he was learning what it meant to stand alone with God. Not only did Pharaoh refuse his request, but he essentially called Moses a liar. And the Israelites went around Moses by taking their case directly to Pharaoh. It was one thing to be rejected by Pharaoh, an unbeliever, but it was quite another thing to be rejected by his own people. Moses experienced a bitter and painful lesson in learning to trust God alone. Every vestige of hope in others was ripped away, and he had no other choice than to stand alone with God.

The entire plan of delivering Israel seemed to have backfired. Once again his own people were bitter toward him and accused him of being directly responsible for their troubles, even though Moses had been willing to give his life for them. How those words must have cut deeply into his heart.

One's heart goes out to Moses because his troubles were only beginning. He had been prepared for the rebuff that he received from Pharaoh because he had been warned of this by God. But no warning had been given him concerning the rebuff by his own people, which was much harder to take. How discouraging it is when one is criticized by those he is trying to help. This teaches us, too, that it is easier to take criticism from unbelievers than it is to take it from believers.

He came unto his own, and his own received him not (John 1:11).

LEARNING TO STAND ALONE
EXODUS 6:1–13

After Moses had cast himself completely on the Lord and the Lord had assured Moses of what He would do, "Moses spake so unto the children of Israel: but they hearkened not unto Moses for anguish of spirit, and for cruel bondage" (Ex. 6:9).

This reaction must have been very hard for a leader like Moses to accept, but it only verified that he had to learn to stand alone with God. Every true leader has to come to the realization that at times he will have to stand alone.

Throughout biblical history men have stood alone with God—men like Noah, Abraham, Joseph and Elijah. Although their friends turned against them and they had no one to lean on for support at times, they stood strong for God because they were willing to stand alone. And Moses' successor was no exception. After the death of Moses, Joshua faithfully led the people of Israel, but at the end of his life he presented the people with a decision they had to make. Joshua told the people, "Choose you this day whom ye will serve;... but as for me and my house, we will serve the LORD" (Josh. 24:15). Whether we are in a high position of leadership or not, it is important for us to realize that there will be times when we must stand alone with God for the convictions He has given us through His Word.

Fear thou not; for I am with thee: be not dismayed; for I am thy God: I will strengthen thee; yea, I will help thee; yea, I will uphold thee with the right hand of my righteousness (Isa. 41:10).

UNQUESTIONED OBEDIENCE
EXODUS 7:1–13

Moses went before Pharaoh, and from this point forward we see unquestioned obedience on his part. Total obedience is really recognition of God's absolute sovereignty, and this is what Moses finally recognized.

The complete obedience of Moses is also seen in Exodus 7:10: "And Moses and Aaron went in unto Pharaoh, and they did so as the LORD had commanded." Verse 20 emphasizes the same theme: "And Moses and Aaron did so, as the LORD commanded." Twelve times God gave the orders, and twelve times Moses and Aaron did as God said. Miracles began to happen one after another as they gave unquestioned obedience to the Lord.

This teaches us that we must be where God wants us to be at the time He wants us to be there, and we must do what He says if we expect to see things happen. As the believer desires to act and obey, he will see God work mightily in and through him.

Now therefore, if ye will obey my voice indeed, and keep my covenant, then ye shall be a peculiar treasure unto me above all people (Ex. 19:5).

MAY 7

REFUSING TO COMPROMISE
EXODUS 8:20–32

As the plagues came on Pharaoh and the Egyptians, he began to weaken a little bit. Pharaoh said to Moses, "Go, sacrifice to your God [here] in the land [of Egypt]. And Moses said, It is not suitable or right to do that; for the animals the Egyptians hold sacred and will not permit to be slain are those which we are accustomed to sacrifice to the Lord our God; if we did this before the eyes of the Egyptians, would they not stone us? We will go three days' journey into the wilderness and sacrifice to the Lord our God, as He will command us" (Ex. 8:25–27, Amplified).

This was Pharaoh's first offer, but Moses was bold in faith and refused to compromise. Moses spoke for God and com¬pletely refused anything less than what God demanded. Moses even exposed Pharaoh's false religion as he mentioned that the Egyptians held certain animals to be sacred. Moses made it clear that his firm intention was to obey God completely.

That Moses' faith was becoming bolder and bolder is also seen in that he prayed for an end to the plague of flies. This was not presumption on Moses' part, because he already had assurance from God that such a prayer was in accordance with His will.

Let us hear the conclusion of the whole matter: Fear God, and keep his commandments: for this is the whole duty of man (Eccles. 12:13).

GOD KNOWS THE HEART
EXODUS 9:22–35

Against the backdrop of this awful judgment is a verse that reveals God's protection of His own: "Only in the land of Goshen, where the children of Israel were, was there no hail" (Ex. 9:26). Goshen was part of Egypt, but God controlled the circumstances so that the Israelites were untouched by the judgment that Egypt experienced.

Notice what Pharaoh's response was to this awful judgment: Although Pharaoh seemed to be conscious of his wickedness before God, it was only a feigned confession made in order to escape judgment.

Moses was not fooled by Pharaoh's false confession. God had given Moses insight so he knew what was in Pharaoh's heart and was not fooled in any way. This reveals how hardened Pharaoh really was; it did not bother him even to fake a confession of sin to God. But God knows what is in each person's heart, and He was not deceived for one minute.

God had showered His mercies on Pharaoh, but Pharaoh had refused to respond positively in any way. So in the remaining plagues God further hardened Pharaoh's heart so as to fulfill His plan of total revelation of Himself as absolutely sovereign.

Shall not God search this out? for he knoweth the secrets of the heart (Ps. 44:21).

RESISTING GOD

EXODUS 10:12–29

When the judgment of darkness came on Egypt, Pharaoh called for Moses and told him, "Go, serve the LORD; only let your flocks and your herds be detained. Even your little ones may go with you" (Ex. 10:24, NASB). This was Pharaoh's fourth and final compromise offer. Pharaoh wasn't dumb; he realized that people are attached to their property and that if the Egyptians could keep the property of the Israelites, then they could be assured that the Israelites would return. But Moses was not about to accept a compromise offer. He said, "Not a hoof shall be left behind" (v. 26, NASB).

Pharaoh was now past feeling, and the omniscient God also knew that he was unchangeable. Thus, the Bible says again, "But the Lord made Pharaoh's heart stronger and more stubborn, and he would not let them go" (v. 27, Amplified).

Then the proud king, unchanged by all of these judgments, said to Moses, "Get away from me! See that you never enter my presence again, for the day you see my face again you shall die!" (v. 28, Amplified). Moses answered Pharaoh, "Thou hast spoken well, I will see thy face again no more" (v. 29).

What terrible grief results when people set their wills against God as Pharaoh did.

This is an evil among all things that are done under the sun.... yea, also the heart of the sons of men is full of evil, and madness is in their heart while they live (Eccles. 9:3).

GOD'S JUDGMENT ANNOUNCED
EXODUS 11

Moses' announcement of the final plague is recorded in Exodus 11. Verse 1 is the key to understanding its purpose: "The LORD said unto Moses, Yet will I bring one plague more upon Pharaoh, and upon Egypt; afterwards he will let you go hence; when he shall let you go, he shall surely thrust you out hence altogether." Not only would Pharaoh be willing to let the Israelites go, he would actually push them out of his country. This reveals the folly of fighting against God, because He finally brings a person to his knees. The creature is impotent before his omnipotent Creator.

As the Israelites prepared to leave Egypt, God instructed, "Let every man borrow of his neighbour, and every woman of her neighbour, jewels of silver and jewels of gold" (Ex. 11:2). The word "borrow" does not accurately convey the meaning of the Hebrew word from which it is translated. The Hebrew word is *shaal*, which basically means "to ask." The Israelites were to ask the Egyptians for the back wages owed them.

God had waited and waited on Pharaoh, and Moses had been patient as he warned Pharaoh of coming judgment. But both God and Moses were to be vindicated. Moses, however, only announced this final judgment, which was entirely from God. The Passover lamb speaks of salvation, and salvation is only of God, although men are used to announce the message.

For God shall bring every work into judgment, with every secret thing, whether it be good, or whether it be evil (Eccles. 12:14).

A NEW BEGINNING
EXODUS 12:1–14

That the time of the Exodus was also the time of the birth of Israel as a nation is evident from what God told Moses and Aaron in the land of Egypt. This was actually a fulfillment of what God had told Jacob: "Fear not to go down into Egypt; for I will there make of thee a great nation" (Gen. 46:3).

The month referred to in Exodus 12:2–3 is the month of April, known to the nation of Israel as "Abib." From that point on Israel was to keep the Feast of the Passover during this month. Deuteronomy 16:1 refers to this: "Observe the month of Abib, and keep the passover unto the LORD thy God: for in the month of Abib the LORD thy God brought thee forth out of Egypt by night." The Feast of the Passover was a remembrance of the beginning of the nation of Israel. As such, the Passover reminded the Israelites of everything that was foundational to the nation itself.

Just as the Israelites needed to be reminded of their beginning as a nation, those of us who know Jesus Christ as Saviour need to be reminded of the deliverance we have experienced. Colossians 1:12–14 refers to this deliverance: "Giving thanks unto the Father.... who hath delivered us from the power of darkness, and hath translated us into the kingdom of his dear Son: in whom we have redemption through his blood, even the forgiveness of sins."

This one thing I do, forgetting those things which are behind, and reaching forth unto those things which are before (Phil. 3:13).

SAVED BY BLOOD

HEBREWS 9:11–22

The Israelites were not spared judgment in Egypt because they prayed or because they fasted or because of their own merits but only because they applied the shed blood as God instructed. They were in houses behind the blood that had been applied to the doorposts; thus, their firstborn were spared from death.

In order for the firstborn to be spared, a lamb had to be killed and its blood applied to the doorposts. Death would be inflicted either on the firstborn or on the substitute for the firstborn. But the death of the lamb alone would not do; its blood had to be applied as God instructed. God said, "They shall take of the blood, and strike it on the two side posts and on the upper door post of the houses" (Ex. 12:7). Nothing was left to chance or to man's ingenuity. Salvation was, and is, totally of God.

Although Christ shed His blood for the sins of the world (1 John 2:2), no one is saved from condemnation unless he personally trusts Christ as Saviour (John 1:12). Receiving Christ as Saviour is appropriating to oneself what Christ has made available. Not until the blood has been applied does it actually provide safety. It is not enough to know that the blood of Jesus Christ was shed for the forgiveness of sin—one must personally trust Him as Saviour.

Forasmuch as ye know that ye were not redeemed with corruptible things, as silver and gold.... but with the precious blood of Christ, as of a lamb without blemish and without spot (1 Pet. 1:18–19).

GOD LEADS HIS OWN
EXODUS 13:17–22

The route God chose for the Israelites to leave Egypt was not by an easily traveled road but was a detour through the wilderness. The other road led through a populated area; it was easier and much more traveled, but in His wisdom, God chose the long road for the Israelites.

On this long route there were no highways, no bridges, no resources to supply their needs and no signs to direct their paths. In fact, it took them two years to reach Kadeshbarnea, which was on the southern extremity of the land of Canaan. But even this teaches us that God chooses the way His people should go. There is a very important lesson to be learned from this incident. We should not only realize that God chooses the way, but we should recognize that it is for our best if we respond to His direction.

When God began to lead them by a pillar of cloud by day and a pillar of fire by night, Israel's walk of faith really began. They were to move when the cloud moved, and they were to stay when the cloud remained stationary. They were to depend totally on the Lord for leadership.

Just as the cloud went before the Israelites, the Lord goes before those who are His own. The Bible says, "When he putteth forth his own sheep, he goeth before them, and the sheep follow him: for they know his voice" (John 10:4).

I will instruct thee and teach thee in the way which thou shalt go: I will guide thee with mine eye (Ps. 32:8).

RELEASED FROM BONDAGE!
EXODUS 14:5–9, 21–31

Just as the crossing of the Red Sea completed the deliverance of Israel from Egypt in order that they could begin their journey toward the Promised Land, so also when a person trusts Christ and has complete salvation, he is to progress in his Christian walk.

The crossing of both the Red Sea and the Jordan River illustrate what was accomplished for the believer in the death of Christ. At the Red Sea there was separation from Egypt; at the Jordan River there was an entering into the place of rest. The place of rest for the believer is referred to in Hebrews 4:9–10: "There remaineth therefore a rest to the people of God. For he that is entered into his rest, he also hath ceased from his own works, as God did from his."

For the believer, the death of Christ not only separates him from this present evil world, but it also makes him spiritually alive and seats him with Christ. What a glorious truth this is! We are on the resurrection side. We have much more than the forgiveness of sin; we have been associated with the risen Christ so that we may be united with Him forever and live the heavenly life. He who was dead is now alive! And this same Jesus indwells the bodies of believers in order to live His life in them (1 Cor. 6:19–20). What a glorious privilege is ours!

Verily, verily, I say unto you, He that heareth my word, and believeth on him that sent me, hath everlasting life, and shall not come into condemnation; but is passed from death unto life (John 5:24).

FROM SINGING TO COMPLAINING
EXODUS 15:1–7,22–27

In the Israelites' song recorded in Exodus 15, the word "Lᴏʀᴅ" occurs 11 times, and various personal pronouns referring to Him occur more than 30 times. So it is clear that the song was sung to Him and about Him. All the honors of the victory were reverently laid at His feet.

In this song of assurance and praise, Moses is not mentioned once. This indicates that the Israelites now had complete confidence in the trustworthiness of God. Only three days after the Red Sea experience, however, the Israelites were grumbling against Moses and against God. Why such a change of attitude in just three days? They had overlooked the fact that the cloud had led them in this direction, and since God was leading them, He would supply their needs.

When the people murmured against Moses (v. 24), they were actually murmuring against God. Every complaint against circumstances, every grumbling about the daily trials of life is directed against the One who "worketh all things after the counsel of his own will" (Eph. 1:11). Although the Israelites did not have this verse at the time, they had seen enough of God's work to know that He did not make mistakes and that He could perform anything necessary to provide for them. And remember, what happened to Israel is to serve as an example to us (1 Cor. 10:11).

Wherefore (as the Holy Ghost saith, To day if ye will hear his voice, harden not your hearts, as in the provocation, in the day of temptation in the wilderness) (Heb. 3:7–8).

FEEDING ON GOD'S PROVISIONS
EXODUS 16:11–36

As the manna fell in the wilderness for the Israelites, each person was to gather what he needed. The Lord instructed, "Gather of it every man according to his eating, an omer for every man, according to the number of your persons; take ye every man for them which are in his tents" (Ex. 16:16). The Bible records that the Israelites "gathered every man according to his eating" (v. 18). From these statements we see that there was personal responsibility to gather the food that each one needed; some gathered more, others gathered less, but each was to gather according to his particular need.

Think of the parallel this has for our feeding on God's Word. Each one must gather spiritual food for himself. A believer cannot live on another person's experience. Testimonies are interesting, and it is wonderful to have a pastor who preaches good messages, but a believer cannot live on those things alone. Each Christian must gather his own spiritual food according to his own need. If each one is feeding himself individually, then the testimonies and messages of others will be of encouragement to him, and he will be of much encouragement to others.

How much appetite for the Word of God do you have? Do you come to the Word with a hungry heart to learn all you can in order that you might know God better? The more we learn about Him, the more we will want to learn.

Neither have I gone back from the commandment of his lips; I have esteemed the words of his mouth more than my necessary food (Job 23:12).

LIFE TO ALL WHO DRINK
EXODUS 17:1–7

The water flowing from the rock indicates the provision for life. The psalmist said, "Behold, he smote the rock, that the waters gushed out, and the streams overflowed" (Ps. 78:20). The smitten rock pointed to the smitten Christ who paid the penalty of sin. The gushing streams of water picture the gracious supply of life through the Holy Spirit.

God smote His Son and raised Him from the dead, thereby sending forth the life-giving stream, but man must come and drink. Although Jesus Christ has paid the penalty of sin for all (1 John 2:2), only those who personally receive Him as Saviour have forgiveness of sin and eternal life (John 1:12; 5:24).

When God provides, He provides abundantly. When God provided water for the Israelites, the psalmist said, "He opened the rock and the waters gushed out; they ran in the dry places like a river" (Ps. 105:41). Concerning the life that the Lord Jesus Christ provides, He said, "I am come that they might have life, and that they might have it more abundantly" (John 10:10). This coincides with the way Jesus compared the Spirit to the abundance of running water (John 4:14; 7:37–38). So the rock in the wilderness prefigured Jesus Christ.

But whosoever drinketh of the water that I shall give him shall never thirst; but the water that I shall give him shall be in him a well of water springing up into everlasting life (John 4:14).

DELEGATING RESPONSIBILITY
EXODUS 18:13–27

As I have studied the Word of God concerning leadership, I have come to certain conclusions about spiritual principles of good leadership. These principles can be applied not only by leaders of organizations but by Sunday school teachers or by anyone with responsibility.

First, God uses people to do His work. When He has a job to do, He calls an individual to do it. Remember, however, that it took Moses a long time to become prepared for his task, and it sometimes takes leaders today a long time to be prepared for their tasks.

Second, when the task becomes too much for the one person God originally called, He calls others to work with the first individual.

Third, God holds the first individual responsible for the work done by the other individuals. This principle applies especially to the spiritual aspects of the work. This principle was particularly evident in Moses' leadership. Even though responsibility and authority could be delegated to others, he was still directly responsible before God.

God knows what work He wants accomplished, and He gives individuals responsibilities in order to accomplish that work. The only way that God's work can be done effectively is for individual believers to know what God wants them to do.

But now hath God set the members every one of them in the body, as it hath pleased him (1 Cor. 12:18).

PREPARING TO GIVE THE LAW
EXODUS 19:1–8, 16–25

Exodus 19 and 20 record an event that was a great turning point in the life of the Israelites as well as all mankind. These chapters record the giving of the Law by God through Moses to the nation of Israel.

Exodus 19:1–2 says, "In the third month, when the children of Israel were gone forth out of the land of Egypt, the same day came they into the wilderness of Sinai. For they were departed from Rephidim, and were come to the desert of Sinai, and had pitched in the wilderness; and there Israel camped before the mount."

God fulfilled His promise to Moses. When God had called Moses at the burning bush in the wilderness of Sinai, He said, "I will be with thee; and this shall be a token unto thee, that I have sent thee: When thou hast brought forth the people out of Egypt, ye shall serve God upon this mountain" (3:12). Moses and the Israelites were now at Mount Sinai, thus fulfilling God's promise to him.

At Mount Sinai the covenant by which God would deal with them for about the next 1,500 years was given. In other words, this covenant remained in effect until the Lord Jesus Christ was crucified at Calvary, thus changing the order of God's dealings with mankind.

The law of the LORD is perfect, converting the soul: the testimony of the LORD is sure, making wise the simple (Ps. 19:7).

LAW REVEALS NEED OF GRACE
EXODUS 20:1–17

The Mosaic Law was not given to produce salvation. The purpose of the Law was to help people see how far short they had fallen of God's righteous demands so they would cast themselves on the grace of God. Even during the time of the Law, grace was made available through the specified sacrifices for sin. These pointed forward to the Lord Jesus Christ, who was the sacrifice for sin. But because Jesus Christ came and offered Himself as the sacrifice for sin, the Law is no longer needed.

According to Romans 5:20, the Law was given so that God could reveal more of His grace: "Moreover the law entered, that the offence might abound. But where sin abounded, grace did much more abound."

When the people gathered at Mount Sinai and heard God speak, they became frightened and "stood afar off" (Ex. 20:18). This is also the result of today's preaching of the Law apart from the context of the grace of God.

Law set forth what man ought to be; grace sets forth what God is. We behold the face of Christ in the Holy Scriptures, and we see who God is by beholding Christ, "for in him dwelleth all the fulness of the Godhead bodily" (Col. 2:9). We know and understand what Christ has done for us as we study the Scriptures and see Him revealed in even the Mosaic Law.

Wherefore the law was our schoolmaster to bring us unto Christ, that we might be justified by faith (Gal. 3:24).

TRUST IN GOD, NOT MAN
EXODUS 32:1–18

Aaron and Hur had been left to look after the affairs of Israel while Moses was absent. Joshua, Moses' servant, had gone partway up the mountain with Moses, so he was not with the people at the time of this sin. But while Moses was on the mountaintop speaking to God face to face, the people wanted some likeness to worship as a substitute. The people were never allowed to see God face to face, but they knew He was on the mountaintop because of all the evidences they saw. But they wanted something they could feel with their hands, something they could see.

The religion of the natural man demands something he can perceive with his eyes. That is why so many people today—even Christians—go after things that are earthly. They need the security that is provided only by what they are able to touch and see.

The Israelites were no different; they wanted a god they could see. Moses was gone, and because their eyes had been on him rather than on God, they wanted an image. Perhaps this is why God took Moses away from them for a time. God not only wanted to talk to Moses face to face, but He also wanted to reveal to the Israelites that they were not really trusting God as they thought they were. What a lesson this is for believers today! Our trust should be in God, not in man.

It is better to trust in the LORD than to put confidence in man (Ps. 118:8).

STAND UP FOR JESUS!
EXODUS 32:19–35

The people were terror-stricken and awed by the irrefutable power exercised by Moses. He stood, one man against more than 600,000 soldiers (Num. 1:46), and commanded that those who were guilty of this sin be put to death. Moses had just been in the very presence of God, and no one was able to resist his authority and power.

As the people viewed the threatening cloud on the mountaintop above them, revealing God's presence, they could offer no resistance, and 3,000 were slain because they had repudiated God. Every person must have been weighed down—some with remorse for their sin, others with dread that the wrath of God would destroy even more of them. They undoubtedly remembered the awful voice of God they had heard about six weeks earlier, specifically prohibiting them from making any graven images. They had been quick at that time to say they would do everything God commanded, but they had committed a terrible sin. They had not feared God as they should have.

May those of us who know Jesus Christ as Saviour determine within our hearts to fix our eyes on Christ and to serve and honor Him, regardless of the apostasy that is everywhere about us. Remember Moses' searching question: "Who is on the LORD's side?" (Ex. 32:26).

But sanctify the LORD God in your hearts: and be ready always to give an answer to every man that asketh you a reason of the hope that is in you with meekness and fear (1 Pet. 3:15).

DESIRING TO KNOW GOD BETTER

EXODUS 33:12–23

Having succeeded in receiving several answers to his prayers, Moses then evidenced his greatest boldness in what he requested of God. Moses said, "I beseech thee, shew me thy glory" (Ex. 33:18). Moses had been so encouraged by God's answers to his prayers that he sought for the ultimate. The one desire that burned within Moses was to know God better. There is a tremendous need for each believer to have this same desire.

God is spirit, so no one is actually able to see Him. If a person could see God, he would be unable to stand the awesomeness of His glory. Thus, even Moses was able to see God only by what He is and by what He does. In effect, God was telling Moses, "I can't show you My face, because if I did, you would not live. But I will show you My goodness, which reveals who I am and what I do." God was going to reveal Himself to Moses by showing His grace and mercy to him.

As the believer walks in close communion with God, there is always the desire to know Him better. If this is not the desire of the believer, something is seriously lacking in his spiritual life.

That I may know him, and the power of his resurrection, and the fellowship of his sufferings, being made conformable unto his death (Phil. 3:10).

REFLECTING GOD'S GLORY

EXODUS 34:1–4,26–35

Moses was changed when he came down from the mountain. Earlier, he had asked to see the glory of the Lord, but when he came down from the mountain with the two tablets of stone, he did not know "that the skin of his face shone while he talked with him" (Ex. 34:29). Moses did not realize that his face reflected the glory of God. This was proof of the closeness between Moses and God, and it revealed to those who saw him that he had truly been in the presence of God's glory.

"When Aaron and all the children of Israel saw Moses, behold, the skin of his face shone; and they were afraid to come nigh him" (v. 30). Moses still did not realize the extent to which his face reflected the glory of God. He was not glorious in his own eyes, but he was in the eyes of others.

Every day before you go out to meet the world, spend some time with God by reading His Word and talking to Him in prayer. Spending time in His presence will bring the sunshine of heaven to your face, and others will observe this in you throughout the day.

But we all, with open face beholding as in a glass the glory of the Lord, are changed into the same image from glory to glory, even as by the Spirit of the Lord (2 Cor. 3:18).

MOVING AHEAD!

NUMBERS 10:1–13

The 11 months at Sinai had brought about many changes in the life of Israel. The people had arrived at Sinai a fugitive and unorganized people; they left a well-organized nation, molded into a commonwealth of 12 tribes. All was beautifully ordered.

Moses had spent the first 40 years of his life being trained in the courts of Pharaoh as a possible successor to Pharaoh. As such, Moses was trained in organization and was the general of the Egyptian army. He learned all that would be necessary to lead the greatest nation on earth at that time. Moses used all the knowledge he had accumulated in leading the Israelites. It was not, however, the unaided genius of Moses that God used. God leads through minds competent to receive and transmit His teaching. In Moses' case, his mental abilities were used to transmit to the Israelites an order of organization that was second to none. What Moses had learned in the world was translated into use for the glory of God.

The Israelites left Sinai as a mighty nation in battle array. They had been furnished with a code of laws, including sanitary regulations, which have been a model for civilized peoples of the world. They had also been provided with a system of sacrifices that continued for centuries. These sacrifices prophetically pointed to the priesthood of the Lord Jesus Christ for believers.

Be strong, all ye people of the land, saith the LORD, and work: for I am with you, saith the LORD of hosts (Hag. 2:4).

COMPLAINING IS CONTAGIOUS

NUMBERS 11:1–15

The mixed multitude (Num. 11:4) was probably a group of Gentiles who left Egypt with the Israelites. Although the complaining was started by the mixed multitude, the Israelites were also guilty of complaining. This indicates how infectious a complaining attitude can be. Because every person has a sin nature, it does not take long even for believers to become disheartened and to develop an attitude of complaining against the goodness of God. After salvation, Christians too often remember what they enjoyed in the world and occasionally long for the pleasures of sin. When this happens, the believer is guilty of leaving his first love.

Christians who have not grown spiritually as they should, through the reading of God's Word and applying it to daily life, find it easy to murmur as the Israelites did. Only a small minority may begin the complaining, but the Christian who is not mature is also susceptible. Just as the bark of one dog can start a whole group of dogs barking, one complaining believer can affect an entire group.

Many pastors have had their hearts broken, and church work has been greatly hampered by a few disgruntled people who influence the entire church. Every church group seems to have a few people who find it easy to complain about anything. Unless the other believers are mature, they will soon follow the pattern of the murmuring, weak believer.

Do not complain, brethren, against one another, that you yourselves may not be judged; behold, the Judge is standing right at the door (James 5:9, NASB).

JEALOUSY USES SPIRITUAL CLOAK
NUMBERS 12:1–16

Miriam and Aaron were Moses' older sister and brother. But even they took issue with Moses' leadership, although at first their complaints concerned his wife. Numbers 12 does not specifically say what Miriam and Aaron found objectionable about Moses' wife, but jealousy must have been the main problem.

This jealousy took its usual hypocritical turn. Miriam and Aaron did not talk to Moses about his wife; instead, they complained about his authority. How easy it is to disguise jealousy beneath a cloak of zeal for the law of God or to think of oneself as pure while rebuking somebody else's faults. Real jealousy originates from power hunger, and it usually breaks out in faultfinding, just as it did in this case.

We need to spend time in the Word and be alone with God until we are more concerned about His honor than our own. We do not have to worry about competition from other believers; our concern is only to glorify the Lord in all that we do. When a Christian is more concerned about God's honor than about his own, God will take care of his worries about competition from fellow believers. Granted, it is much easier to say this than to really live it, but we must come to grips with this problem if we are going to have victory in our Christian lives. We must be aware of the indwelling Christ and rely on Him to give us victory in these areas.

"For where jealousy and selfish ambition exist, there is disorder and every evil thing" (James 3:16, NASB).

WALKING BY SIGHT, NOT BY FAITH

NUMBERS 13:1–3,25–33

In addition to being characterized by unbelief, the Israelites were also characterized by self-will. Concerning the Israelites, the psalmist said, "They quickly forgot His works; they did not wait for His counsel, but craved intensely in the wilderness, and tempted God in the desert. So He gave them their request, but sent a wasting disease among them" (Ps. 106:13–15, NASB). The King James Version translates this last verse: "He gave them their request; but sent leanness into their soul" (v. 15). This reveals that God sometimes permits what is not in His direct will. It also reveals that the individual loses out spiritually.

What a paradox! The Israelites were to walk by faith, but they wanted to send spies into the land (see Deut. 1:19–23). What does faith want with spies? Apparently they were more concerned about walking by sight than by faith.

Many believers today find it extremely difficult to take God at His word. Instead of walking by faith, they want proofs about the future beyond what God has said and the power He has demonstrated. They are just like the Israelites who wanted to send spies into the land so they would know what it was like and how strong it was. Then they would choose whether or not to go in. Every believer should remember 2 Corinthians 5:7: "(For we walk by faith, not by sight.)"

As ye have therefore received Christ Jesus the Lord, so walk ye in him (Col. 2:6).

GOD'S JUDGMENT FALLS
NUMBERS 14:26–38

Even Joshua and Caleb, who dared to believe God, had to return to the wilderness with the others. Joshua and Caleb had to suffer along with them for 38 more years. This is an example of the way decisions affect other people. But the faith of Joshua and Caleb was characterized by great patience. Because they believed God, they were able to endure even the experiences of the desert without losing hope.

After God pronounced that none would enter the land except Joshua and Caleb and the younger generation, the Bible records God's judgment on the ten spies. They were judged by physical death right there and then. "The men, which Moses sent to search the land, who returned, and made all the congregation to murmur against him, by bringing up a slander upon the land, even those men that did bring up the evil report upon the land, died by the plague before the LORD" (Num. 14:36–37). Surely this judgment caused the others to realize that the Lord was not to be trifled with. This surely underscored in their minds that God expects to be taken at His word and not mocked by unbelief.

It is a fearful thing to fall into the hands of the living God (Heb. 10:31).

CHRIST OUR ROCK
NUMBERS 20:1–13,22–29

The rock mentioned in Exodus 17 foreshadowed Christ on the cross because there He was smitten. However, the rock of Numbers 20 foreshadowed the ascended Christ, who now intercedes as a High Priest for believers. The significant difference in the rocks of Exodus 17 and Numbers 20 is also indicated in that a different word for "rock" is used in these two passages. Although both rocks speak of Christ, God was endeavoring to communicate two different things to us concerning the Person of Christ.

In Exodus 17 the rock was smitten, just as Christ was "smitten of God" (Isa. 53:4) and was "bruised for our iniquities" (v. 5). The rock of Numbers 20 foreshadowed Christ in the heavens, as referred to in Hebrews 9:24: "For Christ is not entered into the holy places made with hands, which are the figures of the true; but into heaven itself, now to appear in the presence of God for us."

In the incident of Numbers 20 the rock foreshadowed the exalted Christ, and that is why it needed only to be spoken to. It is so important that this distinction between the smitten Christ and the exalted Christ as He is foreshadowed in the two rocks be maintained. Since the Lord Jesus Christ has been judged on the cross by having all of the sins of the world placed on Him, those of us who have received Him as Saviour need now to speak to Him for our needs.

And did all drink the same spiritual drink: for they drank of that spiritual Rock that followed them: and that Rock was Christ (1 Cor. 10:4).

THE DEATH OF A SAINT
DEUTERONOMY 34

Alone Moses worked, suffered, met God and legislated for his people. But never was this aloneness as apparent as when he was unattended—even by Joshua, his ever-faithful servant—as he walked up Mount Nebo to die. Alone he climbed the craggy steep. Alone he gazed on the landscape before him. And alone he lay down to die. At the moment of death he was absolutely alone—no one in Israel stood by him.

Yet God was with Moses. In a sense, God was Moses' undertaker, and the angels were his pallbearers. God was also the custodian of the grave, for no one knew where Moses was buried.

No tombstone was placed on Moses' grave—no monument to indicate the remains of this great man of God. The epitaph of Moses was not on a tombstone but was recorded in God's eternal Word, written there by the Holy Spirit Himself. No finer epitaph for Moses could be recorded than what is stated in Deuteronomy 34:10–12.

Hebrews 11:27 could also be an epitaph of Moses' life: "He endured, as seeing him who is invisible." What a eulogy! One reads of what many accomplished in the temporal and visible realm, but this man was ruled by the invisible. What a man of faith!

Precious in the sight of the Lord is the death of his saints (Ps. 116:15).

JUNE

The course of Joshua's life (the subject for June) is quite fully disclosed in the Bible, and it shows his conduct was not marred by some special sin as were some of Israel's other leaders.

By today's standards, Joshua should have been on the retirement list long before he was appointed Israel's leader. He was 85 years of age at the time, but—like Moses at 80—he was of unusual vigor of mind, body and spirit.

Joshua had weaknesses, but he lived on a high spiritual level. It is evident that the principle he stated at the end of his life was one that he had followed most of his days. He said, "As for me and my house, we will serve the LORD" (Josh. 24:15). Thus, Joshua's record is that of a man who actively sought God's control for his life and willingly followed wherever God led.

The readings for June are excerpted from *Joshua: Victorious by Faith*.

WORKMEN DIE, BUT GOD LIVES
JOSHUA 1:1–9

The first statement made in Joshua 1:2 is "Moses my servant is dead." Moses was dead but not God. The work of God is in no way hindered by the death of His servants, no matter how eminent they may be. The workman may be removed, but the work goes forward as ordained by God. This is God's doing.

I think of a remarkable organization that God has raised up in this century, starting it through one man. There came a day when God called that man home, and many people wondered if the organization would continue. I can say to the glory of God that it is not only going on, but it is larger than it ever was.

When we recognize that the spiritual life is God's doing, we will begin to grow. Until we do, we will not grow. God can change servants in order to show that He may use whatever instrument He pleases. He is not tied down by, or to, any certain individual. God is sovereign and can terminate the ministry of any of His servants when He pleases. He may change His principle of working any time He desires. A Moses can die, but God is eternal. He never dies.

Before the mountains were brought forth, or ever thou hadst formed the earth and the world, even from everlasting to everlasting, thou art God (Ps. 90:2).

QUESTIONABLE SEPARATION
JOSHUA 1:10–18

A rather sad note enters in with regard to some of the tribes of Israel. They did not all have the same degree of separation from the evil around them or the same degree of surrender to God. The background for this lies in the fact that while Moses was still leader, the Israelites conquered some of the kings on the east side of Jordan and took possession of their lands. It was good land with strong, walled cities and a countryside ideal for the raising of cattle. Two and a half of the tribes, Reuben, Gad and half of the tribe of Manasseh, asked to stay on that side of the Jordan.

It must be said on behalf of these two and a half tribes that their warriors were willing to help the other tribes take the land across the river and possess it. But the Reubenites and Gadites wanted to return to the other side of Jordan where things were more appealing to the eye and where there was ease, comfort, plenty and riches as the world would look at it. They tasted of the blessings of the Promised Land and helped the others to secure it, but they themselves longed for the world—its pleasures and indulgences—and were eventually trapped and ensnared by it. This is always the danger of those who would live on the border and not get into the land.

Wherefore seeing we also are compassed about with so great a cloud of witnesses, let us lay aside every weight, and the sin which doth so easily beset us, and let us run with patience the race that is set before us (Heb. 12:1).

A PAGAN TESTIFIES

JOSHUA 2:1–14

When the King of Jericho commanded Rahab to give up the two men she hid in her house, she lied to him. She said they went out at dark and she did not know which direction they took. Rahab's lie cannot be condoned. Such deceit cannot be justified as far as Christians are concerned. We must remember, however, that she was a pagan woman whose heart and mind were just being opened to spiritual things.

In spite of the fact that she lied, God used her to help preserve His servants. God used an enemy of His people to shelter two of them. This is in line with Proverbs 16:7, which says, "When a man's ways please the LORD, he maketh even his enemies to be at peace with him."

Something of what was going on in Rahab's mind is disclosed in her conversation with the two men after she brought them out from their hiding place. What a testimony this was coming from the person who was not saved in the way we use that terminology! For 40 years the Canaanites had been in fear of the Israelites. This must have been a revelation to these men of the terror that had laid hold of the whole population of Canaan, leaders and people alike. They knew that they could not stand against Israel's God.

The king's heart is in the hand of the LORD, as the rivers of water: he turneth it whithersoever he will (Prov. 21:1).

FAITH IN ACTION

JOSHUA 2:15–24

It is significant that it was a scarlet cord, or rope, that Rahab was to display in her window. This was symbolic of the blood of Christ, which, according to 1 John 1:7, cleanses us from all sin. In Hebrews 9:22 we are told that "almost all things are by the law purged with blood; and without shedding of blood is no remission." The protection that came to Rahab's household reminds us also of the incident of the Passover in Egypt. God instructed His people to sprinkle blood on the doorposts of their houses. He assured them that when the death angel came to slay the firstborn in Egypt, the houses protected by the blood would not be entered. They would be spared. The scarlet cord in Rahab's window protected her household just as the blood on the doorposts protected the Israelites in Egypt.

The New Testament makes special mention of Rahab with regard to this. James wrote: "Likewise also was not Rahab the harlot justified by works, when she had received the messengers, and had sent them out another way?" (2:25). Rahab had a faith that worked. She aided the spies in their escape from Jericho and hung a scarlet cord from her window. This was faith in action.

Now faith is the substance of things hoped for, the evidence of things not seen (Heb. 11:1).

PREPARING TO MOVE OUT
JOSHUA 3:1–8

There is a time for action, and there is also a time for waiting. There are times when we get in too big a hurry and are too impatient to wait on the Lord's time. On the other hand, there are some who lag behind and are not ready to move forward when they should. We need to remember that God is never too late. If we really want to do His will, He will always do His part on time.

So there was a three-day delay when the people reached the Jordan River. This gave them the opportunity to become quiet before God and made it possible for Him to give them final instructions. It was when they were ready to hear that the orders were given.

The same is true in our spiritual experiences. We must make a decision and then act upon that decision. After we have acted on our decision, it may be that God will have us wait for a while. This may sound like a paradox, but it is not. We need to learn to be calm before the Lord and await His time and timing for the events in our lives. The reason for Israel's delay at the Jordan, and often the reason for a delay after God has made plain to us that we are to move ahead, is in order to see if we are in earnest. When this is evident, then further instructions are given us.

Go ye therefore, and teach all nations, baptizing them in the name of the Father, and of the Son, and of the Holy Ghost: teaching them to observe all things whatsoever I have commanded you: and, lo, I am with you alway, even unto the end of the world (Matt. 28:19–20).

A STEP OF FAITH

JOSHUA 3:9–17

It is a never-to-be-forgotten experience when we hear a promise of God and step out on it in faith and then see God doing things on our behalf. The priests who carried the Ark of the Covenant into the Jordan River saw God work. It would not have been enough for them to have stood close to the edge of the water and to have believed in the great ability of God to stop the flow several miles upstream and pile up the waters as though there was a great dam there. If we were asked, "Is God able to do such a thing?" we undoubtedly would answer yes. But if each of us had to answer the question "Will God do this for me?" what would our answer be?

Every Christian is as precious in God's sight as the people of Israel were precious in His sight. What He promised them He did for them, and what He has promised you and me He will do for us. If we step out in faith, God will work on our behalf.

The Israelites did not make the mistake at the edge of Jordan of merely reckoning on God's ability to do what He promised. They did not stand to see what God would do. When they received their marching orders to go into the river and the priests led with the Ark, then the waters parted. Those priests got their feet wet. That is the only way faith operates.

Your faith should not stand in the wisdom of men, but in the power of God (1 Cor. 2:5).

MEMORIALS OF FAITH
JOSHUA 4:1–11

Gilgal was not only established as a home base for Israel during the conquest of the land; it also became a place of remembrance. Joshua was instructed to establish a memorial at Gilgal. Later on in the chapter we read of the setting up of another memorial, this time in the river itself.

These two memorials made of stones were to be reminders to Israel of their safe passage through the Jordan River. From the standpoint of the types involved, these two memorials remind us of the two aspects of our identification with Christ. First of all, the stones in the Jordan speak of the Israelites' having died to the past. Whenever an Israelite came into that area, he would see the stones and would be reminded that it was there Israel passed through the place of death as it were. The second set of stones was set up at Gilgal, the place of Israel's first night's lodging. They speak of new life out of death. These stones were taken out of the river as the Israelites marched through, then brought with them to the camping site. They therefore speak of Israel's new life on the other side of Jordan—a resurrection life.

Therefore we are buried with him by baptism into death: that like as Christ was raised up from the dead by the glory of the Father, even so we also should walk in newness of life (Rom. 6:4).

A PLACE OF SPIRITUAL RESURRECTION

JOSHUA 4:12–24

Gilgal marks the place of spiritual resurrection. Christ not only died, but He was buried and rose again and then ascended to the right hand of the Father. Very little is said in many Christian circles these days concerning the resurrection life, and practically nothing at all is said about the life of ascension. But we find in the Bible that these are spoken of very clearly. We read in Joshua 4:19–20 that the people came up out of Jordan and camped in Gilgal, and the 12 stones that they took out of the river were piled together in Gilgal by Joshua.

The Jordan River speaks of the place of death and Gilgal the place of life. We repeat this because we need to remember it. The corresponding New Testament truth is found in Ephesians 2:5–6 and is very important for our learning and growth. Even when we were dead in sins, God quickened us together in Christ and raised us up together and made us sit together in heavenly places in Christ. This is our ascension, not for the future but for the present. There is a time in the future when He will come and resurrect these bodies of our humiliation and give us resurrection bodies. But even now in our spiritual life we have already been raised together with Him and seated with Him in the heavenlies. In our position before God we are not only delivered from the self and sin life, but we are identified with Christ in His new life.

For ye are dead, and your life is hid with Christ in God (Col. 3:3).

EVIDENCE OF SEPARATION
JOSHUA 5:1–15

As far as Israel was concerned, there was no inheritance possible to them until they were circumcised. This was clearly stated in Genesis 17 where the covenant concerning the land was given. So now, as the nation stood at the edge of Canaan, it was necessary that they follow through on the sign of separation, which for them was circumcision. This was the sign God made with Abraham, and it was to be continued by his posterity.

The people renewed their separation through circumcision and also renewed their relationship by celebrating the Passover. Egypt with its bondage was behind them; the desert wanderings were over; Jordan, the place of decision, was crossed; and the nation was now ready to conquer Canaan. A new kind of food was necessary as Israel went against her enemies and took possession of the country.

Joshua soon discovered that he was face to face with the Captain of the Lord's hosts, the commander of the Lord's armies. Here was the Warrior and Leader, coming not to help but to take charge.

The Captain of the Lord's hosts came not only to direct the armies of Israel but also to fight for Israel and with Israel and through Israel. This is the same truth as is taught in Ephesians 6:10 where we are told to "be strong in the Lord, and in the power of his might."

For we are the circumcision, which worship God in the spirit, and rejoice in Christ Jesus, and have no confidence in the flesh (Phil. 3:3)

A KEY TO FUTURE VICTORIES

JOSHUA 6:1–14

Israel was assured of victory over Jericho. It was the key city to the whole campaign in Canaan. Once that obstacle was removed, the armies of Israel could spread out in all directions. So it is no wonder that we find in this incident of history an abundance of spiritual lessons.

Israel herself could not retreat. They had no alternative except to go forward in victory or suffer death. The death the Israelites might have suffered would have been that of dying at the hands of their foes. In the spiritual realm our danger is in succumbing to the enemy because we do not apply the victory.

Humanly speaking, Jericho was so strongly fortified as to be almost incapable of being taken. It guarded all the passes to the interior of the land of Canaan. Consequently, so long as Jericho held out, the land was safe from invasion.

We find that the same experience meets us once we choose to go on in Christian warfare. Invisible forces rise up to try to stop us and will succeed unless we follow our Captain implicitly. The enemy, Satan, will get us to consider our weaknesses, such as temperament or lack of ability or self-control, but these are the very things over which the Lord will give us victory.

I can do all things through Christ which strengtheneth me (Phil. 4:13).

A SHOUT OF FAITH

JOSHUA 6:15–27

According to Hebrews 11:30, the walls of Jericho fell down by faith. Some people want to attribute the collapse of the walls to an earthquake. It makes no difference to us what means God used. Whatever He did was timed so that after Israel had passed around the city the 13ᵗʰ time, and when the trumpets blew and the shout was made, then the walls fell. It took place just when God said it would.

God will speak again, and this time to the whole world. Just as the shout of the Israelites preceded the judgment on Jericho, so the Lord Jesus will come for His saints, descending from heaven with a shout and with the voice of the archangel and the trump of God, and the dead in Christ shall rise first (1 Thess. 4:16). Then will follow the Great Tribulation, the time of awful judgment for the earth.

Hebrews 12:26 prophesies of this when it says of God, "Whose voice then shook the earth: but now he hath promised, saying, Yet once more I shake not the earth only, but also heaven." Peter described it in 2 Peter 3 in these words: "But the day of the Lord will come as a thief in the night; in the which the heavens will pass away with a great noise, and the elements shall melt with fervent heat, the earth also and the works that are therein shall be burned up" (v. 10).

In a moment, in the twinkling of an eye, at the last trump: for the trumpet shall sound, and the dead shall be raised incorruptible, and we shall be changed (1 Cor. 15:52).

A WRONG TIME TO PRAY

JOSHUA 7:1–12

A failure to pray always makes us insensitive to sin. If we do not take time to pray, we will often not recognize sin for what it is. When we pray in the time of victory, we will not have to plead in the time of defeat.

When Joshua bowed his head in prayer following Israel's defeat, the Lord told him to get up and do something. This may sound like a contradiction to all the teaching we have had on prayer, but it is not. God was simply telling Joshua that it was not the time to pray in the way he was praying. Israel had sinned; it was Joshua's responsibility as leader to erase this sin from Israel's life. The fault for this military reversal did not lie with God but with Israel.

How often we, like Joshua and the elders of Israel, are inclined to blame God when things go wrong. We sometimes say when reverses come that God has forsaken us. Some people harden their hearts against God and blame Him that things are not going as they thought they should go. Yet had these individuals gone to God in the first place, they would have been directed in the proper way. God knows from the very beginning what He is doing and why He is doing it. He knows all the underlying causes that are related to all the incidents in our lives. There is nothing hidden from Him.

He did that which was right in the sight of the LORD, but not with a perfect heart (2 Chron. 25:2).

DEALING WITH SIN
JOSHUA 7:13–26

Several steps were involved in this account that are a guide with regard to the handling of sin and the cure of it in the believer's life. First of all, the stolen goods were brought out from hiding. Sin, whatever its nature, has to be brought into the open. The person who attempts to hide his sin cannot prosper. In the second place, they brought Achan to Joshua, who in this case stands in the position of Christ. Our Lord is both the Saviour from sin and the Judge of sin. In the third place, this sin of Achan's was laid before the Lord, for all sin is directed against Him. If in the process of our sin we have affected others, then they, too, should hear our confession. Public sin should be publicly confessed. It was only after this that Achan and his family were taken and stoned to death, then their bodies and possessions were burned. It is clear from this that the family was party to the father's sin, not innocent victims of it.

God's way of curing sin among believers in our day is given in 1 John 1:9: "If we confess our sins, he is faithful and just to forgive us our sins, and to cleanse us from all unrighteousness." The word "confess" means to "bring out into the open." We lay our sins out before the Lord and agree with Him concerning them. So we lay our sin out before the Lord completely and judge it. Thus the word "confess" also means "I agree with the Lord in this matter."

Purge out therefore the old leaven, that ye may be a new lump, as ye are unleavened. For even Christ our passover is sacrificed for us (1 Cor. 5:7).

NEW ORDERS AND METHODS

JOSHUA 8:10–30

With regard to the continuing effort to subdue Ai, Joshua received new orders. He was to follow a different method than what was used to bring Jericho down. The Lord does not always do things the same way. The method followed for Jericho's capture was not repeated for any other city or fortress in Canaan. So for Ai there was a new plan. God never changes in His character, but He does not necessarily follow the same plans in everything He does.

In our own personal lives God has made it plain that He is not stereotyped in the way He does things. We are told in 1 Corinthians 12 that God has diversities of operations. The passage reads: "Now there are diversities of gifts, but the same Spirit. And there are differences of administrations, but the same Lord. And there are diversities of operations, but it is the same God which worketh all in all." (vv.4–6) There is but one Holy Spirit, and He guides and plans in your life and mine and in the work of God today. The glory belongs to the Lord and not to us. It is God who gives the strategy to retake what has been lost in our lives just as He formulated a new strategy for the capture of Ai.

The way back may seem to be hard at times. We don't like to travel that road. We don't like to face our sins. The devil makes us ashamed, but God says the only way is to go back, as He has planned the way for us and that way only.

The steps of a good man are ordered by the Lord: and he delighteth in his way (Ps. 37:23).

DECIDING WITHOUT PRAYING
JOSHUA 9:1–15

The Gibeonites wanted Israel to make a league with them, which was contrary to God's instructions. God had said all the Canaanites were to be destroyed. Unfortunately, the leaders of Israel believed the lying Gibeonites and did as they suggested.

We are no match in ourselves for Satan's subtle ways. We can defeat him only as we remember the admonition of Proverbs 3:5–7 to trust in the Lord with all our hearts and to lean not on our own understanding. We are to acknowledge God in all our ways, and He will direct our paths. It is when we turn to Him that He gives us wisdom.

Israel's problem was that they were presumptuous, acting on the basis of their own wisdom. In our case Christ has been made unto us wisdom, but we must watch.

Be especially careful of decisions that have to be made under pressure. This is an area I have been careful about with regard to my own life, and it has paid off. When someone comes along and tells me that I have to make a decision right now because the opportunity might be gone by tomorrow, then I am even more on the alert. That kind of argument, particularly with spiritual things involved, could be Satan's subtle way of deception. Many persons have been led from the work of the Lord into side issues because they made decisions suddenly without consulting God.

"See then that ye walk circumspectly, not as fools, but as wise, redeeming the time, because the days are evil. Wherefore be ye not unwise, but understanding what the will of the Lord is" (Eph. 5:15–17).

LEARNING FROM MISTAKES
JOSHUA 9:16–27

Once the league was made by Israel and the Gibeonites, God held Israel to it. He would not let them destroy the cities or the people.

God works on this principle in other areas in our lives today. Even when we make mistakes, we are still under obligation to carry through our part of the transactions we have entered into. Where we involve ourselves and God's Word in our testimony, we have to stick by the promise made. Take for example the subject of marriage. Paul says in 1 Corinthians 7:12, "But to the rest speak I, not the Lord: If any brother hath a wife that believeth not, and she be pleased to dwell with him, let him not put her away." If a mistake has been made in marriage by a believer's marrying an unsaved person, the Christian is to make the best of it and trust God for the rest. If the unsaved partner wants to continue on in the marriage, the marriage must not be broken up.

Israel and Joshua had made a mistake. This mistake drove the Israelites to prayer. The presence of the Gibeonites among them was a constant reminder of the mistake made. The mistakes at Ai and Gibeon were not made again during Joshua's lifetime.

Satan was not able to discourage the Israelites from going on in their conquest of Canaan. Neither should a mistake we have made cause us to give up. Let us confess it to God, forsake it and go ahead.

Providing for honest things, not only in the sight of the Lord, but also in the sight of men (2 Cor. 8:21).

GOD IS SOVEREIGN
JOSHUA 10:1–15

Whatever God did either to the sun or the earth or whatever else was involved, the result was that there was light for a period extending about the length of another day. God, who is the God of the impossible, aided the Israelites by prolonging the daylight and by showering hailstones upon the Amorites. Concerning that day, Joshua 10:14 says, "And there was no day like that before it or after it, that the LORD hearkened unto the voice of a man: for the LORD fought for Israel."

Joshua knew his God. He had become acquainted with Him personally. This was especially true at the time he met the Lord as the Captain of the Lord's hosts. Joshua's knowledge of the Lord, however, must have begun with his years in Egypt, then increased during the 40 years he spent under the tutorship of Moses in the desert. Serving as Moses' minister, Joshua saw the mighty miracles of God and was introduced to some of the more personal aspects of God's dealing with Moses and His people. Joshua was one of the two men who dared to believe God the first time the spies were sent into Canaan. He knew that God was sovereign and accepted God's sovereignty for his own life.

When reading in the prophets for my devotions, I am constantly impressed by the presentation of God's sovereignty, His limitless might and the finality of His Word. What He says He will do, He does. Time in no way limits Him. Do you know this God as the Bible presents Him?

In whom also we have obtained an inheritance, being predestinated according to the purpose of him who worketh all things after the counsel of his own will (Eph. 1:11).

POSSESSING AN INHERITANCE

JOSHUA 11:16–23

We read in Joshua 11:23: "So Joshua took the whole land, according to all that the LORD said unto Moses; and Joshua gave it for an inheritance unto Israel according to their divisions by their tribes. And the land rested from war." The important word in this verse is "inheritance." Joshua gave Israel the land for an inheritance. But in chapter 13 we read "Now Joshua was old and stricken in years; and the LORD said unto him, Thou art old and stricken in years, and there remaineth yet very much land to be possessed" (v.1). This appears on the surface to be a contradiction with what chapter 11 says.

God had given all the land to the Israelites, but they were responsible to go in and possess it. They were promised, according to Joshua 1:3, "Every place that the soul of your foot shall tread upon, that have I given unto you." We also know now that God gave them the land for an inheritance. It was divided among the tribes as is outlined for us in the Book of Joshua. Nevertheless, each tribe had to go in and possess the land in order to enjoy its benefits.

So is it with our possessions in Christ. These must be appropriated on an individual basis. The Church as a whole is blessed only as we individuals possess what is ours in Christ. Our inheritance is in Him. In fact, He is our inheritance. A good illustration is given us in 2 Samuel 3. "Now then do it." See also Colossians 3:1–3.

And if children, then heirs; heirs of God, and joint-heirs with Christ; if so be that we suffer with him, that we may be also glorified together (Rom. 8:17).

 **JUNE 19**

FAILING TO APPROPRIATE
JOSHUA 18:1–10

Joshua 18 starts on a sad note. We read in verse 1: "And the whole congregation of the children of Israel assembled together at Shiloh, and set up the tabernacle of the congregation there. And the land was subdued before them." The land was conquered. The hard battle for it was over. Yet we learn, "And there remained among the children of Israel seven tribes, which had not yet received their inheritance" (v.2). That means they had not gone into the land to possess it. It had been given to them, but they had not gone in to receive it. No wonder Joshua admonished them, saying, "How long are ye slack to go to possess the land, which the LORD God of your fathers hath given you?" (v. 3).

In Joshua 21:43 we read, "And the LORD gave unto Israel all the land which he sware to give unto their fathers; and they possessed it, and dwelt therein." The thought is that they had a home in which they could settle. The Lord gave them rest from their enemies, and "there failed not ought of any good thing which the LORD had spoken unto the house of Israel; all came to pass" (v. 45). But they did not go in to possess it. They subdued the people and made them pay tribute. This was coexistence, not dispossession. This program was a fruitful source of trouble for Israel. It is also a dangerous one for us to follow with regard to sin and the failure to appropriate our possessions in Christ.

Now the just shall live by faith: but if any man draw back, my soul shall have no pleasure in him (Heb. 10:38).

COURAGEOUS IN GODLY LIVING

JOSHUA 23:1–8

To be courageous in the face of dangers confronting them was not only God's will but also His command. This is equally true with regard to us today. We are to be courageous in godly living as we seek to live according to the Word of God. All three members of the Trinity are working in our behalf so that all we have to do is by faith accept and appropriate what has been provided.

We may face defeat at times, but we are not to dwell upon our defeat. We are to return to the Lord, confess our wrongdoing, forsake it and go on with Him. We are to forget those things that are behind. There is more land to be possessed.

A negative admonition follows. Joshua said, "That ye come not among these nations, these that remain among you" (v.7) There were still many pagan people remaining in Canaan, but the Israelites were not to have fellowship with them. God's people were not to copy the heathen forms of worship but to be completely separated from them. There was to be no coexistence with the enemy.

This is also true in the Christian life. There is to be a putting off of what is evil and a putting on of the armor of God (see Eph. 6:1–17). The Israelites were to cleave to the Lord their God and put off the ways and beliefs of the Canaanites.

In whom we have boldness and access with confidence by the faith of him (Eph. 3:12).

THE WAY TO VICTORY
JOSHUA 23:9–13

We learn in Joshua 23:9–10 that nothing can stand before the person who will dare to trust God. Everything is in the favor of those who trust Him. With God on their side, total victory is assured. This is true with regard to us in our spiritual warfare. The enemies are great and more powerful than we are, but they are helpless when we go in the strength of the Lord Jesus Christ.

Admonition was added to these assurances as Joshua spoke to the people. He warned them that they must be careful how they conducted themselves and that they, above all, must love the Lord. This positive and then negative approach would serve to alert the Israelites to their blessings and also to their dangers.

We, too, must not turn back in defeat but go forward in Christian victory. There are evil things that will entangle us and ensnare us, so we must get rid of them. These may be but little things in our lives, but the little things can destroy us.

We are warned in Hebrews 12:1 to "lay aside every weight, and the sin which doth so easily beset us, and let us run with patience the race that is set before us." Nothing is to be allowed to hinder us. The weights spoken of in this passage may not be sins, but they could lead to sin or at least they could hinder us. There is a danger of losing what we have gained. We can be sure of this: Our sin will find us out.

For whatsoever is born of God overcometh the world: and this is the victory that overcometh the world, even our faith (1 John 5:4).

NOT ONE THING HAS FAILED

JOSHUA 23:14–16; HEBREWS 6:16–20

Recognizing that his death was imminent, Joshua told the Israelites that he was going the way of all the earth and then reminded them, "Ye know in all your hearts and in all your souls, that not one thing hath failed of all the good things which the LORD your God spake concerning you; all are come to pass unto you, and not one thing hath failed thereof (Josh. 23:14). What a faithful God! What He promised He fulfilled.

As I think back over my own life and God's dealing with us at *Back to the Bible* Broadcast, I, too, have to say that not one thing God has promised has failed. I have failed at times to appropriate what God has for me, but He has never failed. It is this very fact that should cause us to press on with Him. He is faithful and willing, in fact eagerly desirous, to see us go on to the end in victory. So why not appropriate all things that God has provided for us?

A serious warning is also given. God was faithful in keeping His promises to the Israelites. He was faithful in blessing. He was equally faithful in judgment when that was necessary.

The same warning is needed by us. God has offered us everything in Christ. He will not fail, but if we go back in our Christian experience, we will be the losers. To know truth and not obey it is to retrogress. God wants us to grow in the knowledge of Christ and appropriate by faith all that has been provided for us.

If we believe not, yet he abideth faithful: he cannot deny himself (2 Tim. 2:13).

ALL OF GRACE
JOSHUA 24:1–13

In this final part of his discourse, Joshua rehearsed God's wonderful deliverances of Israel, beginning with God's calling of the people in Abraham and His protection and leading of the patriarchs, Isaac and Jacob. Israel's deliverance from Egypt, the opening of the Red Sea and the destruction of Pharaoh's army are briefly retold. God's protection and provision for them in the wilderness, His deliverance of them from the Amorites, from those who would have enslaved them and tried to curse them, and His bringing Israel safely into Canaan, giving them a glorious land as a gift, are recounted. Then Joshua added that God did not give them the possessions in Canaan because they deserved them. They did not merit His gifts. God said, "I have given you a land for which ye did not labour, and cities which ye built not in them of the vineyards and oliveyards which ye planted not do ye eat" (Josh. 24:13).

This is true, too, with our eternal salvation. We do not merit it by good works (Eph. 2:8–9) or by keeping the Law (Rom. 3:20–22). Salvation becomes ours only as we believe in the finished work of Christ on the cross. "Believe on the Lord Jesus Christ, and thou shalt be saved" (Acts 16:31).

But if it is by grace, it is no longer on the basis of works, otherwise grace is no longer grace (Rom. 11:6, NASB).

WE MUST CHOOSE

JOSHUA 24:14–15; 2 CORINTHIANS 6:14–18

Joshua admonished the people first of all to fear the Lord. This does not mean to be afraid of Him but to place reverential trust in Him. With such trust in the Lord they would follow Him with confidence. With such fear of the Lord there would be a hatred for evil. So what he was asking the Israelites to do was to have an attitude of heart of complete trust in God. Because of this, then, they would avoid evil and walk in faith.

The second admonition was to serve the Lord. Israel was to serve Him in sincerity and in truth. After a proper attitude of heart comes the activity of the mind and the body. To serve in truth means to serve in perfection and with stability. For us this means to serve the Lord now with a perfect heart. We must put on the whole armor of God so that we can stand against the wiles of the devil. We need this in order to fight the battles of the Lord successfully.

Joshua warned the Israelites, in the third place, to put away those things that God did not allow. The idolatry so characteristic of Canaan, with all its attendant evil, unbelief, carelessness and backsliding, was to be put away. It was not a matter of following majority opinion but of finding out what God wanted and doing it. Joshua made it very plain that the Israelites had to choose whom they would serve. We, too, face the same issue.

Jesus saith unto him, I am the way, the truth, and the life: no man cometh unto the Father, but by me (John 14:6).

THE PEOPLE'S CHOICE
JOSHUA 24:16–33

The people were decided and definite in their reaction to Joshua's admonition. They responded with a definite decision to follow the Lord.

Warning the people that they were making no light decision, Joshua said to them, "Ye cannot serve the LORD: for he is an holy God; he is a jealous God; he will not forgive your transgressions nor your sins" (Josh. 24:19). They needed this reminder. God is holy and cannot coexist with sin. He is a jealous God and will not take a secondary place. We cannot serve God and live in sin.

The Israelites assured Joshua that they would obey the Lord, for they said, "Nay; but we will serve the LORD. And Joshua said unto the people, Ye are witnesses against yourselves that ye have chosen you the LORD, to serve him. And they said, We are witnesses" (vv. 21–22).

There was even a covenant made, and Joshua took a great stone and placed it under an oak as a witness of the people's intention to serve God.

The generation that made the promise was true to its word. We learn in verse 31: "And Israel served the LORD all the days of Joshua, and all the days of the elders that overlived Joshua, and which had known all the works of the LORD, that he had done for Israel." This was a good beginning, and what a different history we would have had if each succeeding generation of Israelites had reached the same decision and stayed with it.

For the gate is small and the way is narrow that leads to life, and few are those who find it (Matt. 7:14, NASB).

INCOMPLETE VICTORY
JUDGES 1:1–2,27–36

We have seen before that we cannot possess what we do not first dispossess. We cannot possess what someone else has control of. Israel could not possess that portion of Canaan where they coexisted with the Canaanites, even though the Canaanites were their slaves. Instead of destroying the Canaanites or driving them out as God had commanded, the Israelites in many areas allowed them to live in their midst. It was not a complete victory for God's people. Time after time we are told how they failed to go all the way to accomplish God's purpose. Passage after passage tells us the same story.

This is the story of the seven tribes of Israel that did not completely dispossess the inhabitants and thus possess the land for themselves. God said to drive out these Canaanites, for their cup of sin was full. Israel was to get rid of them and then to dwell where they had dwelt.

There are things that God has told us to get rid of in our lives. And there is no need for us to protest that we cannot because Christ died and rose again to make it possible for us to do so. Furthermore, we have the Holy Spirit indwelling us so that Christ now indwells us through the Holy Spirit to live out His life in us. Thus day by day we can, by faith, overcome in the spiritual warfare and be victors through Christ.

For sin shall not have dominion over you: for ye are not under the law, but under grace (Rom. 6:14).

RESULTS OF REBELLION
JUDGES 2:11–23

What follows when we fail to do God's will is pictured for us in Israel's experience recorded in Judges 2. The people of Israel did what was wrong in the sight of the Lord and forsook Him who was the God of their fathers. They followed the gods of the heathen around them and thereby provoked the true God to anger.

Their spiritual condition was up and down, a condition that lasted some 400 years while God dealt with them in grace and mercy. He was long-suffering and sent them judge after judge to deliver them. Then we have the account in Judges 2:20–23, which is the sad condition into which the people of Israel were plunged because they would not follow the Lord.

The lesson is obvious for us. If, after we know the truth of the victory provided for us in Christ Jesus (for the Lord always causes us to triumph in Christ Jesus), we do not follow, then chastisement must fall. If we do not take a definite stand against sin and the self-life, we must face the consequences. It is this rebellious attitude of mind and heart that is the root cause of much of the useless kind of Christianity we see today. There are Christians who have a ticket to heaven but who are useless to God, failing to accomplish anything for Him.

"But if ye will not obey the voice of the LORD, but rebel against the commandment of the LORD, then shall the hand of the LORD be against you, as it was against your fathers" (1 Sam. 12:15).

A THREEFOLD ENEMY

ROMANS 6:6–18

The Bible teaches that the Christian's enemy is a threefold one: the flesh, the world and the devil. The flesh is the old self life, the fallen nature in each one of us. The world is the world of mankind around us that is alienated from God and opposed to His rulership. The devil, or Satan, includes also the fallen angels whom he controls.

The basis for our victory over this threefold enemy has already been laid for us in Christ. With regard to the flesh, we read in Romans 6: "Knowing this, that our old man is crucified with him, that the body of sin might be destroyed, that henceforth we should not serve sin. For he that is dead is freed from sin" (vv. 6–7).

With regard to the world, we read in Galatians 6:14: "But God forbid that I should glory, save in the cross of our Lord Jesus Christ, by whom the world is crucified unto me, and I unto the world." This is why the Lord could tell us in John 16:33, "In the world ye shall have tribulation: but be of good cheer; I have overcome the world." Further light is thrown on this subject in 1 John 5:4–5: "For whatsoever is born of God overcometh the world: and this is the victory that overcometh the world, even our faith. Who is he that overcometh the world, but he that believeth that Jesus is the Son of God?"

For I know whom I have believed, and am persuaded that he is able to keep that which I have committed unto him against that day (2 Tim. 1:12).

 **JUNE 29**

BECOMING SPIRITUALLY AGGRESSIVE
1 CORINTHIANS 9:24–27; HEBREWS 12:1–4

Canaan, the Promised Land for the Israelites, is not a type of heaven as some have thought and as some hymns portray it. Rather it is a type of the Christian's battle against sin and his victory over it as he seeks to live for the Lord. Canaan was a scene of conflict, not of complete peace and rest as heaven will be. The nations in Canaan become types of the principalities and powers we read about in Ephesians 6:12, where the apostle Paul tells us, "We wrestle not against flesh and blood, but against principalities, against powers, against the rulers of the darkness of this world, against spiritual wickedness in high places."

When Joshua led the people of Israel into Canaan, he and they not only had to overcome the human leaders and their armies in the land of promise but also the evil spiritual forces under the direction of Satan who were the actual rulers of these heathen kings.

I have drawn more spiritual lessons for myself and the *Back to the Bible* Broadcast from Joshua's experiences and the Book of Joshua and its New Testament counterpart, Ephesians, than from any other person or portions in the Bible. We as believers are warned to put on the whole armor of God, according to the Book of Ephesians, if we are going to enter victoriously into spiritual warfare against the powers of Satan. If we are to avoid a stalemate in our Christian lives, an experience similar to Israel's 40 years in the desert, we will have to choose to become spiritually aggressive.

I press toward the mark for the prize of the high calling of God in Christ Jesus (Phil. 3:14).

WHERE DO WE STAND?

1 CORINTHIANS 10:1–13

There is a parallel in the experience of Israel and Christians. While the Israelites were in the desert, they were largely controlled by the flesh, or the old self-life. Consequently, they were always on the defensive. Murmuring and quarreling characterized their experience. A Christian who is marked by the same qualities or a church that is noted for its murmuring and quarreling is not on the offensive for the Lord. Theirs is a desert life experience.

Another aspect of Israel's experience was when they entered the land. Then they faced the need of entering into offensive warfare. They came in as invaders with the objective of conquering. It was necessary that they destroy the enemy if they were to take possession of the land for themselves and their posterity.

We need to ask ourselves where we stand with regard to these experiences. Are we still in the world, enduring its bondage? Are we caught up in worldliness? Or are we in a desert experience in which we are on the defensive, making no headway? Or have we entered into spiritual warfare, seeking to take possession of the things the Lord has for us? (See Eph. 6:10–17.)

Examine me, O Lord, and try me; test my mind and my heart (Ps. 26:2, NASB).

JULY

David, Israel's great king (the subject for July), was an outstanding man in many ways. Concerning David, God said, "I HAVE FOUND DAVID the son of Jesse, A MAN AFTER MY HEART, who will do all My will" (Acts 13:22, NASB). What made David a man after God's heart? It is this side of David's life that helps to explain why he was outstanding as a military strategist, prophet, psalm writer, king—and above all, as a humble believer in the Lord.

The members of David's own family were not always cordial toward him, yet he was gracious in his treatment of them. Many of the psalms came out of the bitter waters through which David passed, and these inspired hymns have been repeating their messages to every generation of believers from that time to this.

The readings for July are excerpted from *David: A Man After the Heart of God*.

A MAN AFTER THE HEART OF GOD

1 SAMUEL 16:1–13

When Samuel was sent to the house of Jesse to anoint one of his sons to be king, the old prophet apparently assumed that since Saul (the present king) was a man of striking physical appearance, God would choose another like him. As Eliab, Jesse's oldest son, stood before him, Samuel said in his heart, "Surely the LORD's anointed is before him" (1 Sam. 16:6). Then God showed Samuel that the divine standard was not according to a man's physical appearance but according to his heart attitude toward God. "Look not on his countenance," the LORD said, "or on the height of his stature; because I have refused him: for the Lord seeth not as man seeth; for man looketh on the outward appearance, but the LORD looketh on the heart" (v. 7).

Paul referred to this fact when he said in Acts 13:22–23, "And when he [God] had removed him [Saul], he raised up unto them David to be their king; to whom also he gave their testimony, and said, I have found David the son of Jesse, a man after mine own heart, which shall fulfil all my will. Of this man's seed hath God according to his promise raised unto Israel a Saviour, Jesus." So God's choice was a heart choice. It is clear from this that God's thoughts are not our thoughts, and our ways are not God's ways (see Isa. 55:8–9). God looked for a man whose heart was right toward Him and found him in David.

Know that the LORD hath set apart him that is godly for himself (Ps. 4:3).

A LIFE THAT BLESSES OTHERS
1 SAMUEL 16:14–23

Having been anointed king of Israel, David's life could never be the simple life of a shepherd boy again. He was able to return to his flocks for brief periods, but those times soon ceased. As Psalm 23 indicated, David never forgot that the Lord was his Shepherd. The reminders of the Lord's majesty and care and the benefits of the quiet pastures and still waters steadied David in many a crisis. And they helped bring about the restoration of his soul when he sinned.

The quality of David's life was such that when he first appeared at the royal residence, Saul "loved him greatly" (1 Sam. 16:21). David came to dispel with his sweet music the evil spirit that often troubled Saul. He, of course, did not know that David was to be his successor. On the other hand, David behaved so well and was so humble that Saul had no reason to dislike him; rather, he admired and loved him. He made David his armor-bearer and sent word to Jesse that his son was now attached to the inner circle of the king's bodyguard.

Do our lives give off a sweet fragrance that is a blessing to others? Others should see Christ's life reflected in our lives as believers in Christ.

By this shall all men know that ye are my disciples, if ye have love one to another (John 13:35).

JULY 3

THE WAY OF VICTORY
1 SAMUEL 17:17–37

Saul stated that David was not able to go against the Philistine. Saul said, "Thou art but a youth, and he a man of war from his youth" (1 Sam. 17:33). Here was a man of gigantic stature and who had been trained for war from his adolescent years. In this way, Saul sought to discourage David just as Eliab had tried to discourage him with criticism and slander. But David knew his God and would not be put off. Many centuries later, Paul put into words the truth that God does not choose the great things of this world to do His work, but He calls on those things that the world considers as nothing to confound the world's wisdom (see 1 Cor. 1:26–29). Herein lies a basic difference between human reasoning and God's reasoning. David knew his God and had already seen the hand of God upon his own life in a remarkable way.

David said to Saul, "Thy servant kept his father's sheep, and there came a lion, and a bear, and took a lamb out of the flock: and I went out after him, and smote him, and delivered it out of his mouth: and when he arose against me, I caught him by his beard, and smote him, and slew him" (1 Sam. 17:34–35).

All of us face lions and bears and Goliaths who defy the living God and scorn His people. But where is the Lord God of David? He is still the same today, and those of us who put our trust in Him will be victorious.

God is our refuge and strength, a very present help in trouble (Ps. 46:1).

STANDING STRONG FOR GOD

1 SAMUEL 17:38–51

God's own program for the ages calls for the complete subjugation of all enemies. "Then cometh the end, when he shall have delivered up the kingdom to God, even the Father; when he shall have put down all rule and all authority and power. For he must reign, till he hath put all enemies under his feet. The last enemy that shall be destroyed is death. For he hath put all things under his feet" (1 Cor. 15:24–27).

When Goliath died, the Philistine army began to run in terror, and the people of Israel followed them to take the spoils. This is always true. Wherever the faithful servant or servants of God carry through some project to victory, the unbelieving and faithless crowd will always come in, seeking what it considers its share.

That same crowd may have held back the victory for a time through envy and jealousy, but as soon as the victory is won, they want to climb on the bandwagon.

May God give us grace to believe Him and, through faith, not to be defeated Christians but victorious children of the living God. May God stir our hearts so that we will not be ashamed of Jesus Christ our Lord.

What time I am afraid, I will trust in thee (Ps. 56:3).

THE PRICE OF POPULARITY
1 SAMUEL 18:1–16

Popularity has its attractive side, but it carries with it spiritual dangers. There is always a price to pay for it, and sometimes it is too high. Some can handle popularity and not be hurt by it; others cannot. Pride arising in the human heart for any reason is not good. Then there are always those who become jealous of anyone who seems to be well liked by others. Perhaps these dangers, internal and external, help keep a person on the alert. The Lord knows how much any of us can take of these things and always provides a way of escape (see 1 Cor. 10:13).

David knew the source of his strength, so that praise only caused him to give God the glory. It did not change his humble attitude toward life. On the other hand, Saul's reaction to the praise given David changed Saul for the worse.

Let us not become discouraged if, after we surrender our lives to God, He permits testings and trials to come. They will always come. Young people write to me or speak to me in services about this. One of their most common questions is why things are so adverse after they have given themselves completely to the Lord. We know first from the Scriptures and then from experience that testings are essential for our spiritual training. They are needed before God can trust us with the responsibilities of spiritual leadership.

Set your affection on things above, not on things on the earth (Col. 3:2).

"PERSECUTED, BUT NOT FORSAKEN"

1 SAMUEL 19:1–18

When David realized he had to flee, he naturally went to his own house. But his home was not a safe place for him. Being human, David had his weaknesses, and one of those weaknesses showed itself in some of the women he married. It is doubtful if Michal was a true believer, and his marriage to her was a source of trouble to him.

Out of this experience he wrote Psalm 59. In it he poured out his heart for deliverance (vv. 1–2) and declared his innocence, saying, "Strong men are banding together to attack me, not for my transgression, nor for my sin, o Lord. Without any wrong of mine, they run and prepare themselves" (vv. 3–4, Berkeley). He felt keenly the pressure of the lies and persecution by his enemies.

This is a good psalm for us to read when we are being pressured by foes or hounded or criticized because of belonging to the Lord. Perhaps our troubles have been financial; but whatever they are, let us learn from David how to triumph in them. He cast himself on the deliverance of God, and his Lord provided the way of escape.

We are troubled on every side, yet not distressed; we are perplexed, but not in despair, persecuted, but not forsaken; cast down, but not destroyed (2 Cor. 4:8–9).

THE EFFECTS OF SIN
1 SAMUEL 21:1–10

When he fled to Ahimelech, the priest, David resorted to an untruth. Ahimelech was afraid that David's presence before him was the beginning of trouble, but David sought to quiet the priest's fears by saying, "The king hath commanded me a business, and hath said unto me, Let no man know any thing of the business whereabout I send thee, and what I have commanded thee: and I have appointed my servants to such and such a place" (1 Sam. 21:2).

This was a sad chapter in David's life, but he was not forsaken. God permitted these tests in order to teach David some very valuable lessons. The Lord was preparing him for the throne where he would have to meet much greater tests.

David did not know that his lies would bring trouble to Ahimelech. David was hungry and asked for food. While conversing with the priest, he saw Doeg, chief herdsman for King Saul, near the sanctuary. This man was an Edomite, not an Israelite, who wore a cloak of religion to cover up the true condition of his heart. He was a tool of Saul's, cruel and unscrupulous, and it is likely that David's heart skipped a beat when he saw this wicked man.

Had David stayed with Samuel no harm would have come to Ahimelech and his fellow priests; but David's presence among them, of which they were entirely innocent, proved to be their death warrant (1 Sam. 22:9–18). One person's sin can sometimes have far-reaching effects on others.

For he that soweth to his flesh shall of the flesh reap corruption; but he that soweth to the Spirit shall of the Spirit reap life everlasting (Gal. 6:8).

REJECTED BUT STRONG

1 SAMUEL 22:1–5; PSALM 34:8–22

We find in 1 Samuel 22 that David has stopped hiding among his enemies and has returned to his own land. It was during this period in his experience that he wrote Psalms 34, 57 and 142.

David was God's anointed king in exile. These men gathered around him, recognizing him as God's chosen one. They were willing to wait for God's time with him and were willing to suffer with him if necessary. They did for David what we are admonished to do for Christ in Hebrews 13:13: "Let us go forth therefore unto him without the camp, bearing his reproach." Paul reminded us in Romans 8:17 that we are "heirs of God, and joint-heirs with Christ; if so be that we suffer with him." Our Lord is now rejected but is gathering together a group to reign with Him. This is only a small army. They are equipped to fight, not with carnal weapons but with the spiritual weapons that are mighty through God. With Christ as Captain this army will conquer.

We can only do great things in the future as we learn to do the right things now. We learn from Ephesians 2:6 that God has "raised us up together, and made us sit together in heavenly places in Christ Jesus." This is something that is true of us now. We are being trained by our Lord now and can learn to say as Paul did, "I can do all things through Christ which strengtheneth me" (Phil. 4:13).

Though he fall, he shall not be utterly cast down: for the LORD upholdeth him with his hand (Ps. 37:24).

BEWARE OF CIRCUMSTANCES!
1 SAMUEL 23:6–14

We learn from this chapter that people who intend evil can also speak of the Lord and His work in a very pious way. Saul was told that David had delivered Keilah, and he said, "God hath delivered him into mine hand; for he is shut in, by entering into a town that hath gates and bars" (1 Sam. 23:7). This was Saul speaking, a man who had been so disobedient to God that the Spirit of God had departed from him. He was a man who, no matter how he prayed, received no answer from God because his heart was not right toward God. Yet here he was saying that God had delivered David into his hands.

We must always be careful of our interpretation of circumstances. On a number of occasions I have counseled with different persons who were very obviously following a selfish path. Their one strong argument was that the circumstances favored the course they wanted to take; but it was obvious to me, at least, that they were viewing circumstances in a false light. I was able to check the subsequent history of some of these people and found them miserable in heart with no joy in the Lord. If our wills are not wholly submitted to the Lord, we are bound to misinterpret the circumstances around us.

There is a way that seemeth right unto a man, but the end thereof are the ways of death (Prov. 16:25).

FAITH WAITS ON GOD

1 SAMUEL 24:1–15

No sooner had Saul dealt with the Philistines than he turned and followed David into the wilderness of Engedi. With an army of 3,000 chosen men, Saul went into the area of "the rocks of the wild goats" (1 Sam. 24:2). When Saul decided to enter the cave, he did not know that David and his men were hiding in its recesses.

David's men jumped to the conclusion that these circumstances were designed by God so that David could take the life of Saul. It does not take a strong imagination to picture how they must have argued and pleaded with him to get rid of his enemy once and for all.

Had David reasoned about this—and he possibly did—he would have recognized that this was a golden opportunity to get rid of his enemy. But David had been learning that reason alone was not sufficient. He decided to wait on God. What his men urged could be true, but it would be at the sacrifice of faith and of a humble will that was submissive to God if David took matters into his own hands.

My soul, wait thou only upon God; for my expectation is from him (Ps. 62:5).

 **JULY 11**

CAN OTHERS TRUST YOU?
1 SAMUEL 24:16–22

When Saul realized how close he had come to death and how David's integrity had kept him from taking his life, the king said, "Thou art more righteous than I" (1 Sam. 24:17). Irritating Saul all the time was this thought: "Behold, I know well that thou shalt surely be king, and that the kingdom of Israel shall be established in thine hand" (v. 20). Though Saul was momentarily stopped in his evil intentions, he had not bowed his heart to the will of God with regard to David's succeeding him on the throne.

Would our enemies be able to rest on our promises as Saul did on David's? Unbelievers have often had good reason to point an accusing finger at Christians for their lack of consistent living. Some Christians have even observed that it is easier to work with unbelievers than it is to work with some professing Christians. If others should ever have reason to distrust us, the fault will lie in our failure to keep a proper relationship with God.

David, of course, first gained the victory over himself before he triumphed over Saul. This cannot be done at a church altar, though we can make very momentous decisions there. But the decisions only open the door to a life of walking in victory with God. The life of victory is accomplished through a moment-by-moment fellowship with God.

Moreover it is required in stewards, that a man be found faithful (1 Cor. 4:2).

YESTERDAY'S VICTORY INSUFFICIENT
1 SAMUEL 25:2–13, 23–27, 32–35

While David and his men had been hiding from Saul in the southern part of the land of Canaan, they were not idle. They contributed in a great measure to the peace and security of the people in that area. David, with his 600 men, was very active in protecting these Israelites.

Nabal acted as though he did not know who David was, though he undoubtedly knew a good deal about him but was using this method of showing his contempt. David did not meet this testing as he had met the testing concerning Saul. Then he was gracious and noble and kindhearted, but now he was ready to destroy a whole family.

Abigail was of different stuff than her husband. She decided to do what her husband failed to do and had donkeys loaded with all kinds of food and then went out to meet David. She recognized that David was fighting the Lord's battles and that he had a right to be incensed against Nabal for his churlishness, selfishness and greed.

God did not permit David to fulfill his basic intention of killing all the males of Nabal's household. God used Abigail to perform this special service to David and to bring him back into fellowship with God. This should remind us that yesterday's victory is not sufficient for today. We must have a moment-by-moment walk with the Lord so that when each testing comes, we will be victorious for Christ.

"You therefore, beloved, knowing this beforehand, be on your guard so that you are not carried away by the error of unprincipled men and fall from your own steadfastness (2 Pet. 3:17, NASB).

SIN MUST BE JUDGED
1 SAMUEL 26:5–14,17–21

David had taught his men two years earlier that it was not right to kill God's anointed. But Abishai looked on this as a deliverance by God for David and thought that Saul's life should be taken. Abishai offered to do this for David, but David refused. He would not allow his companion to touch the life of the man who was God's anointed.

With complete reliance upon God, David crept into the midst of this hostile force and took away the spear and water jug from Saul's side. Early the next morning David awakened Saul and his men by calling to them from a safe distance. David reminded Saul that he had driven David from God's inheritance, and that was just as good as saying he should serve other gods. He was not allowed to come near the tabernacle and was hunted like a flea or a partridge.

Saul had not gotten over his jealousy. It came over him again and again because he did not judge it properly as sin. This was one of the factors that made such a great difference between Saul and David. David thoroughly judged his sin. Read, for example, Psalm 51, which was written several years following this incident. If we do not confess and forsake sin, it will lead to more sin and ultimately to death.

Even as I have seen, they that plow iniquity, and sow wickedness, reap the same (Job 4:8).

ACTING IN PANIC
1 SAMUEL 27

David was in very difficult circumstances because Saul was constantly hounding him. David had 600 men with him, and undoubtedly there were many families also that had to be provided for. How do you hide 600 men and their families? It is no wonder, from the human standpoint, that David said, "I shall now perish one day by the hand of Saul" (1 Sam. 27: 1).

For the second time David fled to Israel's enemies, thinking he would find a safe place among them. Apparently his reasoning was that if he went to the land of the Philistines, he would be safe from Saul because Saul was afraid of them. That sounds like good reasoning, but it was only human reasoning. It led David into difficulties that could have been avoided had his trust remained strong in the Lord.

David had acted in panic when he had said in his heart that there was no hope for his safety while he stayed in Judah. This is something all of us need to be aware of. We should never act in panic. When troubles strike, let us carry them to God and let Him bring peace and quietness of heart to us. We cannot quiet ourselves, but we can be quieted in God's presence. His mercy is there for us at any time.

The LORD is good, a strong hold in the day of trouble; and he knoweth them that trust in him (Nah. 1:7).

THE DILEMMA OF THE DISOBEDIENT

1 SAMUEL 28:1–19

David and his men became bodyguards to Achish, king of Gath, and this soon put David in a dilemma. The Philistines decided to go against the Israelites, and David apparently could see no way out of going along and fighting against his own people. He had a weakness for telling lies when doubts came into his heart. This was one of his besetting sins. He had lied to Jonathan and, through Jonathan, to Saul. He had lied to Ahimelech, and that had brought death to 85 priests.

When Saul saw the Philistines, he desperately wanted help to know what to do. The story of his visit to the witch of Endor is well known. Samuel had been dead for some time, and Saul had no one he could turn to who would reveal to him God's will. It was in keeping with Saul's character to have issued orders to destroy everyone who sought contact with the dead, such as the witch of Endor, and then, when he found himself facing a real difficulty, to seek the help of just such an evil person.

The witch of Endor was terrified when she discovered that it was not the evil spirit for whom she was a medium who appeared to Saul. It was Samuel himself. Once again we see that Saul's great sin was the sin of rebellion against the will of God. May we always seek to know God's will in order that we may do it.

But the wicked are like the troubled sea, when it cannot rest, whose waters cast up mire and dirt. There is no peace, saith my God, to the wicked (Isa. 57:20–21).

A BELIEVER OUT OF PLACE
1 SAMUEL 29

Now we can see how God delivered David from the dilemma sin had gotten him into in Gath. He must have been a troubled man when Achish told him that he and other Philistine princes were going against Israel. But when those princes came, they were alarmed and indignant to find Hebrews in the army of Achish. They said, "What do these Hebrews here?" (1 Sam. 29:3). That was a good question and is a question the world has a right to ask when Christians are out of place. Worldly people seem to know better than some of us who claim the name of Christ that we ought to have standards different from theirs.

We often think that we must mix with the world in order to win the people of the world. We think that by compromising we will win them to the Lord. This is often an argument given by Christian young people who marry unbelievers. They feel that after they are married they will be able to win their mate to Christ. But it rarely works out that way. Disaster often follows.

God in His mercy has His way of keeping a person from going completely to ruin. David was dismissed from the army by Achish, and this dismissal was his way out. Achish was satisfied with him, but the other princes of the Philistines were not. This was how God made it possible for David to escape from this great dilemma. God kept David from falling into the greater tragedy of actually fighting against his own people.

Do not be deceived: "Bad company corrupts good morals" (1 Cor. 15:33, NASB).

SEEKING GOD'S WILL
1 SAMUEL 30:1–8,18–26

When David and his men found Ziklag burned with fire and their wives and their children gone, they wept. This was a bitter blow to all of them. David in particular, however, tasted the bitterness of being without God's protection. He had been miraculously taken care of on many other occasions, but now that protection had been removed for the time being. David had exchanged the king of Gath and a walled city for the Spirit of the Lord and found no protection in man. It is the Spirit of the Lord who protects God's people. How often we forget this.

Some of us might be inclined to think that the normal thing would have been for David to start out after the Amalekites without even asking the Lord about it. We might think this was the obvious thing to do. But remember, David had had enough of his own reasoning. He had followed his own reasoning in going to Gath and by it had escaped from the hand of Saul, but he got himself into more difficulties than he ever expected. The seemingly natural thing to do may not always be the right thing as far as God is concerned. When David's fellowship with the Lord was restored, he let the Lord guide his steps.

God's Word admonishes us; "Trust in the LORD with all thine heart; and lean not unto thine own understanding" (Prov. 3:5). David sought God's will, and God eventually gave victory.

But whoso hearkeneth unto me shall dwell safely, and shall be quiet from fear of evil (Prov. 1:33).

GOD DOESN'T NEED HELP

2 SAMUEL 1:1–16

Second Samuel opens with the account of a messenger coming to David and telling him that Saul and Jonathan and many others were dead. Thinking to gain David's approval and possibly receive a reward from him, this messenger, who was an Amalekite, told David that it was at his hands Saul had died. He said he had come upon Saul, who was still alive even after falling on his own sword. Saul had pleaded with him to kill him before the Philistines came upon him and mutilated his body while he was still alive. The young man claimed he did as Saul requested. Some Bible students believe the young man told the truth; others believe he lied, but whatever the correct version is, he took his story to the wrong man.

David had always had a strong aversion to raising his hand against God's anointed. Neither would he permit any of his own men to do it. So when this young Amalekite claimed to have killed Saul, David had him put to death. David did not want what the Lord did not give to him. He would not take by force what God had promised.

So many of us make the mistake of feeling we have to help God fulfill His promises.

Thine, O Lord, is the greatness, and the power, and the glory, and the victory, and the majesty: for all that is in the heaven and in the earth is thine; thine is the kingdom, O Lord, and thou art exalted as head above all (1 Chron. 29:11).

WAITING FOR GOD'S TIME
2 SAMUEL 2:1–11

Second Samuel 2 opens with these words: "And it came to pass after this, that David inquired of the LORD, saying, Shall I go up into any of the cities of Judah? And the LORD said unto him, Go up. And David said, Whither shall I go up? And he said, Unto Hebron" (v. 1). David found, as we will, too, that we never lose anything by believing God and then patiently waiting on Him. But we will surely suffer if we take things into our own hands and rush blindly ahead.

The word "Hebron" means "alliance" or "communion" in contrast to Ziklag, which refers to self-will. Being allied with God and being in communion with Him, David was in a place to be led in the will of God.

David's reign began by reigning first over Judah. It was not necessary for David to take the throne; God saw that he received it. God moved him back to Hebron, and his own tribe anointed him king.

Seven and a half years went by, however, before the whole kingdom was put under his hand. David still had to wait, but it was God's time he was waiting for, not people's.

"For there is a time for every purpose and for every work (Eccles. 3:17).

"NOW THEN DO IT"
2 SAMUEL 3:1,7–18

David's waiting on the Lord indeed paid off. At the end of seven and a half years, God began to arrange events so that David was finally crowned king of all Israel. Abner, who was general of the armies of Israel, had put Ishbosheth on the throne of Saul to reign over 11 tribes. However, when Ishbosheth quarreled with him concerning one of Saul's concubines, Abner retaliated by scheming to turn the kingdom over to David.

A very practical admonition comes from a statement made by Abner that we can apply to our own hearts. Abner went to the people of Israel and said that they had sought for David in the past to be their king, and he added, "Now then do it" (2 Sam. 3:18).

Make Christ king in your life. He is God's appointed King as David was appointed and then anointed for the kingship of Israel. Remember, the name "Christ" means the "anointed of God," and as such He has been appointed and anointed to be king in our lives. So make Him king today.

The work of redemption that Christ did for us is a finished work. The work of the Holy Spirit, on the other hand, which is forming Christ in us, is progressive. Have we ever progressed beyond Calvary?

Therefore leaving the principles of the doctrine of Christ, let us go on unto perfection (Heb. 6:1).

THE KING GIVES VICTORY
2 SAMUEL 5:1–10

So impregnable did the Jebusites think their fortress to be that they jeered at David and his men, saying that the blind and the lame could hold it against David's army. "Nevertheless," we are told, "David took the strong hold of Zion: the same is the city of David" (2 Sam. 5:7). David then moved into the city and made it the headquarters for his government, and later on it became the central place of worship for God's people. Eventually Solomon's great temple was erected in Jerusalem. From this city the Lord Jesus Christ will rule in the Millennium and establish His New Jerusalem of which the Prophet Ezekiel spoke.

There is a rich spiritual lesson for us here. Some habits of sin are so deeply entrenched in our minds and bodies that we have struggled in vain against them from the day of our new birth. We may have felt it was no use to try to overcome these habits and that we might as well give up. What we need, of course, is to let the King, the Lord Jesus Christ, lead us in the battle against this entrenched sin. We can never defeat the enemy by ourselves. It must always be done through the strength of Christ.

What shall we then say to these things? If God be for us, who can be against us? (Rom. 8:31).

WHEN GOD SAYS NO

2 SAMUEL 7:1–13

Nathan commended David for his desire to build a temple and then went to his own house. That night God spoke to the prophet, and as an obedient servant, Nathan brought the word to David. The message was no. God was not going to allow David to build a house of worship for Him. The Lord, however, was pleased with the intentions and the attitude of David's heart in this matter. Years later, after David's death, Solomon built a magnificent temple and in his dedication message said, "It was in the heart of David my father to build an house for the name of the LORD God of Israel. And the LORD said unto David my father, Whereas it was in thine heart to build an house unto my name, thou didst well that it was in thine heart" (1 Kings 8:17–18).

Though God said no to David's building a temple, He was so pleased with David's attitude that He made a covenant with him in which He promised to establish the house of David forever.

Can you take a no from God? He knows what is best for all of us. Remember, His promise to David was "I will be with thee for ever" (see 2 Sam. 7:16). This promise is ours also, for He has said He will never leave us nor forsake us (see Heb. 13:5).

As for God, his way is perfect (2 Sam. 22:31).

FACING SIN

2 SAMUEL 11:1–5

We have seen before that God does not gloss over the sins of His children. David, though a man after God's own heart, was not sinlessly perfect. We come now to the darkest hour in this great man's life. It seems that the higher the peak of victory, the deeper the fall a believer can sustain. Though David was one of God's choicest men, he gave way to selfish desires that have left a blot on his name that time has not erased.

David's sin of adultery was not the end of his fall. It led him to commit murder also. David sank into spiritual deadness with no apparent thought of repentance until God shook him to the very depths of his soul, and then he returned to his senses and sought God's forgiveness.

David's sin was recorded for our learning. The Bible does not hesitate to reveal and denounce sin. God's Word conceals nothing. When necessary, it pulls aside the curtain and discloses the human heart. We are stunned as we think of a man like David, wondering how he could have fallen so low. Will God be able to consider him the man after His own heart following this terrible incident? But can we point the finger at David and excuse ourselves?

Are we able to face sin in our own lives, not just in David's life?

He who conceals his transgressions will not prosper, but he who confesses and forsakes them will find compassion (Prov. 28:13, NASB).

THE UNCHANGING FLESH NATURE

2 SAMUEL 11:6–15

David's scheme was to bring Uriah home on a military furlough, hoping that he would be considered the father of Bathsheba's child. Uriah was much more righteous than David in this. He would not permit himself to relax until the war was over.

David then resorted to extreme measures. To the sin of adultery he added the sin of murder. He wrote a letter to Joab and sent it with Uriah. It contained instructions that Uriah must meet death in battle. Uriah—honest, upright and fully dedicated to his nation and to his king—was given a letter with his own death warrant in it to be handed to Joab, the leader of Israel's army. If David could not cover up his sin by his plots, then he would seal Uriah's lips so that he could not accuse David of being the father of Bathsheba's child.

Some of us think that when a person such as David falls into such terrible sin, the reason must be that he was not a true believer. We must never forget that the evil nature inherited from Adam, or the flesh, in the believer is no different than in the unbeliever. Until we see this, we will never understand the sovereign grace of God and God's sovereignty in the methods He uses in our lives.

The heart is deceitful above all things, and desperately wicked: who can know it? (Jer. 17:9).

 **JULY 25**

SOWING AND REAPING
2 SAMUEL 12:1–10

David's harshness and lack of pity were due to his being out of touch with God. No wonder he failed to remember the judgment prescribed by the Law. At this point the Holy Spirit gave Nathan boldness to say to David, "Thou art the man" (2 Sam. 12:7).

Through Nathan, the Lord reminded David of His sovereign choice of David, of His protection of him through the years of Saul's bitter enmity, of his elevation to the throne and of the abundance of God's provision for him. In spite of God's mercies, David had despised God's commandment. God hid nothing from His servant. David was forced to face his sin.

Nathan's message to David not only reminded him of God's tender mercy, love, abundant gifts and honor but also warned David that, because he had sinned, he would reap a harvest of sorrow. "Now therefore the sword shall never depart from thine house; because thou hast despised me, and hast taken the wife of Uriah the Hittite to be thy wife" (v. 10).

The Lord made it very plain in the New Testament that believers cannot escape reaping the kind of harvest they sow. We cannot hide our sin; we will not get away with it. The secrets of the night are not hidden from God.

Be not deceived; God is not mocked: for whatsoever a man soweth, that shall he also reap (Gal. 6:7).

GETTING RIGHT WITH GOD
PSALM 51:1–17

David asked God to create in him a clean heart (see Ps. 51:10). With regard to the unbeliever, this would be a matter of regeneration, but for the Christian it involves renewal and restoration. David said, "Cast me not away from thy presence; and take not thy holy spirit from me" (v. 11). This is Old Testament doctrine and has to do with the fact that when a person had the Spirit of God and was disobedient, the Holy Spirit might leave him as He left Saul. David did not want this to happen to him.

In this Church Age, the Spirit of God comes into the believer's life to stay. Nevertheless, many Christians, some of them Christian workers, have been put on the shelf and are useless to God because of some sin that they have allowed to control, or dominate, their lives. Our position before God in Christ is assured, but our condition, or experience, if it is to be victorious, must be one of living in fellowship with the Lord. Then the grace of God comes into full view as we see David saying, "Then will I teach transgressors thy ways; and sinners shall be converted unto thee" (v. 13). Once the individual has been restored to fellowship, then, by the grace of God, he can effectively share the Gospel with others.

If we confess our sins, he is faithful and just to forgive us our sins, and to cleanse us from all unrighteousness (1 John 1:9).

GOD'S PURPOSE IN CHASTISING
HEBREWS 12:1–13

God's purpose in chastening us is so that we might learn not to sin. We cannot expect forgiveness and then be turned loose to go on living in the sin that brought God's displeasure. God fixed a gulf between sin and righteousness. This must be maintained. Absolutely no compromise is possible. No attempt should ever be made by us to reduce or detract from the absolute holiness and purity of God. Sin is always sin, and righteousness is always righteousness. There can be no blending of them in any way, shape or form. God cannot forgive us at the expense of lowering His standard of righteousness.

In order to teach us to hate sin, God chastens us. If He did not, we would be crawling to Him every five minutes for more pardon because of our continuing to live in sin. God's people are taught by Him to hate sin by its bitter consequences and are also taught to love righteousness, or holiness. God chastens us as He pleases "for our profit, that we might be partakers of his holiness" (Heb. 12:10).

God does not want us to come to heaven with nothing to show for our spiritual lives and service. He wants to see abundant spiritual fruit.

As many as I love, I rebuke and chasten: be zealous therefore, and repent (Rev. 3:19).

RESTORATION FOLLOWS FORGIVENESS

2 SAMUEL 12:11–23

When God forgives, He at once restores. He never carries a grudge. Nevertheless, we must expect to face consequences because of our sin. The Lord uses the rod of discipline on His children, and one aspect of that discipline is to let us reap what we sow. While He restores us to fellowship, the bitter cup we have brewed for ourselves has to be drunk. David lived for 20 more years, but the seeds of murder and lust that he had planted bore fruit in his own family.

Another son was born to David and Bathsheba, and David "called his name Solomon: and the LORD loved him. And he sent by the hand of Nathan the prophet; and he called his name Jedidiah [beloved of the LORD], because of the LORD" (2 Sam. 12:24–25).

David and Bathsheba's first son was taken from them because of their sin. But in the grace of God, their second son was chosen of God to succeed David on the throne. Surely this was an indication of God's complete forgiveness of David and a fresh evidence of God's mercy. On one hand we see the severity of God. On the other, we see His grace, since the lesson He taught His child had been learned.

I acknowledged my sin unto thee, and mine iniquity have I not hid. I said, I will confess my transgressions unto the LORD, and thou forgavest the iniquity of my sin (Ps. 32:5).

 **JULY 29**

RESULTS OF NEGLECT
1 KINGS 1:5–14, 28–31

David's last years, possibly eight or nine after the death of Absalom (2 Sam. 18), were comparatively quiet. But there came a moment toward the last days of his life, after he had reigned almost 40 years, that a crisis began because he had been careless in making known his choice of a successor.

This crisis occurred when David was ill and about to die. His two oldest sons, Amnon and Absalom, were both dead. A third son possibly died in his youth, for very little is known of him. The fourth son, who was then David's oldest living son, was Adonijah, the son of Haggith. He set himself up as king and prepared chariots and horsemen and 50 men to run before him (see 1 Kings 1:5). David had not displeased this son at any time. He had never said to him, "Why hast thou done so?" (v. 6).

What factors led to Adonijah's attempt to take over the throne? There was only one—neglect on David's part. He had not done what God had ordered him to do. David was careless, not rebellious, yet that carelessness opened the door for Satan's counterfeit. Our enemy is always looking for opportunities to control our lives. Where he cannot stir us up to revolt against God, he will seek to make us careless so that before we realize what is happening, we are dominated by our fallen natures.

For what shall it profit a man, if he shall gain the whole world, and lose his own soul? (Mark 8:36).

A MISPLACED CONFIDENCE
2 SAMUEL 24:1–14; 1 CHRONICLES 21:1

This last attack of Satan upon David took place about 38 years after David had ascended the throne and about two years before his death. Satan was successful for a brief time in enticing David into sin, which should remind us all that we are never free from being tested. At the same time we can have God's victory. If we fall, we can find forgiveness and restoration if we are genuine in our repentance.

Ordinarily nothing would be wrong with numbering people. Census taking is done periodically by any alert government. But numbering the Children of Israel was a matter of pride. David wanted to know how strong his nation was militarily. His strength really was in God, but David was putting his trust in his armies when he numbered the people. God's advice was, "You do not need to number the people. I have taken care of this situation." The strength of Israel's army meant nothing if God was not with them.

The same is true in our spiritual life. Until we can say with true conviction, "I am nothing," God cannot do much for us. He has chosen that which is nothing to confound the wisdom of the wise (see 1 Cor. 1:26–29). Our sufficiency is of God, not of ourselves (see 2 Cor. 3:5).

It is better to trust in the LORD than to put confidence in man (Ps. 118:8).

WHEN IS IT A SACRIFICE?

2 SAMUEL 24:18–25

The Lord not only stayed the plague, but through Gad He also instructed David to build an altar to the Lord on the threshing floor of Ornan, the Jebusite (1 Chron. 21:18). The Lord was very specific about this and left no alternative in the matter. Why this particular spot was chosen does not appear in the narrative, but later on in 2 Chronicles 3:1 we have this statement: "Then Solomon began to build the house of the Lᴏʀᴅ at Jerusalem in mount Moriah, where the Lord appeared unto David his father, in the place that David had prepared in the threshingfloor of Ornan the Jebusite."

If David had been a grasping, selfish man, he might have looked on this as an opportunity to fulfill the will of God without any cost to himself. He had been passed over when the plague struck men in Israel, and now a rich man had offered him a threshing floor for an altar and animals and grain for the offerings. But David refused to bring before the Lord that which cost him nothing. "And the king said unto Araunah [Ornan], Nay; but I will surely buy it of thee at a price: neither will I offer burnt offerings unto the Lᴏʀᴅ my God of that which doth cost me nothing" (2 Sam. 24:24).

What a tremendous lesson for us. It is one thing to serve on boards and committees that handle the affairs of others; it is quite another to make decisions that affect us personally. It is not a sacrifice to the Lord if we give of that which costs us nothing.

The sacrifices of God are a broken spirit: a broken and a contrite heart, O God, thou wilt not despise (Ps. 51:17).

AUGUST

The devotional readings for August are taken from the lives of Elijah and Job.

Elijah was a prophet to Israel in the days of Ahab, one of the most wicked kings who ruled the Northern Kingdom. Elijah stood strong for God before Ahab and was victorious before the prophets of Baal. Elijah was not a superhuman being, however. The Bible tells us he was "a man with a nature like ours" (James 5:17, NASB).

Job experienced the loss of his family and possessions and endured intense physical suffering as God allowed Satan to afflict him. And remember—he did not have the Book of Job to read to bring him comfort! God proved He could hold on to Job in spite of what Satan did to try to get Job to curse God.

The readings for August are excerpted from *Elijah: A Man of Like Nature* and *Job: A Man Tried As Gold*.

GOD LIVES!
1 KINGS 17:1; JAMES 6:16–18

Elijah was a man with a nature like ours. He had a remarkable ministry, but he was still human. He had special gifts from God and was set apart to perform a special ministry. The difference between him and us is due to the special work God had for him and the fact that he was fully submitted to God. When he relied on his own resources, he became as weak as a child. At one period in his life he was discouraged almost to the point of death. Renewed by God, he was as bold as a lion.

He dared to stand before King Ahab and pronounce the judgment of God on him and his kingdom. The prophet showed no hesitancy and expected God to do what He said He would. The basic principle behind this is given in the New Testament.

The first thing that Elijah did when he stood before Ahab was to remind the king that the God of Israel is a living God. Jezebel had brought Baal worship into Israel and had 850 priests leading in the worship of idols. So the first thing Elijah said was, "As the Lord God of Israel liveth" (1 Kings 17:1).

Elijah was unafraid when he stood before Ahab because he had knelt in humility before Almighty God. The Lord gives grace to the humble, but He resists the proud. For this reason we are to submit ourselves to God, but we are to resist the evil one, and he will flee from us. When we are right with God in our hearts, then we will ask for the things that please Him, and He will answer us.

I am the living bread which came down from heaven: if any man eat of this bread, he shall live for ever: and the bread that I will give is my flesh, which I will give for the life of the world (John 6:51).

ONE STEP AT A TIME
1 KINGS 17:2–7

Obeying God always comes first, then He reveals the next step. Too many of us, in doing the work of God, want to see the end result immediately. But that is not trusting God, that is trusting sight. Faith does not see; it trusts and obeys. When Elijah had delivered His message to Ahab, the Lord told him what his next step was to be. Tradition says that this brook ran into the Jordan about 15 miles above Jericho. Its waters came from the mountains of Ephraim from a spring concealed under a high cliff and shaded by a dense jungle. It is probable that it was in such a spot that God hid His servant—a place of safety made known after Elijah's first step of obedience.

The ravens were to bring Elijah his food at Cherith. Suppose, however, he had thought he knew a better hiding place and had gone back to some spot in the mountains of Gilead? He could have starved to death, for the ravens had not been commanded to go there. The ravens were told by God to go to the Brook Cherith, by those high cliffs near the Jordan River where a special stream was fed by a spring. There God would protect Elijah from Ahab. The brook bordered the land of Samaria, the very land over which Ahab was king. There God protected His servant.

Behold, to obey is better than sacrifice, and to hearken than the fat of rams (1 Sam. 15:22).

SUFFICIENT FOR EACH DAY
1 KINGS 17:8–16

Because Elijah was a man like us, he undoubtedly wondered what God had in store for him when he saw the brook beginning to dry up.

Since he was trusting in God, however, he believed and help arrived. God did not send a sudden squall of rain for that immediate neighborhood, nor did he provide some supernatural source of water in that place. Instead, Elijah was to arise, go to Zarephath and dwell there. Only at Zarephath would a widow provide food for him.

Few of us have faced the extremity this widow experienced. It seemed as though each day she might face starvation; yet each day by faith she trusted God to meet her need. The result was that she and her house "did eat many days" (1 Kings 17:15). God supplied not a year at a time but a day at a time.

This is what we need with regard to God's grace. We do not need a great stockpile of it for future use but a daily appropriation of it, which God supplies freely. The manna was gathered daily, not in the evening but in the morning, and each one gathered for himself. So must we accept grace from God. We cannot hoard today's grace for tomorrow or call on yesterday's grace for today. We cannot gather enough on a Sunday to last a whole week. We need to have daily contact with God, particularly in the morning.

Give us this day our daily bread (Matt. 6:11).

NEW LIFE
1 KINGS 17:17–24

The death of her son apparently reminded the widow of some past sin. Her conscience was aroused, and she wanted to vindicate her character in her own eyes. Under such circumstances a person wants to turn the blame, if there is any, on someone else.

Perhaps our reaction to some sorrow or loss or problem is "Do I deserve this?" or "Why has God treated me so harshly?" If we have lost a loved one, perhaps we ask why God took that loved one. We wonder why we have to suffer and why our neighbors do not. This is the carnal nature expressing itself, not the spiritual nature.

Elijah's one purpose in bringing this young boy back to life was to honor God. The psalmist said, "Delight thyself also in the LORD; and he shall give thee the desires of thine heart" (Ps. 37:4). God could easily give new life to this lad.

Life flowed into the boy's body again, and Elijah put him in his mother's arms. She said, "Now by this I know that thou art a man of God, and that the word of the LORD in thy mouth is truth" (1 Kings 17:24). Perhaps others could say that of us if we would only trust and obey God, showing the same spirit of trust and submission that Elijah did.

I give unto them eternal life; and they shall never perish, neither shall any man pluck them out of my hand (John 10:28).

A SECRET BELIEVER
1 KINGS 18:1–7

As Elijah, in obedience to God's command, set out to meet Ahab, he saw that the famine was very severe in Samaria, one of the areas ruled by Ahab and inhabited by the Israelite people. Apparently it extended beyond Ahab's kingdom, but Samaria seemed to be getting the brunt of it. This, of course, was in line with God's judgment. He was disciplining His people. The prophet Isaiah wrote: "If ye be willing and obedient, ye shall eat the good of the land: but if ye refuse and rebel, ye shall be devoured with the sword: for the mouth of the LORD hath spoken it" (Isa. 1:19–20). This principle was literally fulfilled before Elijah's eyes. The people had rebelled, and they were not eating of the good of the land.

Obedience to God is the key to His blessings upon us. The Israelites had suffered for three and a half years because of their disobedience, but because of the obedience of a man of God, the Lord's judgment would be lifted.

The first man Elijah met, however, was not Ahab but Obadiah, the governor of Ahab's household.

Obadiah held a position of prestige and influence in overseeing Ahab's household and possessions. But instead of Obadiah's lifting up Ahab, apparently Ahab tended to drag Obadiah down so that he was more concerned about herds and possessions than about the will of God.

Does this speak to our hearts? Perhaps God allowed this man's life to be included in the Scriptures to teach us this lesson.

In whom we have boldness and access with confidence by the faith of him [Christ] (Eph. 3:12).

WHERE DO WE STAND?

1 KINGS 18:7–16

Elijah commissioned Obadiah to tell Ahab that he was looking for him. Obadiah's response was one of fear. This man seems to have lacked moral strength and spiritual backbone. When the commission was given, he was reluctant to obey.

The similarities between Obadiah and Elijah are few, and the contrasts are many. They were both God-fearing men, and both had a commission. Elijah had a commission to show himself to Ahab, and Obadiah had a commission to tell Ahab that Elijah was coming. But this was about as far as their similarities went.

These two men contrasted greatly with regard to obedience. When God told Elijah to do something, he did it without hesitation. Obadiah, on the other hand, hesitated, fearing for his life. He lacked faith in the power of God.

Why not check our own lives against the lives of these two men. Where do we stand? Are we where God wants us? Is God able to use us, or are we rejoicing only in what He is doing through others? Let us learn to know Him. Let us take time to do so, for this knowledge does not come overnight. Time spent in the presence of God brings eternal results.

Search me, O God, and know my heart: try me, and know my thoughts (Ps. 139:23).

CHARGE AND COUNTERCHARGE
1 KINGS 18:17–19

The monarch's first words were "Art thou he that troubleth Israel?" (1 Kings 18:17). I am not sure how Ahab said that, but I have a feeling he was shaking in his boots. He was standing before a man who had been in the presence of God. Though Ahab could say to his servants, "You do this and do that" and though he was surrounded by his bodyguards, I am sure he was awed in the presence of Elijah.

The king's accusation was false, and under such circumstances the normal reaction is for a person to justify himself. The Spirit-filled person, on the other hand, has surrendered all his rights and has no self to justify. Elijah might have moderated the king's displeasure by telling him that rain was on the way, but that was not the message Ahab needed at that moment. The king and his people had to be humbled before God. God's glory was at stake, and His honor had to be vindicated. Thus, Elijah's answer was fearless. He sought no favor from the king.

Even though Ahab's bodyguards were with him and would have slain Elijah at the king's command, the prophet minced no words. These soldiers held no terror for him. The language he used is seldom heard in our day to rebuke leaders of nations who are doing wrong. "I have not troubled Israel; but thou, and thy father's house, in that ye have forsaken the commandments of the LORD, and thou hast followed Baalim" (v. 18).

Charge them that are rich in this world, that they be not highminded, nor trust in uncertain riches, but in the living God, who giveth us richly all things to enjoy (1 Tim. 6:17).

MAKE A DECISION!
1 KINGS 18:20–24

God worked not only in Ahab's heart but also in the hearts of the Israelites. He subdued the king so that he obeyed Elijah's orders, and He also made the people of Israel willing to gather at Mount Carmel. Even the 450 prophets of Baal attended, though the 400 prophets of the goddess Asherah may have anticipated what was to follow, for apparently they did not respond to the command to meet at Carmel. It is very possible that all of the Israelites, those of the king's household and the false religious leaders who came to Carmel had contempt in their hearts for Elijah; nevertheless, a power beyond themselves caused them to come.

Seven times during the course of that great day, Elijah spoke, and his words were the true index of his heart. His first words were addressed to the people of Israel, not to the prophets of Baal: "How long halt ye between two opinions?" (1 Kings 18:21).

Elijah demanded a definite decision on their part. There was only one true God, the God of Abraham, Isaac and Jacob, the great I Am. There was no other God. He will not accept a divided heart on the part of His people.

We, too, have a decision to make in this day. We must decide between the god of materialism and the God of grace. We cannot serve God and money or other material objects. The individual who is not for Christ is against Him.

Choose you this day whom ye will serve (Josh. 24:15).

THE MAJORITY CAN BE WRONG
1 KINGS 18:25–29

As the majority group, the worshipers of Baal had been given first chance. Because there were so many of them, it took them only a very short time to prepare the sacrifice. As is often the case in matters that pertain to God, however, the majority was on the wrong side.

When Elijah admonished these idolatrous priests not to put any fire under their offering, he was warning them that he would not stand for any tricks. They had often deceived people, but what they were now doing was out in the open with many eyes watching them. There was no opportunity given to these tricksters and imposters to use fire on the altar to Baal.

The frenzy of Baal's prophets reached its height at noon. In the excitement generated by the rhythm and speed of the priests' action, it would not have taken a great deal for the people watching them to have been swept off their feet emotionally and to have joined in the wild orgy. But Elijah was ready for this very thing. He very effectively used the weapon of sarcasm to expose the intentions of these evil men and at the same time to insure emotional stability among the observers.

It is possible that Israel had never seen such earnestness and enthusiasm at any previous time. But such things are no proof that the cause is good and true. Some people assume that such a display of zeal and fervor is evidence of spirituality; however, this can be far from the truth.

The king is not saved by a mighty army; a warrior is not delivered by great strength (Ps. 33:16, NASB).

THE FIRE FALLS

1 KINGS 18:30–39

By having water poured over the sacrifice as often as he did, Elijah prevented any human counterfeiting or trickery. Then he began to pray.

This short prayer has only 63 English words (even fewer in Hebrew), and it takes about 20 seconds to speak them. But the prophets of Baal had prayed to their idol for several hours and had received no answer at all. Elijah prayed for 20 seconds, and God answered by fire.

Elijah's prayer differed in character and sincerity from that of the prophets of Baal. James described it when he said, "The effectual fervent prayer of a righteous man availeth much" (James 5:16).

Even some Christians seem to misunderstand what this verse means. They shout in prayer as though God were deaf. They put on a demonstration as though they had to attract God's attention. Earnestness in prayer does not involve physical gestures but a condition of the heart and will with regard to the purposes of God.

Perhaps here we may learn to examine our own prayers. Since Elijah's prayer was motivated by his desire to see God honored, God answered His servant. In writing concerning prayer James said, "Ye ask, and receive not, because ye ask amiss, that ye may consume it upon your lusts" (4:3). Right motives are essential if our prayers are to be answered.

For our God is a consuming fire (Heb. 12:29).

RAIN AT LAST!
1 KINGS 18:40–46

To have allowed the prophets of Baal to continue living and exercising all their evil practices would have exposed the Israelites to further corruption. It would have left the impression in the minds of these priests, as well as the Israelites, that the prophets of Baal, though agents of apostasy, were immune from judgment. God said that they were all to be destroyed. Not one of them was to escape.

When Elijah declared that there was the sound of abundance of rain, no rain had as yet fallen. There were no clouds in the sky, no thunder and lightning, nothing that gave visible proof that rain was imminent. There was not a physical sign anywhere that rain was on the way. Elijah's statement was based on his faith in the Word of God.

The scene, as depicted in 1 Kings 18, is remarkable. Ahab was probably still surrounded by his nobles, riding in all his pomp to Jezreel—at least 16 miles away. Then the rain began to fall, and ahead of the king ran Elijah in the power of the Lord. The countryside that had seen so much sun and so little rain was dry and hot and showed the ravages of the drought. Then suddenly the sky was filled with dark clouds, the lightning flashed, the thunder rolled, and the rain poured down. The hand of the Lord was on His prophet, and Elijah outran the chariot to the gates of the city!

For ye have need of patience, that, after ye have done the will of God, ye might receive the promise (Heb. 10:36).

A MIGHTY MAN FALLS

1 KINGS 19:1–8

Elijah traveled on foot about 95 miles to the southern border of Judah. Then he went another day's journey into the wilderness. By that time he was completely exhausted. He had remarkable physical strength and endurance, but he had extended himself to the breaking point. He had first prepared for the "showdown" with the prophets of Baal at Mount Carmel. Then it was necessary to kill the prophets of Baal. Such invasion of Satan's territory is not done easily. Then Elijah prayed for rain with great earnestness, and finally he ran about 16 miles to Jezreel to see what results would follow the great triumph at Mount Carmel. All of this took place in one day.

Satan knows that a tired body is an added opportunity for him, and he took advantage of it in this case. When Jezebel threatened Elijah, he seemed to lose control and continued running until he sat under the juniper tree in the wilderness. Then he requested that he might die.

Elijah had lost hope of seeing the people of Israel return to the Lord. Thus life no longer was attractive to him. When hope is gone, life is not worth living. Perhaps it seemed to Elijah that the Lord had given up also, but this was not the case. The Lord did not answer the prayer of His discouraged servant when he asked to die.

The present world has no answer to the turmoil and strife going on in its midst, but the Church is not without hope. Our hope lies in the coming of our Lord. This we must never forget.

Hope deferred maketh the heart sick: but when the desire cometh, it is a tree of life (Prov. 13:12).

GOD IS STILL IN CONTROL
1 KINGS 19:8–18

Perhaps we have felt like Elijah and said, "What is the use?" Perhaps we have given the best of our lives to accomplish something for the Lord and feel that we have been left stranded. Perhaps we feel that the enemy is seeking to destroy all traces of Christianity and belief in the true God and that he is after our soul, too. Perhaps we feel we are the only one left of all God's people. If so, we need to be reminded, as Elijah was, that God still had 7,000 who had not bowed their knee to Baal. And God still is the Almighty God. He is still on His throne. People cannot dethrone Him, no matter how hard they try. All we need for life and godliness and Christian service is found in Him.

Perhaps we have tried hard to overcome temptations and to rise above our testings. Perhaps we have fought against the overwhelming odds of modernism in our church. Perhaps we have done so and have found few, if any, standing with us, and we are about ready to give up our belief in the fundamentals of the Word of God. Do not give up. God is still in control of this world and this universe.

Perhaps we have tried hard to live for the Lord and have failed. Perhaps we fail today as we failed yesterday and the day before and are asking, "What's the use?" Let us come out of the cave of darkness and listen to the still, small voice of God. He tells us that He has given us all that pertains to life and godliness (see 2 Pet. 1:3). Every provision has been made for us.

In whom also we have obtained an inheritance, being predestinated according to the purpose of him who worketh all things after the counsel of his own will (Eph. 1:11).

BYPASSING DEATH
2 KINGS 2:1–11

The closing incident in Elijah's life was perhaps the most touching in his whole history. He was translated to heaven without having to die. His ministry may have covered 15 or 20 years, but the public aspect of it was much briefer than that. At a time of great depression in his life, when lying under a juniper tree, he had prayed for death, but when the time of his translation came, he was thankful that God had not answered that prayer.

The prophet's translation was to be at a specially designated place. Elijah had learned long ago that absolute obedience to God's directions was necessary for God's blessings.

Elijah began his journey from Gilgal to the place of his ascension, and Elisha insisted on going with him. This journey involved a great test for Elisha, who was to be Elijah's successor. From the account you may be led to think that Elijah was reluctant to have Elisha go with him, but this may well have been part of the test for the younger man. Elijah was alone in his ministry, and he was humble, and he may have felt that his coming translation was too sacred a matter to be witnessed by others.

We can learn valuable lessons from this experience. If we wish to behold the glory of God and to be fit vessels to participate in God's work, we must go on to maturity in Christ.

Then we which are alive and remain shall be caught up together with them in the clouds, to meet the Lord in the air: and so shall we ever be with the Lord (1 Thess. 4:17).

WE CAN DO IT ALSO
JAMES 5:16–18

The Bible says Elijah was a man subject to like passions, or as another translation says it, "A man of like nature" (James 5:17, RSV). God permits us to see where Elijah failed so that we need not think we are dealing with a perfect man. He was human just as we are; what sets him apart from most of us is that he fully believed God.

What Elijah accomplished is possible to us today if God should call us to such a ministry and if we will believe and trust Him for it. It is true that we know nothing of Elijah's family background or of his life before his public ministry began. He appeared suddenly, and he went away suddenly. Yet he was a man who had the same fallen nature that we have; he was subject to temptations similar to ours; he faced the same tests and trials that all humans face. He walked with the same God we have the privilege of walking with. He sought the Lord for the same things that you and I seek Him for. We may seek the Lord as Elijah did, for our Saviour made God's will very plain: "Ask, and it shall be given you; seek, and ye shall find; knock, and it shall be opened unto you" (Matt. 7:7). The apostle Paul said, "I can do all things through Christ which strengtheneth me" (Phil. 4:13).

The eternal God is thy refuge, and underneath are the everlasting arms (Deut. 33:27).

QUALITIES THAT PLEASE GOD
JOB 1:1–5

In brief but pointed phrases Job is described in the first verse in the book: "There was a man in the land of Uz, whose name was Job; and that man was perfect and upright, and one that feared God, and eschewed evil" (Job 1:1).

First of all, he is said to be "perfect." This word does not refer to sinless perfection but to the fact that Job wholeheartedly wanted to please God.

Second, Job is described as an upright man. He had a good relationship with other human beings, which was due to his having a right relationship with God. He was a man of unusual piety.

Third, Job was a man who feared God. In the Old Testament context, this refers to a man who had a reverential trust of God coupled with a hatred for evil. "The fear of the Lord is the beginning of wisdom" (Ps. 111:10; Prov. 9:10). With that trust in God grows a sensitivity to sin and a hatred of it.

Fourth, Job was a man who eschewed evil, which means that he turned away from it. He abstained from evil and shunned it. His manner of life corresponded to his relationship with God.

Through trust in Jesus Christ, we have been cleansed from sin. Its guilt has been removed, and we are counted righteous in God's eyes. We are born again, but does our conduct before other people indicate what our relationship is before God? Job's conduct did.

Fear God, and keep his commandments: for this is the whole duty of man (Eccles. 12:13).

A GLIMPSE THAT STRENGTHENS
JOB 1:6–11

In the first two chapters of the Book of Job, God gives us a look behind the scenes so that we can see events on earth from the standpoint of heaven. There is no doubt that if Job could have seen into the councils of heaven before and during his trial, he would have answered his friends quite differently. But God did not allow him to know about this heavenly scene presented to us. Nor did God explain it to him at the close of his experiences. He may have learned about it after he went to heaven but not before.

God's eternal purpose for Job would have been thwarted if Job had been given the explanation for his trial. If he had known all that went on behind the scenes in heaven, there would have been no place for faith. Without faith, Hebrews 11:6 tells us, it is impossible to please God. Job could never have been purified, as gold is purified by fire, if he had not gone through the situation in which he had to trust God implicitly.

God has permitted us to see these things to help strengthen our faith when we face baffling afflictions. His purpose is that we might place implicit faith in Him and in His counsel and His goals for us, believing that the hard experiences in life are permitted for a good purpose. This is the teaching of Romans 8:28–29: "All things work together for good" for the believer.

For our light affliction, which is but for a moment, worketh for us a far more exceeding and eternal weight of glory (2 Cor. 4:7).

VICTORIOUS FAITH DEFEATS SATAN

JOB 1:12–22

According to Job 1:12, the Lord gave Satan permission to afflict Job up to a certain point.

God told Satan that he could do what he wanted with all Job had, but he was not to touch Job himself. So Satan set out to prove that Job was not what God claimed him to be, but God's purpose was to show that Job was a man of God.

When the great calamities fell upon Job, it was not Satan's lightning nor Satan's whirlwind that brought destruction. The lightning and the wind belong to God. Satan merely had permission from God to use them. Even Job saw this, for he said, "The LORD gave, and the Lord hath taken away; blessed be the name of the LORD" (v. 21).

The character of a person is generally revealed at a time of sudden crisis. When there is no time for reflection, our true nature is revealed. This is especially true when someone is under as much pressure as Job was.

Satan was defeated by Job's turning to the Lord. The evil one failed in everything he tried to do against Job. Instead of driving Job away from God, Satan had driven him closer to God. Here was a man who could be faced with all that Satan could cast at him and still stand firm in his faith.

Is this how we react when Satan brings trials and testings into our lives? Or do we cringe and ask why? Do we shake and tremble under the terrible trial?

My grace is sufficient for thee: for my strength is made perfect in weakness (2 Cor. 12:9).

QUESTIONING GOD'S LOVE
JOB 2:1–10

Satan did not give up easily. He did not succeed the first time, but he would try again. He had removed Job's possessions and his family, but now he was going to touch Job where he thought every person was vulnerable. Satan's proposition now was to add physical suffering to the problems of this man whom he thought was strained to the breaking point.

God had given His permission, so Satan brought a terrible disease on Job. Some think it was a form of black leprosy, said to be the worst kind of leprosy.

Even after all this, Satan was not through with Job. Another blow was still to come. Job's wife came to him and said, "Dost thou still retain thine integrity? curse God, and die" (Job 2:9).

She must have thought that God, whom Job served, had forsaken him. Possibly she thought God could not be a God of love since He had let such suffering come upon a man who had served Him so well.

Isn't such an attitude familiar to us? Haven't we even thought these things ourselves?

"'For I know the plans that I have for you,' declares the Lord,' plans for welfare and not for calamity to give you a future and a hope'" (Jer. 29:11, NASB).

NEEDED: TRUE FRIENDS
JOB 2:11–3:5

Friends can be very valuable. The right kind of friends can help us over the difficult spots in life. But the quality of friendship expressed by these three men left much to be desired.

When they saw Job's plight, they were shocked. They hardly knew what to think. The man whom they had known as the greatest man in their part of the world was ill and sitting on an ash heap. They were silent for seven days, having no comfort to give him. They said nothing, and apparently Job said nothing in all that time. But Satan kept up the pressure, and finally at the end of the seven days Job opened his mouth and cursed the day he was born.

In the wake of all these combined losses, now had come the crowning loss—he began to doubt that God really cared about him. This was a most crucial moment in Job's experience. He cursed the day of his birth, but he did not curse God. He doubted God's care, but he did not lose faith that God existed.

This was when his friends should have helped him. This was when they should have encouraged him, but they did not.

Are we friends to those in need? Do we stand by fellow believers when they experience times of difficulty and stress? Or do we find someone in difficulty and add to their troubles?

A friend loveth at all times (Prov. 17:17).

COUNSEL BASED ON HUMAN EXPERIENCE

JOB 4:1–7

Eliphaz was possibly the eldest of the group and supposedly the wisest also. However, superior age does not mean superior wisdom. The philosophy of Eliphaz was based on what we will call general observations and spiritual illumination. He claimed to have some kind of vision, on which he laid a great deal of stress. Several times in Job 4 he stressed what he had seen and experienced.

Eliphaz used what is today called the psychological approach—he commended Job before he condemned him. Eliphaz then leaned heavily on his observations, which were all related to his experience. No one, as far as he had seen, had ever perished if he was innocent. Suffering, according to his experience, was always the result of God's judgment of sin. His conclusion was that Job was no exception to this rule and was being punished for some sin he had committed.

Some people have this idea today. They believe that if a person or a family is going through severe trials, such trials are deserved and are the result of sin.

If this were true, why did David suffer as he did before he became king? He had to run for his life, not because he had done wrong but because Saul was jealous of him.

And what about our Saviour Himself? He did not sin. In fact, He could not sin. And yet He suffered.

It is easy to see that the argument of Eliphaz was not correct.

For I will give you utterance and wisdom which none of your opponents will be able to resist or refute (Luke 21:15, NASB).

COUNSEL BASED ON TRADITION

JOB 8:1–10

Bildad made no appeal to the revealed will of God but only to whatever wisdom the fathers may have taught.

He asked if God perverted justice. The answer, of course, is no. Then Bildad used this premise to argue that Job must have lost his children because of some transgression on their part. He also charged Job with lack of purity and uprightness.

This was little help to a man who, according to Job 1, had offered sacrifices to God just in case his children had offended God in something they had said or done. Then to have them accused of some sin that was so great that they all died because of it was a terrible charge to make.

The arguments of Bildad were all from appearance and based on suppositions. He used many "ifs." He did not really know, but he supposed many things. This was the way he interpreted the situation, but his interpretation was wrong.

Christians need to learn to distinguish between facts and how the facts are interpreted. Just because we read something does not mean we may assume that something else is also true. Just because one person interprets a set of facts a certain way does not mean that his interpretation is correct. All the facts may not be given. And often the withholding of one essential fact can change the interpretation.

Beware lest any man spoil you through philosophy and vain deceit, after the tradition of men, after the rudiments of the world, and not after Christ (Col. 2:8).

COUNSEL BASED ON LOGIC ALONE

JOB 11:1–7

Zophar is the most dogmatic of the three. He assumes many things, based on his own intuition, or common sense, and then states his conclusion with a finality that permits no opposition. For Job to differ with Zophar's conclusions is proof, in Zophar's eyes, that Job is a sinner.

Some people are like that today. They are so sure of what they say that anyone who disagrees with them calls forth their scorn or anger.

Zophar was a legalist and a formalist. He did not understand God's character at all. He knew a certain amount of truth, but it was distorted because it was not complete.

When men like Zophar assume what is untrue and call for repentance on the basis of their false assumptions, they only stir up anger. God, of course, allowed these men to use their arguments against Job. The Lord wanted to help him see that though his calamities were not the result of sin, his character needed to be refined. Job needed to be made humble, for he was proud. But we cannot force people to see this by sheer dogmatism on our part.

For my thoughts are not your thoughts, neither are your ways my ways, saith the Lord (Isa. 55:8).

CONFIDENCE IN GOD, NOT MAN

JOB 13:4–15

As we read in Job 13, Job again spoke quite forcibly of his refusal to let his "friends" arbitrate his case for him. He declared he would take it to God himself. Job brushed his "friends" aside and told them that what they knew he knew, that he was not a bit inferior to them.

It goes without saying that Job's words to his friends and some of their words to him are hardly patterns for believers to use. A great deal of bitterness was evident on both sides.

Job was suffering greatly in body and mind, and the discourses of Eliphaz, Bildad and Zophar added torment to his already overburdened heart. Job forcefully expressed his resentment against their unfair treatment. At times he "blew off steam," and yet intermingled with his strong words were often statements of remarkable truth concerning God. From what we have already seen in chapter 13, Job stated that even if God were to kill him, he would trust Him. Would we be able to make such a statement in the midst of intense suffering?

It is better to trust in the LORD than to put confidence in man (Ps. 118:8).

WHEN THE HEAVENS SEEM AS BRASS

JOB 31:6–8,33–35

Job was an unusual man. He had done many noble deeds. He was outstanding in many ways. He was the kind of man who, once he humbled himself before God, could be trusted with more responsibility. The Scriptures say that the person who is faithful in little things will also be faithful in great things (see Matt. 25:23; Luke 16:10). Job's pride, however, was still keeping him from enjoying the best that God offered.

It was no light decision for Job to ask God to weigh him in the balances. Job was a chaste man, God-fearing, kind and sincere. He was ready to put his signature on the list of his own virtues. And he wanted his adversary to put his charges down in writing. Job thought that since he had always pleased God before, everything was all right. He was worthy of the best God could give him. This was his personal evaluation, however.

In and of himself, no one is ever worthy of anything from God. The more we realize our unworthiness, the better position we are in for God to use us. Then we must yield ourselves to Him to do with us and through us what He pleases.

That ye would walk worthy of God, who hath called you unto his kingdom and glory (1 Thess. 2:12).

LET GOD BE JUSTIFIED
JOB 32:1–12

The great principle underlying Job's spiritual problem was given centuries later by our Lord: "If any man will come after me, let him deny himself, and take up his cross daily, and follow me. For whosoever will save his life shall lose it: but whosoever will lose his life for my sake, the same shall save it" (Luke 9:23–24). Job was trying to hang on to his reputation and his past victories. If we want God's best, we must be willing to lay aside everything that might be counted dear to us so that God can really do for us what He wants to do.

I can almost see Elihu as he listened to the various speeches, getting a bit warm on the inside. "Why don't they get down to the facts? Why don't they speak the truth? Why does Job seek to justify himself? Why doesn't he see himself as God sees him?"

Elihu sized up the matter very clearly. The reasons given for his anger (Job 32:2–3) are of more value than what was said in the 29 chapters of discourses. He recognized that Job was trying to justify himself rather than God. Then he pointed out the problem of the three men: They had condemned Job instead of leading him to condemn himself.

When we justify ourselves, we condemn God. But when we condemn ourselves, we "justify" God. We do this by admitting that God is right in what He is doing and praising Him for it.

He is the Rock, his work is perfect: for all his ways are judgment: a God of truth and without iniquity, just and right is he (Deut. 32:4).

GOD IS GREATER THAN MAN
JOB 33:1–12

Elihu's first thought in approaching Job and his problem was to make very clear that God is greater than man. This is a fact that we must clearly understand if we are to have the right answers in our times of trouble. Elihu uncovered Job's faults without stirring up his opposition. This is an art that the Spirit of God imparts if we allow Him to take charge of our helping others. Nothing wounds an upright person as much as unfounded suspicion and any charges that may grow out of it.

Bible-believing churches and pastors could well apply this principle of pointing out faults without offending. We need to be careful that we do not let a carnal spirit divide us and hurt us so the Lord finds it difficult to use us.

Job's problem was pride, self-will and doubting God's goodness. This is what Elihu brought to Job's attention. He told Job this was not right and then emphasized the fact that God is greater than man. For this reason man has no right or authority to ask God for an explanation of His actions.

God does things that are incomprehensible to us. He is infinite and we are finite. He is the Creator and we are the creatures. His ways are higher than our ways and His thoughts than our thoughts (Isa. 55:9). We must clearly understand this fact if we are going to have any peace of mind with regard to the everyday happenings of life and God's control over this universe.

Except the LORD build the house, they labour in vain that build it: except the LORD keep the city, the watchman waketh but in vain (Ps. 127:1).

WHEN GOD SPEAKS

JOB 38:1–11

God spoke to Job out of a whirlwind at this point, and what He said had an immediate effect. God's voice made Job conscious of the presence of God, whom he had not seen and said he could not find. Before this the discussion had been about God as if He were absent. Now Job was suddenly made aware of His nearness.

When a person suddenly realizes he is in God's presence, his life can be profoundly affected. At one time Peter said to Jesus, "Depart from me; for I am a sinful man, O Lord" (Luke 5:8). He realized that since he was in the presence of the Lord Jesus, he was in the presence of God.

God did not immediately restore Job's health or possessions. He did not even argue with Job. Why should He? Instead, He asked Job a series of questions that were designed to bring him to proper thinking and believing.

Job had shown some arrogance; he needed to be humbled. In this God used irony to good effect. He did not use sarcasm, for His purpose was not to humiliate Job but to humble him. It is one thing to be brought to the place where we recognize we are nothing; it is quite another to be humiliated—so bullied or made fun of or made to look cheap that we inwardly cringe at the treatment we receive. People can easily humiliate each other, but that is not the way God works.

God, after He spoke long ago to the fathers in the prophets in many portions and in many ways, in these last days has spoken to us in His Son (Heb. 1:1–2, NASB).

NOTHING MORE TO SAY
JOB 40:1–5

Job had contended with God. He had argued against God's dealing with him, which was the root of his problem. He, the creature, had sat in judgment against God, the Creator. He had even accused God of doing the wrong thing.

Now God had spoken to Job and made His presence known. From nature He had emphasized very obvious lessons so that Job could not fail to catch the moral principles involved. No wonder Job replied that he was vile.

How could Job really answer God after this revelation of God's care for His creatures? Job realized how contemptible he had been in speaking as he did of the Lord. He had thought the Lord cruel and unjust; in reality God had shown His love to Job. Job decided all he could do was put his hand on his mouth, say nothing more and just listen to God.

How do we face times of suffering? Do we wonder after a long period of testing if God really cares? We seek for love and care, and God in His grace is ready and willing to love us and care for us; but above all we must remember that God has permitted this testing and has a purpose in it. God is both sovereign and righteous; therefore, He always does what is right.

When a believer does wrong, he may suffer for the wrong done. On the other hand, much suffering in the life of a believer is for discipline, not punishment. Through such suffering God molds him into the image of His Son (see Rom. 8:28–29).

Now we know that what things so ever the law saith, it saith to them who are under the law: that every mouth may be stopped, and all the world may become guilty before God (Rom. 3:19).

TWO INSEPARABLE TRUTHS

JOB 42:1–6

Job had a new comprehension of God, which brought a new comprehension of himself. He acknowledged that he was vile.

Many believers think they have reached the end of themselves when they give mental assent to the doctrine of human depravity and say we are all depraved. But it is one thing to speak of vileness and depravity in general; it is quite another for us to know deep within that we are vile. To say before the Lord, "I am the one," is the place Job came to and the place we need to come to. This is a personal, intimate thing—a private matter between ourselves and God. It is not something that one believer can reveal to another. It comes as the result of the work of the Spirit in our hearts.

These two things always go together: "Mine eye seeth thee" (Job 42:5) and "I abhor myself" (v. 6). To catch a new vision of God and His righteousness is to bring us to the place where we hate what we are in ourselves. When God's light shines into our hearts, we cannot help but abhor ourselves.

Self-abhorrence is expressed by a humble spirit and a gracious attitude. It is of little use to profess humility if we are quick to resent any injury we may suffer or to feel insulted when someone has slighted us or discouraged us.

The true secret of a broken and contrite heart is to abide in the presence of Almighty God and then to maintain a correct attitude toward those around us.

Then said I, Woe is me! for I am undone; because I am a man of unclean lips, and I dwell in the midst of a people of unclean lips: for mine eyes have seen the King, the LORD of hosts (Isa. 6:5).

VINDICATED BY GOD

JOB 42:7–17

The vindication of Job was a vindication before his "friends." God called him "my servant" and had him act in the capacity of a priest for the three who had so cruelly slandered him. We not only need to see what God was able to do with Job, we also need to see the God of Job for ourselves.

We learn from Job, and this is part of the vindication, that the suffering of the godly always includes a compensation, or a reward. It may not come in this present life. It did in Job's life, and we can be assured that it will eventually come for us. The Bible says so, and that settles it. Job's reward had to come during his lifetime in order to complete the object lesson the Lord was presenting through him. Life for the believer does not end with his life on earth; it continues on into heaven. All believers have an inheritance reserved in heaven.

The Bible tells us in many places that we cannot avoid suffering here on earth. The suffering will not endure forever, though, and we must look beyond it to the rewards God will give for faithfulness.

"Behold, we count them happy which endure. Ye have heard of the patience of Job, and have seen the end of the Lord; that the Lord is very pitiful, and of tender mercy" (James 5:11). God does not delight in our being afflicted, yet through these afflictions His very gracious purposes are realized. This is what James called "the end of the Lord"; the outcome of the Lord's dealings with us includes vindication.

And he shall bring forth thy righteousness as the light, and thy judgment as the noonday (Ps. 37:6).

SEPTEMBER

The New Testament Books of Romans, Galatians and Ephesians provide spiritual food for the month of September.

Romans emphasizes that salvation is obtained by trusting Christ alone, for only His finished work on the cross has paid the penalty for sin. The book also urges Christians to live a victorious life.

Galatians stresses that a person is not saved by the works of the Law nor is he made spiritually mature by keeping the Law. Both Romans and Galatians make it clear that "the just shall live by faith" (Rom. 1:17; Gal. 3:11).

Ephesians is a rich treasure chest of spiritual truths, revealing that every believer can have an abundant life by recognizing his position in Christ and living accordingly.

The readings for September are excerpted from *How God Makes Bad Men Good: Studies in Romans; Flesh and Spirit in Conflict; Practical Studies in Galatians;* and *Living Abundantly: Studies in Ephesians.*

ONE MAN'S TESTIMONY
ROMANS 1:13–17

In Romans 1:14–16 Paul made three significant statements about himself. First, he said, "I am debtor" (v. 14). He realized he had an obligation because he had seen the truth concerning Jesus Christ. Those of us who have been reconciled to God through the blood of Jesus Christ have a ministry of reconciliation—we have an obligation to take the message to others (see 2 Cor. 5:18–20). When we stand before Christ to give account, our faithfulness to this type of ministry will no doubt be one of the chief concerns.

Second, Paul stated, "I am ready" (Rom. 1:15). It's one thing to sense an obligation and even to be willing, but it is another thing to be ready. Readiness involves a mental attitude—putting ourselves at God's disposal to do His will.

Third, Paul said, "I am not ashamed" (v. 16). He was not ashamed of the Gospel of Jesus Christ. This is a clear and strong reference to the great doctrine that the Holy Spirit, through Paul, established by irrefutable logic in the succeeding chapters of Romans; that is, the doctrine of justification by faith. Or one may simply call it the doctrine of salvation by grace.

But sanctify the Lord God in your hearts: and be ready always to give an answer to every man that asketh you a reason of the hope that is in you with meekness and fear (1 Pet. 3:15).

GOD HATES SIN! DO WE?
ROMANS 1:18–25

There must be no misunderstanding of what God's wrath is. It should never be confused with man's wrath, which is sinful. God's wrath is not a sudden fit of temper; neither is it a desire for revenge. These things are sin, and we cannot attribute sin to God. God's wrath is a fixed attitude of opposition toward all unrighteousness. This attitude never changes. It will culminate in righteous judgment on all who finally and completely reject God's offer of love.

God abhors sin, but He loves the sinner. This was clearly manifested when He made a way for the sinner to escape the consequences of sin and provided such a wonderful salvation in Christ. God's attitude toward the sinner is seen in such passages as John 3:16: "God so loved the world, that he gave his only begotten Son."

His attitude toward sin, however, is entirely different. Sin is of the devil, and God in His wrath is against it. He will never tolerate it, regardless of the circumstances. If a sinner continues in sin, refusing to accept God's gift of eternal life, then God's unchanging attitude of wrath toward sin will be revealed against the sinner. This is the truth stated in John 3:36: "He that believeth on the Son hath everlasting life: and he that believeth not the Son shall not see life; but the wrath of God [His unchangeable attitude against sin] abideth on him."

In other words, when the sinner clings to his sin and refuses God's offer of mercy, then sin and the sinner are one so far as the wrath of God is concerned.

This then is the message which we have heard of him, and declare unto you, that God is light, and in him is no darkness at all (1 John 1:5).

DOING AND TEACHING GO TOGETHER
ROMANS 2:17–29

We need to ask ourselves if our lives are good illustrations of what we teach. We teach that people should not steal, but do we steal? We may never rob banks, but are we guilty of withholding money that rightfully belongs to others? Are we totally honest in preparing our income tax returns? And stealing involves more than just money—it can also involve time. Are we stealing God's time by doing things with our schedules and energies that God never intended? Are we placing God first in our lives, not only concerning our finances but also concerning our time? Or do we give God only the finances and the time that are left over? We should never think that once we have given some money and time to the Lord that the rest is ours to do with as we please. All that we have belongs to God, so He should be taken into consideration in everything we do.

Each of us needs to come to God with an open heart and ask Him to do what David asked of Him: "Search me, O God, and know my heart: try me, and know my thoughts: and see if there be any wicked way in me, and lead me in the way everlasting" (Ps. 139:23–24). God has given believers the responsibility of spreading the Gospel to all the world, and we need to use all at our disposal to accomplish this task. How serious it will be if, when we stand before the Lord, we must admit that we did far less than we could have.

If we say that we have no sin, we deceive ourselves, and the truth is not in us (1 John 1:8).

LIFE'S MOST IMPORTANT FEAR
ROMANS 3:9–18

Romans 3:18 is not speaking of a reverential fear of God that a person has who recognizes Him as the great Potentate of all ages and as the Almighty God we serve. Rather, this verse refers to those who have no concern for the existence, character or attributes of God. They do not think that God merits any thought at all. They completely fail to recognize their accountability to Him.

People's basic problem—the root cause of all their trouble—is that they do not know God, and they do not fear meeting God when they die. People speak lightly of death because they do not want to face its realities. People have taken it for granted that God, if He even exists, will overlook what they do and will take care of them, regardless of how they live.

People's refusal to make God the God of their lives is the fountain from which all these evils flow. Solomon said, "The fear of the LORD is the beginning of wisdom" (Prov. 9:10). When people refuse to fear God, or recognize Him for who He is, they lack wisdom, and they experience increasing mental confusion. One needs only to consider the fields of modern music and modern art to see this. And in addition to the absence of wisdom and an increasing mental confusion, there is also moral and spiritual darkness.

The fear of the LORD is the beginning of wisdom: and the knowledge of the holy is understanding (Prov. 9:10).

UNDERSTANDING YOUR STANDING

ROMANS 5:1–5

Our standing before God is in the grace to which we have constant access (Rom. 5:2). We do not need new credentials each time we come to God, because our standing is constant since we come by means of what Jesus Christ accomplished for us. God does not accept us as we are, but as we are in Christ Jesus. God makes His grace abound toward us (2 Cor. 9:8), and we are able to come boldly into His immediate presence (Heb. 10:19). All of this is available to us; our responsibility is simply to act on the basis of what God has made available. We need to follow the principle stated by Jesus: "If any man thirst, let him come unto me, and drink" (John 7:37). Through grace, God has made all the benefits available to us; we now need simply to appropriate them or to act on the basis of what God extends to us.

God's grace is what He is; therefore, our standing is as sure as God is. Inasmuch as justification is by faith, it is already securely ours when we trust Jesus Christ as our personal Saviour. The benefits, or blessings, that accompany justification are also ours, but in order to enjoy them we must appropriate them for ourselves. To fail in appropriating these benefits is like having money in the bank but refusing to use it or having water immediately available but refusing to drink it. Wonderful as these blessings are, they benefit us personally only as we appropriate them.

Stand fast therefore in the liberty wherewith Christ hath made us free (Gal. 5:1).

TRIUMPH IN TRIBULATION
ROMANS 5:3; 2 CORINTHIANS 4:7–18

Humanly speaking, no one likes tribulation. Within ourselves we react negatively to difficulties. The word "glory" means "rejoice." No unbeliever can do this, but the believer's whole outlook is changed because of his relationship with Christ. A true Christian can look tribulation in the face and say, "I thank God for this difficulty; I rejoice in it."

Notice that Romans 5:3 does not say we rejoice in spite of tribulations; rather, it says we rejoice in tribulations. This is sometimes an extremely difficult thing to learn. Have you learned it? If not, you are missing one of the greatest blessings that God has in store for you. You can rejoice and thank God even for the tribulation you are passing through.

Most believers are familiar with Romans 8:28, which emphasizes that God is working all things together for our good and His glory. God is using everything—whether we would call it tribulation or not—in order to mold us into the image of His Son (v. 29). And it takes difficulties to make us like Christ. In order for us to have the qualities of Christ, we need to pass through difficulties. They teach us valuable lessons in the Christian school of experience.

These things I have spoken unto you, that in me ye might have peace. In the world ye shall have tribulation: but be of good cheer; I have overcome the world (John 16:33).

ONE WITH CHRIST!
ROMANS 6:1–10

After an individual is justified by faith in Christ, he discovers that he still has a sin nature. This gives him trouble, and he finds himself committing sins that he does not wish to commit. Soon he may become a believer who is dominated by sin. What does God do about this?

The solution to this problem is our identification with Jesus Christ in His death and resurrection. In this identification God sanctifies, or makes holy, the justified individual (a sinner saved by grace). Whereas justification deals with the guilt of sin, sanctification (identification) deals with the power of sin in the life of the believer. How does God sanctify, or make holy, a believer in daily experience? Romans 6 gives the answer.

The answer is our union, or identification, with Christ. Notice again that everything we have is because of Christ. Being in union with, or identified with, Christ is what is meant throughout the New Testament by the expression "in Christ." Being in Christ simply means that the believer has become one with Christ, or identified with Him.

Christ is not just a partner walking alongside the believer; He actually indwells the believer. Therefore, the believer is identified with Christ because Christ's life is in the believer.

I am crucified with Christ: nevertheless I live; yet not I, but Christ liveth in me: and the life which I now live in the flesh I live by the faith of the Son of God, who loved me, and gave himself for me (Gal. 2:20).

DEAD RECKONING
ROMANS 6:11–14

Reckoning is based on absolute truth. We are not called upon to reckon something to be true that is not really true. It is true that Christ died for us and that when we believed in Him as Saviour we died with Him. That's a fact. In that He lives, we also live. That's a fact. So reckoning is based on facts, not on experience. I do not reckon myself to be dead to sin because I feel dead. I don't reckon myself to be alive to God because I feel alive. Experience is important in its place, but it does not determine truth. But knowing what is true, we must reckon it to be true, and then the proper experience will follow.

Perhaps you say, "But I failed Him after I reckoned on the fact that I had died to sin; therefore, I must not be dead to sin." No, it is still a fact. Even when a believer does not behave as though he were dead to sin and alive to God, these are still accomplished facts. That is what salvation is all about. Being born again means we have passed from death to life.

Our identification with Christ in His death is not progressive; that is, we do not die a little bit at a time. Our understanding of the significance of our identification with Him may come gradually, but the fact of our death with Him has been accomplished once for all. Also, we do not become alive to God a little bit at a time; that, too, is once for all. We passed from death to life the moment we believed (John 5:24) and are transferred from the kingdom of darkness to the kingdom of light (Col. 1:13). We need to take God at His word concerning these accomplished facts.

But God forbid that I should glory, save in the cross of our Lord Jesus Christ, by whom the world is crucified unto me, and I unto the world (Gal. 6:14).

269

DEAD TO THE LAW
ROMANS 7:1–6

Everyone who claims he can keep the Law does not have a proper knowledge about the purpose of the Law. It was not given to save anyone; it was given to show everyone their need of placing faith in Christ. The Law exhibits and expounds God's law of righteousness, but it gives no power to perform it. All it does is condemn us when we fail God. God has set us free, however, through Christ, both from the old adamic nature (Rom. 6) and from the Law (Rom. 7). All of this has been done that we might be free to live unto God.

Not only does the Law itself never die, but also God's standards set forth in the Law can never be lowered. The Law causes the individual to see his sin, and it condemns him because he is a sinner. But it does not help him to live a godly life. It is necessary, therefore, that a person's relationship to the Law be changed. That is exactly what takes place when an individual trusts Christ as Saviour and thereby appropriates his death with Christ. The individual is no longer under the condemnation of the Law but is free from its curse and is free to please Jesus Christ.

God does not free us from the Law in order that we might sin without condemnation; He frees us from the Law in order that He might live out His righteousness in us. God has set us free not only from the sin nature but also from the law of condemnation. This, then, makes it possible for Christ to live His life in us, and thus we live a godly life.

For I through the law am dead to the law, that I might live unto God (Gal. 2:19).

YOUR DEBT TO GOD'S SPIRIT
ROMANS 8:6–17

It is not a sin to be tempted, but it is sinful to allow oneself to be drawn away and to yield to the temptation. So at the time when temptation arises is the moment to apply Romans 8:13—to mortify the deeds of the body through the Holy Spirit. And notice that it is only through the Holy Spirit that we can effectively do this.

This calls for a new attitude. We must recognize that we are personally responsible. We cannot escape our responsibility by saying, "Well, it is the Holy Spirit's job to take over, so I am not responsible." The Holy Spirit will not and cannot work if our minds are not determined to hate sin and to refuse to fulfill what our evil natures urge us to do. It is not just a matter of feeling hatred for sin, but it's a determination of the will. The mind is the seat of the will, and we must use our thinking capacity to choose that which is right and to refuse that which is wrong. God assists even in our willing, or choosing, for Philippians 2:13 says, "It is God which worketh in you both to will and to do of his good pleasure." But God will not bypass our wills. If we choose to do wrong, He will not force us to do right. Our wills must be in complete submission to Him.

The person who knows Jesus Christ as Saviour has "the mind of Christ" (1 Cor. 2:16). By God's Word, through the ministry of the Holy Spirit, we know what Jesus Christ would think about a given matter; therefore, as we seek to honor Him, we think the same way. This is why we should not yield the members of our bodies as instruments of unrighteousness but should yield them to God as instruments of righteousness (Rom. 6:13).

Blessed is the man that endureth temptation: for when he is tried, he shall receive the crown of life, which the Lord hath promised to them that love him (James 1:12).

271

NOT IMITATION BUT INCARNATION
ROMANS 12:1–5

Christ wants to live His life through us. He wants to use our eyes to behold the world situation as it is today. He wants to use our ears to hear the cry of the unsaved and the cry of those who are in need. He wants to use our lips to tell others the Gospel. He wants to use our hearts to express compassion and love to everyone. He wants to use our minds to think through situations and to have something to say to the people involved. He wants to use our hands to do His work and our feet to get to the places He wants to go to help others through us. The body also includes the soul, which is the seat of the intellect, the emotions and the will. God not only wants the physical aspect of our bodies, but He also wants our intellect, emotions and will.

Christ wants to think His thoughts through us, and He wants to bring our minds under His control. Second Corinthians 10:4–5 says, "(For the weapons of our warfare are not carnal, but mighty through God to the pulling down of strong holds;) casting down imaginations, and every high thing that exalteth itself against the knowledge of God, and bringing into captivity every thought to the obedience of Christ." Jesus Christ also wants our emotions so He might express Himself through us to a lost and dying world. The Lord Jesus Christ also wants our wills through which to make decisions that will honor Him.

For as many of you as have been baptized into Christ have put on Christ (Gal. 3:27).

NO ROOM FOR
ENVY IN THE CHURCH
ROMANS 12:6–16

What a shame when there is a spirit of envy among the members of the Body of Christ. Instead, there should be praise for the way God is using each one. One translator paraphrases Romans 12:3: "Now I have a warning for you, prompted by the divine grace bestowed on me—and I address it to all who are among you:—do not be uplifted with unjustifiable notions of your importance. Let your thoughts tend to sober views, proportioned to the measure of faith which God has allotted to each man" (Way).

When we become lifted up with feelings of importance because of the particular gift we have, we should remember that it is a gift. The Holy Spirit sovereignly bestows gifts on believers as He chooses (1 Cor. 12:11), not according to what the individual wishes. So when we criticize a person who is exercising another gift, we are actually criticizing the Lord who gave that gift to the person. The other Christian is also part of the Body of Christ, and we need him just as he needs us. All of us who have accepted Jesus Christ as personal Saviour are members of the Body of Christ (v. 27).

A person should not aspire to be something that is not in the will of God for him, because God has made him what he is and has a particular place for him in the Body. Frequently people are dissatisfied with the gift, or gifts, they have. They wish they had another gift or wish they were like someone else. But each gift, no matter how insignificant we may think it is, is useful and worthy in the Body of Christ. That's why God has given each particular gift to someone. We need to realize that God knows what He is doing when it comes to the distribution of gifts.

Be kindly affectioned one to another with brotherly love; in honour preferring one another (Rom. 12:10).

273

DEALING WITH DISAGREEMENTS

ROMANS 12:14–21

It is not our business to repay people for what they do to us. Vengeance belongs to the Lord, even as it is indicated in Deuteronomy 32:35. Since vengeance belongs to the Lord, we would be presuming to take the Father's business out of His hands if we tried to repay evil with evil. He takes into full account every injustice done to us, and He Himself will settle the account. We are to keep on loving with the love with which God has loved us. That love is shed abroad in our hearts by the Holy Spirit (Rom. 5:5).

When we are misunderstood by others, we need to draw on the Word of the Lord for strength and encouragement. A passage that Mrs. Epp and I have both found extremely helpful over the years is Psalm 37:5–6: "Commit thy way unto the LORD; trust also in him; and he shall bring it to pass. And he shall bring forth thy righteousness as the light, and thy judgment as the noonday." From this passage we see that our responsibility is to commit the whole situation to the Lord. If we have been falsely accused, we can count on the fact that God will eventually bring the true situation to light. I have applied these verses to my life many times, and I know from personal experience that they work. God said it; that's why it works.

Love and forgiveness returned for the evil done to us will often bring a person to his knees and will "destroy" him as an enemy, but it will not destroy his character.

For we know him that hath said, Vengeance belongeth unto me, I will recompense, saith the Lord (Heb. 10:30).

SUBMITTED BUT FAITHFUL

ROMANS 13:1–10

It is possible for a believer to be in a situation where he cannot obey the government, but he is to submit to it. Submission refers to our attitude—how we respond inwardly to those who are in authority; obedience refers to our visible actions—how we respond outwardly to those in authority. For instance, Peter and John were forbidden to teach in the name of Jesus by the government authorities of that day (Acts 4:18). They could not obey these injunctions, because Christ's command for them to proclaim the Gospel superseded the command of the rulers. However, the apostles later submitted to the punishment that the government meted out and then kept right on preaching (5:18–20). They could not obey the government's commands, but they could submit to the power of the government. When confronted with their disobedience (v. 28), Peter and the other apostles answered, "We ought to obey God rather than men" (v. 29). We see their submission by their willingness to obey as far as possible.

A contrast between submission and obedience is also seen in Acts 5:40–42: "When they had called the apostles, and beaten them, they commanded that they should not speak in the name of Jesus, and let them go. And they departed from the presence of the council, rejoicing that they were counted worthy to suffer shame for his name. And daily in the temple, and in every house, they ceased not to teach and preach Jesus Christ."

Submit yourselves to every ordinance of man for the Lord's sake (1 Pet. 2:13).

BE CAUTIOUS WHEN YOU CRITICIZE
ROMANS 14:10–13

When we realize that each of us must give an account to God, it will cause us to be more cautious about criticizing a Christian brother. We will then heed what 1 Corinthians 4:5 says: "So do not make any hasty or premature judgments before the time when the Lord comes [again] for He will both bring to light the secret things that are [now hidden] in darkness, and disclose and expose the [secret] aims [motives and purposes] of hearts. Then every man will receive his [due] commendation from God" (Amplified). This is advice that Paul gave to the Corinthians, and it applies just as directly to each believer today.

We shall all be judged one day—not by each other's standards and not even by our own standards. We shall be judged by the standards of Christ. Before God alone, we shall give an account for our own actions and not for those of the other person. I do not have to give an account for you, and you do not have to give an account for me. Before God, I will have to give an account for myself.

No wonder Paul said, "Let us not therefore judge one another any more: but judge this rather, that no man put a stumblingblock or an occasion to fall in his brother's way" (Rom. 14:13). In other words, we should stop turning critical eyes on each other. This is sometimes a difficult instruction to follow. It is natural to always justify oneself and one's own actions in the face of what others are doing. It is natural to criticize the other person because he does not see or do things our way.

For we must all appear before the judgment seat of Christ; that every one may receive the things done in his body, according to that he hath done, whether it be good or bad (2 Cor. 5:10).

DON'T MINIMIZE GOD'S GRACE!
GALATIANS 1:1–10

The basic error the apostle Paul was dealing with was the mingling of Law with grace. There are three grave errors that arise out of this. First there is what we call "legalism." This is the teaching that people are saved by works or human effort. That, in this case, would include the keeping of the Law and observing the rituals and ceremonies found in the Old Testament covenant God made with Israel. This same error is reflected today when someone claims to have done his best to keep the Ten Commandments. This to him is the way of salvation.

The second error that can undermine true faith in Jesus Christ is what we may call "false liberty." The Christian is called unto liberty, but that liberty is defined for us in the Scriptures and not left to our imagination. Yet there are those who teach that because they are saved by grace, it makes no difference how they live or behave. This Satanic error is answered in the Book of James. He wrote: "Even so faith, if it hath not works, is dead, being alone" (2:17). In other words, a faith that does not produce works is not real faith.

The third error is the one Paul deals with in his letter to the Galatians. In fact, the error itself is often named "Galatianism." This false doctrine teaches that we are saved by grace but are kept saved by the Law. In reality, this makes salvation dependent on our works. Our works of righteousness are to be a supplement to our faith for ultimate salvation. One must endure to the end by keeping the works of the Law if he is going to be saved. This is the error of Galatianism, the error that Paul combats in this brief letter.

And ye shall know the truth, and the truth shall make you free (John 8:32).

THE MARKS OF A CHRISTIAN
GALATIANS 2:1–10

Four marks of a Christian are set forth in the Book of Galatians. First, a Christian is one who has the living Christ living in him. "I am crucified with Christ: nevertheless I live; yet not I, but Christ liveth in me: and the life which I now live in the flesh I live by the faith of the Son of God, who loved me, and gave himself for me" (Gal. 2:20).

Second, a Christian is one who has the Holy Spirit within him, for in Galatians 4:6 we read, "And because ye are sons [if we are born again into His family], God sent forth the Spirit of his Son into your hearts." He is the One who really begets us, or creates us anew, and makes us believers. He also creates in us the new character from which Christian conduct comes. Christian conduct does not make a Christian, but a true Christian, one who is born of the Holy Spirit, will have Christian conduct as well.

In the third place, a Christian is one who has shared the cross experience with Christ as the basic solution of his personal problems. We all have come under this experience of the cross, although we may not all have understood it. The key text on this subject is "I am crucified with Christ: nevertheless I live; yet not I, but Christ liveth in me" (2:20). When Christ died, I died with Him, and when He arose, I arose with Him.

In the fourth place, the Christian is one who is possessed of a life that is so divine, so ideal, that it cannot be pushed into a mold of external regulations. We have a new life, a life from God, which is Christ Himself.

Examine yourselves, whether ye be in the faith; prove your own selves (2 Cor. 13:5).

DYING TO LIVE
GALATIANS 2:11–21

The new life is life "in Christ." The word "in" does not in this connection speak of location, such as "in an automobile," but carries the idea of union. We are in union with Christ. Through Him we are dead to the Law, having been identified with Him in His death and resurrection. On the resurrection side of this experience we have His life. He has come to live in us. It is this that marks the real difference between the old life prior to our salvation and the new life now that we are saved.

It is necessary before the believer can enjoy victory in Christ for the power of the old life to be broken. This is accomplished through union with Christ in His crucifixion. This is not an experience that we must struggle to enter into now. It was accomplished for us in the past. The King James Version is not clear on this point. The American Standard Version of 1901 will help us here. The expression "I am crucified with Christ" is translated in the ASV: "I have been crucified with Christ." God got rid of the old self-life by crucifying it. We were separated from the old self-life when we died with Christ.

That this is a past transaction is clearly demonstrated from Romans 6. In verse 2 Paul says, "We who died to sin, how shall we any longer live therein?" (ASV). In the third verse the apostle says, "Know ye not, that so many of us as were baptized into Jesus Christ were baptized into his death?" Here the verbs are clearly in the past tense and describe the finished transaction.

And they that are Christ's have crucified the flesh with the affections and lusts (Gal. 5:24).

LAW, GRACE AND VICTORY
GALATIANS 3:1–14

The Christian life is a "by faith" life not a "by Law" life. Paul makes a very strong statement at the end of Galatians 2 when he says, "I do not frustrate the grace of God: for if righteousness come by the law, then Christ is dead in vain" (v. 21). If we could save ourselves and if we could live a righteous life by our own efforts, there was no purpose in Christ's dying in the first place. He might as well have stayed alive.

Many things were in vain if the Law was necessary for salvation. Not only was Christ's sacrifice unnecessary, but the sufferings of the Galatians because of their faith in Christ were also unnecessary if Judaism was the way of salvation (3:4). Later on Paul said, "Christ is become of no effect unto you, whosoever of you are justified by the law" (5:4).

We do not downgrade the Law when we put it in the place God has put it. But we frustrate the grace of God if we try to substitute Law for grace. When faith is given its proper place with grace, we find that a person is justified by faith without the deeds of the Law. The Law is not set aside by faith but is established. The Law was never given to save people's souls, so whatever being "established" means, it is not that. The sinner establishes the Law by confessing his guilt and acknowledging he is justly condemned. Furthermore, by Christ's assuming the sinner's place and enduring the penalty of the Law, He establishes the Law. The Law is righteous and condemns the sinner to death. When that death takes place, the Law is satisfied. Christ through His death, then, established the Law.

For the law was given by Moses, but grace and truth came by Jesus Christ (John 1:17).

280

ADDED, NOT MIXED
GALATIANS 3:15–25

The passage before us says that the Law "was added" (Gal. 3:19). It was added to something already existing. John the Baptist introduced our Lord to the public and said of Him, "The law was given by Moses, but grace and truth came by Jesus Christ." The Law had a definite beginning. It began not with Adam but with Moses. There was not a God-given Law in all those 2,500 years or more between Adam and Moses, but there was sin, and because there was sin there was death. Adam had some very definite instructions from God as to what he was to do or not to do, and he disobeyed. For this he died. But those who lived between Adam's day and the day of Moses died also, not because they had sinned exactly as Adam sinned but because they were sinners.

The Gospel is good news to all, past, present and future. But the Law was never good news. It was bad news. It was added to the good news, but it did not take the place of grace. Neither was it mixed with grace. And it did not supplant grace. Grace was the good news, but the Law was not.

The word translated "added" means "to place alongside of." The Law's being placed alongside of grace does not mean grace was removed. This is wonderful to see, and yet it is all-important. Grace was there so that man could flee to it when the Law had done its work. When man saw himself condemned and cursed by the Law, he could turn to God's grace and find salvation.

Therefore we conclude that a man is justified by faith without the deeds of the law (Rom. 3:28).

BORN FREE!
GALATIANS 4:19–31

The lesson God has for us in Galatians 4:19–31 is that we cannot ever fulfill the commandments of God by our own human efforts. They can be kept only as we accept Christ as Saviour. Then, through the indwelling Spirit, the life of Christ is fulfilled in us. The bringing of Ishmael into the world was all of man's planning. God had nothing to do with it. That which is of the flesh displeases God, and He will not accept it. Ishmael was a child born after the flesh; and since his mother was a slave, he, too, was a slave.

With Isaac it was entirely different. He was born of a freewoman. His coming into the world was due to God's work. So the point made here is that we are considered through faith in Christ to be the brethren of Isaac. We are the children of promise, born through divine power and not through human effort.

There is a strong tendency on the part of those who insist that Law is necessary for salvation to persecute those who preach salvation by grace plus nothing. Those who insist on Law say that we who preach grace are making it easier for people to sin. But this is not the case. Grace does not give people license to sin. It teaches us to deny ungodliness and worldly lusts and to live soberly and righteously in this world. So even though opposition or even persecution comes, we should be ready to endure it.

But what is to be our attitude in this teaching of Law and grace? Are we to go along with the teachers of Law and say nothing? The answer of Scripture is "Cast out the bondwoman and her son: for the son of the bondwoman shall not be heir with the son of the freewoman" (Gal.4:30). The two will not mix. We are saved by grace. We are not in bondage to the Law. We cast it from us.

Stand fast therefore in the liberty wherewith Christ hath made us free, and be not entangled again with the yoke of bondage (Gal. 5:1).

CAST YOUR VOTE FOR VICTORY!
GALATIANS 5:13–26

The flesh and the Holy Spirit are contrary one to the other. Their aims and purposes are diametrically opposed to each other. Each one says no to the other. They checkmate each other. This, of course, results in a stalemate for the Christian. This is why the apostle says, "Ye cannot do the things that ye would" (Gal. 5:17).

A mistake made by many of us Christians is that we try to gain victory over the flesh by our own will and efforts. But this is the same as pitting the flesh against the flesh. We are trying to overcome the flesh by using the flesh. We might as well assign the devil the task of conquering the devil.

Someone has given the following as a solution to this problem: "The Lord has voted for me; the devil has voted against me. Whichever way I vote, so goes the election." If we determine to walk in the Spirit, we are casting our vote in the right way. This is the choice we must make if we are to overcome the lust of the flesh.

The way of deliverance, then, is to walk in the Spirit (v. 16). We are to be led by the Spirit (v. 18). And we are to live in the Spirit (v. 25). If we give the Holy Spirit a free hand, if we let our lives be the practical day-by-day expression of His life in us, we will be victors.

For to be carnally minded is death; but to be spiritually minded is life and peace (Rom. 8:6).

TWO BURDENS
GALATIANS 6:1–10

To speak of bearing one another's burdens and then to say that every man shall bear his own burden appears on the surface to be a contradiction. This really is not the case. Two different words are used in the original language that are translated "burden" in Galatians 6:1–10.

The burden spoken of in verse 2 is a burden caused by circumstances. The first verse in this chapter admonishes the spiritual person to restore a brother caught in a fault. Instead of discouraging the guilty and burdened brother, the Christian counselor is to help sustain his spiritual life. We are to help bear the burdens of such a person. We are to put ourselves in his place and make his burdens part of our burden.

The burden in verse 5 deals with our responsibilities as Christians. The subject of personal work is raised here and is part of our task as members of the Body of Christ.

In such passages as 1 Corinthians 12:18 and Romans 12:5, we are told we are members of the Body of Christ, and the function of members in a body is to work. The life of the Body is His life. So each one of us who is a member of the Body of Christ has a responsibility and must bear it, thus proving his own work. To the sinner the Lord Jesus said, "Come unto me, all ye that labour and are heavy laden, and I will give you rest" (Matt. 11:28). But to us he says, "Take my yoke upon you, and learn of me.... For my yoke is easy, and my burden is light" (vv. 29–30). He wants us to bear our burden of responsibility to God and man.

We then that are strong ought to bear the infirmities of the weak, and not to please ourselves (Rom. 15:1).

BOASTING THAT BRINGS BLESSING!

GALATIANS 6:11–18

It is remarkable to realize that the crucifixion is a way of life, not just a way of death. Christ's crucifixion was not the end of His redemptive work, for He arose from the grave and provided us with the resurrection life. Romans 6:7 says, "For he that is dead [has died] is freed from sin." This means that the person who has died is free from the claims, power, slavery and allurements of sin.

The basis for Paul's glorying is the cross of Christ. The Judaizers had sought their own glory, but this led only to failure. The kind of self-life they lived through imposing rules and regulations ended in accomplishments that produced self-glory. But all of these self-accomplishments were reached in the sphere of the flesh nature and therefore ended in pride. This has always been a danger facing Christians, and it is no less today. There is too much Christian life and testimony on a fleshly level.

Paul's boast and joy and delight was in the One whom the world had crucified. God set His hand of approval on His Son, who was crucified, by raising Him from the dead.

What is your boast today?

And they that are Christ's have crucified the flesh with the affections and lusts (Gal. 5:24).

LIFE, ETERNAL AND ABUNDANT
EPHESIANS 1:1; JOHN 3:13–21

Eternal life is procured by the death, burial and resurrection of Jesus Christ. By His death Jesus paid the penalty for sin; by His burial He took sin away; by His resurrection He lives in the believer. This is all involved in the new birth. On the other hand, the abundant life is procured for the believer through the living, ascended Christ, who is seated at the right hand of the Father. The believer who lives on the basis of what he possesses in Christ has an abundant life. He realizes the indwelling Christ is able to meet any need.

Eternal life is objective in the sense that a person obtains it by placing faith in the fact of Christ's shed blood for the remission of sins. The abundant life is subjective in that it is a personal response to what a believer has in Christ. The one who knows that Christ is able to meet every need and who lives accordingly has the abundant life.

Eternal life is the same for all believers, regardless of their sinful past. It does not matter whether the person was guilty of gross sin, as society measures sin, or whether he was a person of high moral standards. All who receive Christ have eternal life. However, not all believers have abundant life. The abundant life varies in believers according to their individual responses to Jesus Christ.

He that hath the Son hath life; and he that hath not the Son of God hath not life (1 John 5:12).

THE KEY TO THE TREASURY
EPHESIANS 1:2–3; JOHN 15:1–10

The believer's resources—all spiritual blessings—are "in Christ" (Eph. 1:3). Christ is the life of the believer and thus provides for him all that he needs. Before salvation the individual was in Adam, but after salvation he is in Christ. In Adam the individual possessed only a sinful nature, but in Christ he possesses a divine nature. The divine nature of the believer causes him to want to do the will of God.

Apart from Christ, a person has no relationship to God and God has no relationship to him. Before a person receives Christ, he is unable to benefit from the spiritual blessings God has provided. Only after a person becomes "in Christ" are all the resources of God available to him. God's wealth for the believer is deposited in Christ, and it is only when a person receives Christ that this spiritual wealth becomes available to him.

Without Christ one has no spiritual strength, but in Christ he is able to achieve any spiritual victory. However, even the believer must rely on spiritual provisions if he is to experience spiritual victories. Jesus told believers, "I am the vine, ye are the branches: He that abideth in me, and I in him, the same bringeth forth much fruit: for without me ye can do nothing" (John 15:5). Because Paul knew his spiritual resources he said, "I can do all things through Christ which strengtheneth me" (Phil. 4:13).

In Christ a person has position—where He is, the believer is; privilege—what He is, the believer is; possession—what He has, the believer shares. The two words "in Christ" open up all God's treasures for the believer.

He that abideth in me, and I in him, the same bringeth forth much fruit; for without me ye can do nothing (John 15:5).

YOU WERE BORN WEALTHY
EPHESIANS 1:3; ROMANS 8:35–39

The individual who has received Christ as Saviour has been united to Christ, but he is traveling through a world that has an ungodly, hostile atmosphere. Thus, the believer needs a spiritual atmosphere in which to breathe. Just as astronauts have to take along their own atmosphere when they go to the moon, the believer needs spiritual atmosphere to sustain his spiritual life while on earth. The believer needs spiritual food, spiritual companions, spiritual exercise, spiritual strength and spiritual weapons.

God has blessed believers with "all" spiritual blessings (Eph. 1:3). Many of these are mentioned in Paul's letter to the Ephesians.

God has withheld nothing in providing benefits for the believer—all spiritual blessings are available. God has not just given out of His riches, but He has provided for the believer "according to" His riches.

There is not a single benefit that God wants to provide for the believer that He is unable to provide. Every blessing that is needed for the spirit, soul and body; every blessing that is needed for past, present and future; every blessing that is needed for salvation, sanctification and service; and every blessing that is needed for time and eternity has been provided in Christ for the believer. As is seen from 2 Corinthians 9:8, God is able to make His grace overflow to the believer so that the believer has everything he needs to meet any spiritual problem.

According as his divine power hath given unto us all things that pertain unto life and godliness (2 Pet. 1:3).

CHARACTER COMES FIRST
EPHESIANS 1:4; 1 PETER 1:13–21

There is much talk today about "working for Christ" but little about "being like Christ." Being like Christ means more than just following Him as a good teacher or example; it refers to the believer's being molded into the image of Jesus Christ. This is accomplished only as the believer yields to the work of the indwelling Christ.

The term "without blame" in Ephesians 1:4 means "without blemish"; that is, "free from faultiness." The believer is to live above reproach. This is the potential of every believer because he is in Christ, but it is true of the believer only as he appropriates the resources God has made available to him. The believer possesses a nature that is blameless, and he is to live accordingly.

Believers are to be holy and blameless "before him" (v. 4). Notice that this verse is not referring to a future time, such as the believer's judgment, but to the present. The believer should allow God to work in his heart so that his practice might measure up to his position— holy and blameless. As the refiner can see his image in the purified gold, so God works with a believer until He sees His image. Each believer's prayer should be, "Search me, O God, and know my heart: try me, and know my thoughts: and see if there be any wicked way in me, and lead me in the way everlasting" (Ps. 139:23–24).

Who shall also confirm you unto the end, that ye may be blameless in the day of our Lord Jesus Christ (1 Cor. 1:8).

CLAIM YOUR INHERITANCE
EPHESIANS 1:7–15

An inheritance is something that a person comes into possession of because of his relationship with another. It is not something that is earned; it is a gift.

The believer's inheritance includes life itself. By receiving Christ as Saviour, the believer inherits eternal life. Jesus said, "He that heareth my word, and believeth on him that sent me, hath everlasting life, and shall not come into condemnation; but is passed from death unto life" (John 5:24).

The inheritance of the believer also includes everything he needs for his life. The believer is actually a citizen of heaven who is on a pilgrim journey on earth. However, God has made all spiritual blessings available to the believer. Paul told believers, "All things belong to you, and you belong to Christ; and Christ belongs to God" (1 Cor. 3:22–23, NASB). God's riches made available to the believer are also emphasized in Romans 8:32: "He that spared not his own Son, but delivered him up for us all, how shall he not with him also freely give us all things?"

Our present blessings are only a small part of our spiritual inheritance, which is to be received in full in the future. The moment one receives Christ as Saviour he is placed as a mature son into the family of God and becomes an heir of an inheritance that is beyond human comprehension. We are to let Christ reign in our lives now, but our full spiritual inheritance includes being with Christ and reigning with Him throughout eternity.

To an inheritance incorruptible, and undefiled, and that fadeth not away, reserved in heaven for you (1 Pet. 1:4).

YOU ARE PART OF HIS TREASURE

EPHESIANS 1:16–18

From Ephesians 1:18 it is apparent that we are more than a mere inheritance of Christ. Paul emphasized the kind of inheritance we are to Christ in the words "riches of the glory of his inheritance." Believers are an inheritance of glorious riches to Christ.

This reveals to us what God considers to be of greatest value in the universe. It is not the planets or stars; it is people. God created the universe by His might and power, but He purchased mankind by His precious blood. This universe will someday pass away, and God will create a new heaven and a new earth. But man, who has been redeemed by Christ, shall abide forever! This reveals how important believers are to God. No wonder God is going to display the exceeding riches of His grace through us in ages to come (2:7). This is why Jesus desires to present the Church "to himself a glorious church, not having spot, or wrinkle, or any such thing; but that it should be holy and without blemish" (5:27).

When we consider the marvelous truths of what God thinks of us as believers, it causes us to be filled with praise because of our wonderful Saviour. Although there are times when, humanly speaking, there is only despair, we are able to lift our eyes to Christ and know that He is working in us to accomplish that which will bring glory to Him. So it is important that we do not become discouraged with circumstances; these are the very tools that God uses to make us more like Christ.

Knowing that of the Lord ye shall receive the reward of the inheritance: for ye serve the Lord Christ (Col. 3:24).

OCTOBER

During the month of October, the readings are taken from Ephesians, Philippians and Colossians. Because the apostle Paul wrote these three letters from a prison in Rome, they are commonly referred to as "prison epistles."

Ephesians presents doctrine—the believer in Christ; practice—Christ in the believer; and conflict—Christ working through the believer.

Philippians stresses that the believer should put Christ first in everything, just as He put us first by leaving His Father's throne and coming to earth to die for us.

Colossians emphasizes that the believer is insufficient in himself to live the Christian life; he must rely on the all-sufficient Christ.

The readings for October are excerpted from *Living Abundantly: Studies in Ephesians; Christ Preeminent: Studies in Philippians;* and *The All-Sufficient Christ: Studies in Colossians.*

POWER FOR YOU—TODAY!
EPHESIANS 1:19–23

The Scriptures frequently refer to God's power as it relates to the believer. Ephesians 6:10 says, "Be strong in the Lord, and in the power of his might." Philippians 1:6 says, "Being confident of this very thing, that he which hath begun a good work in you will perform it until the day of Jesus Christ." Colossians 1:29 records Paul's testimony: "I also labour, striving according to his working, which worketh in me mightily."

God's power is sufficient for our every need. None of us has to live a defeated life. But those who do not make use of God's available power live miserable, defeated lives. There's more than enough power to break the hold of all sinful habits; more than enough to give deliverance from temptation; more than enough to enable the believer to live above circumstances. Paul said that God's power is "to us-ward who believe" (Eph. 1:19).

God's power is made available to us by His indwelling presence. Paul referred to this when he told the Colossians that God's power "worketh in me mightily" (1:29). So the dynamo of Christian living is within the believer because God is within the believer. Hebrews 13:21 records the prayer, "Make you perfect [mature] in every good work to do his will, working in you that which is wellpleasing in his sight."

The person who has received Christ is a new creation. Referring to himself as a believer, Paul wrote: "I am [have been] crucified with Christ: nevertheless I live; yet not I, but Christ liveth in me: and the life which I now live in the flesh I live by the faith of the Son of God, who loved me, and gave himself for me" (Gal. 2:20).

Now unto him that is able to do exceeding abundantly above all that we ask or think, according to the power that worketh in us (Eph. 3:20).

ENTHRONED AND ENABLED
EPHESIANS 2:1–10

Because we are seated in the heavenlies in Christ, we should have spiritual rest and relaxation. However, many who know Christ as Saviour are characterized by worrying. The Bible says, "Fret not thyself because of evildoers, neither be thou envious against the workers of iniquity" (Ps. 37:1). The believer is commanded, "Rest in the LORD, and wait patiently for him: fret not thyself because of him who prospereth in his way, because of the man who bringeth wicked devices to pass. Cease from anger, and forsake wrath: fret not thyself in any wise to do evil" (vv. 7–8). We need not worry, "for our conversation [citizenship] is in heaven; from whence also we look for the Saviour, the Lord Jesus Christ" (Phil. 3:20).

Paul was writing these great truths from a dungeon in Rome, but he was deeply conscious of his position in Christ. This was the secret of his victorious living. He realized what his spiritual resources were in Christ.

Christ has been set "far above all principality, and power, and might, and dominion, and every name that is named, not only in this world, but also in that which is to come" (Eph. 1:21). He has been raised far above everything and everyone else. He is not contaminated by the things of this world. As we live according to our heavenly position in Christ, we will not be contaminated by the world either. This involves having a proper attitude of the heart and mind and living by faith. As we appropriate what we have in Christ, we will share in the power and conquests of that exalted position.

In the world ye shall have tribulation: but be of good cheer; I have overcome the world (John 16:33).

295

GOD HAS ENDED THE WAR
EPHESIANS 2:11–18

God has reconciled both Jews and Gentiles to Himself. Therefore, when the Jew and the Gentile receive Christ as Saviour, they can be at peace with each other because they are at peace with God. Once God has become their Father, they can gladly call each other "brother." And it is only when individuals are in right relationship with God that they can be in complete harmony with each other. This means that our deepest racial problems can never be completely solved until those involved come to know Christ as their Saviour and yield their lives to His control. Only the Christian has the basis for truly solving the problems that people face.

Jesus Christ reconciled both Jew and Gentile to God "in one body by the cross" (Eph. 2:16). The moment they were united to God through faith in Christ, they were united to one another. They became members of the same body—the Body of Christ.

So all the redeemed of this age are spiritually united on earth as the Body of Christ, and the risen, ascended Christ is in heaven as the Head of the Body. As the Head, He gives life and direction to the members of the Body. Each believer is to no longer consider what he was in the natural realm but is to consider what he is in Christ. Regardless of one's nationality, color or denominational preference, he becomes one in Christ with every other believer when he receives Christ.

For by one Spirit are we all baptized into one body, whether we be Jews or Gentiles, whether we be bond or free (1 Cor. 12:13).

GOD IS BUILDING A TEMPLE
EPHESIANS 2:19–22

Jesus Christ is building His Church. When He was on earth, He said, "I will build my church; and the gates of hell shall not prevail against it" (Matt. 16:18). We are living stones within God's building, and we also have a part as co-builders as we take the Gospel to others so they can receive Christ as Saviour. Christ came and preached peace; now we who know Him as Saviour are to preach the Gospel to others so they may have this peace. Jesus told the Father, "As thou hast sent me into the world, even so have I also sent them into the world" (John 17:18). Just before Jesus ascended to the Father, He gave believers the Great Commission: "All power is given unto me in heaven and in earth. Go ye therefore, and teach all nations, baptizing them in the name of the Father, and of the Son, and of the Holy Ghost: teaching them to observe all things whatsoever I have commanded you: and, lo, I am with you alway, even unto the end of the world. Amen" (Matt. 28:18–20).

Those who receive Christ as Saviour become living stones, precisely fitted into the building of God. Just as there are many shapes and sizes of stones, so individual believers vary from one another, but God has a special place for each in the building. Those in Paul's day knew that it took much work to shape stones so they would fit precisely in a building. So Paul was emphasizing not only that believers are stones in God's building but also that it takes the shaping work of God to make them fit properly into the building. The harder the stone, the longer it takes the builder to make it what

(continued on next page)

GOD'S BUILDING A TEMPLE

he wants it to be. As living stones we sometimes find the process painful, but the end result is good. That's why Romans 8:28 says, "And we know that all things work together for good to them that love God, to them who are the called according to his purpose."

Know ye not that ye are the temple of God, and that the Spirit of God dwelleth in you? (1 Cor. 3:16).

DOES CHRIST FEEL AT HOME IN YOUR HEART?

EPHESIANS 3:14–17

Paul referred to his relationship to the indwelling Christ when he wrote: "I am [have been] crucified with Christ: nevertheless I live; yet not I, but Christ liveth in me" (Gal. 2:20). Thus, as Paul prayed for the Ephesians, he prayed that Christ might dwell in their hearts in the sense of being enthroned in their lives—that He might be truly at home, not just a guest. He will be completely at home in our lives to the extent that He is truly Lord of our lives. When we received Him as Saviour, He came to permanently indwell us, but our need now is to put Him first in everything so that He will be at home in us. When we come to this point, our desire will be the same as Paul's when he said, "That I may know him, and the power of his resurrection, and the fellowship of his sufferings, being made conformable unto his death" (Phil. 3:10).

Notice that the place of Christ's dwelling is "in your hearts" (Eph. 3:17). Christ dwells in the inner man and desires to control the person He indwells. Of course, Christ indwells every person who receives Him as Saviour, but this does not necessarily mean He is in control of the person's life.

In order for Christ to control our lives, we must give up the self-life —we must desire to please Him rather than ourselves. This means we will have to say no to our own desires when they conflict with His. We will have victory in our lives only as we submit ourselves to the Lord and by faith live in dependence on Him. We must not

(continued on next page)

 **OCTOBER 5**

DOES CHRIST FEEL AT HOME IN YOUR HEART?

underestimate the importance of denying ourselves when our desires conflict with His. Jesus said, "If any man will come after me, let him deny himself, and take up his cross daily, and follow me. For whosoever will save his life shall lose it: but whosoever will lose his life for my sake, the same shall save it" (Luke 9:23–24).

Behold, I stand at the door, and knock: if any man hear my voice, and open the door, I will come in to him, and will sup with him, and he with me (Rev. 3:20).

WHOSE PRISONER ARE YOU?

EPHESIANS 4:1–2; ACTS 16:25–31

It is interesting to note the difference between the ways Paul referred to himself in the first half of Ephesians and the last half. In beginning the first half, or doctrinal portion, Paul referred to himself as "an apostle of Jesus Christ" (1:1). Paul emphasized his apostleship because he had a special message to give believers, and that message was given in the first three chapters. In the last half of Ephesians, which emphasizes the practice of Christians, Paul referred to himself as "the prisoner of the Lord" (4:1). This last section of Ephesians is an intense appeal by Paul for believers to walk worthy of their calling, and Paul underscored his appeal by calling himself a prisoner of the Lord.

How interesting that Paul should have this viewpoint. He was a prisoner of Rome and was in a damp dungeon because of preaching the Gospel, but he really considered himself to be a prisoner of the Lord. Paul recognized that the Lord could use him where he was, and this is precisely what the Lord did. During this imprisonment, Paul wrote letters to Philemon, the Colossians, the Ephesians and the Philippians. These letters are now contained in the Scriptures and have had great impact on the world down through the ages.

It is good to ask ourselves, Whose prisoner am I? Do I consider myself a prisoner of circumstances or of the Lord Jesus Christ?

Know ye not, that to whom ye yield yourselves servants to obey, his servants ye are to whom ye obey; whether of sin unto death, or of obedience unto righteousness? (Rom. 6:16).

SPIRITUAL UNITY IS NOT AUTOMATIC

EPHESIANS 2:11–18

The unity referred to in Scripture is a spiritual unity of everyone within the Body of Christ; that is, all who have received Him as personal Saviour. This means that our unity must always be based on the truth of the Scriptures, which tell who Christ is and what we are in Him. Any unity that compromises the teaching of the Scriptures regarding Jesus Christ is not a unity that has God's approval. However, the ecumenism of our day seems far more concerned about unity for unity's sake, than it does about adhering to the truth of the Scriptures. In fact, the teaching of the Scriptures is sometimes de-emphasized so much that for the sake of unity some groups do not even have doctrinal statements. Such groups tend to emphasize God's love and the need of working in harmony with those with whom we disagree. It is naive, however, to emphasize love at the expense of truth—to emphasize God's love but not His holy standards and justice. Organizational unity is not necessarily wrong if only believers are involved. However, it is wrong— no matter how good the cause may be—for believers to compromise their message in order to work with unbelievers.

When Paul said we are to be "endeavouring to keep the unity of the Spirit" (Eph.4:3) the word he used for "endeavouring" was a word that originally meant "to make haste" and then came to mean "to be zealous or eager, to give diligence." Each believer is to give his utmost attention to see that harmony is preserved within the Body of Christ. It is a spiritual unity, or oneness, that exists among all who know Christ as Saviour, but it can be maintained only as we walk in fellowship with Him.

Behold, how good and how pleasant it is for brethren to dwell together in unity! (Ps. 133:1).

WHAT TO DO WITH ANGER
EPHESIANS 4:17–27

It is apparent that we should be angry with sin and come to hate that which would separate us from God or cause loss of fellowship. This means there will be times when we will hate what others do because it goes contrary to the Word of God. Such anger may be referred to as "righteous indignation." However, when self becomes projected into the matter, it is possible for a believer to sin, at least in his attitude toward others. In Ephesians 4:26, Paul was warning against permitting smoldering fires of resentment to remain in anyone's heart: "Let not the sun go down upon your wrath." We should make it our practice never to retire without first being sure that we have confessed known sin of actions and attitudes, "for the wrath of man worketh not the righteousness of God" (James 1:20).

Jesus was angry with those who withstood God. He called the Pharisees and Sadducees a "generation of vipers" (Matt. 3:7). The scribes and Pharisees He called "hypocrites" (23:14). On another occasion He made a whip of small ropes and drove the money changers from the temple (John 2:13–16).

Although the Lord Jesus Christ was able to be angry without sinning, it is difficult for us. That is why Paul gave the command as he did in Ephesians 4:26. Our anger should be stirred when God's name is taken in vain or when He is blasphemed, but we must be careful that we do not sin in the way we react to these incidents. If we speak unkind words or are embittered toward others, we have sinned and it needs to be confessed to the Lord.

But everyone must be quick to hear, slow to speak and slow to anger; for the anger of man does not achieve the righteousness of God (James 1:19–20, NASB).

DON'T ROB YOURSELF!
EPHESIANS 4:28–32

In our relationships with others, we need to be sure that we do not steal from them. We need to be honest in business transactions and be faithful in giving service for which we are paid. If we are paid for a full day's work, we steal from our employer if we do not give him a full day's work. Even such a relatively small matter as taking too long on coffee break is a way of stealing from one's employer. The Bible says, "Provide things honest in the sight of all men" (Rom. 12:17). Each believer needs to examine himself to be sure that he is not stealing from God or others. The Bible says, "Wherefore we labour, that, whether present or absent, we may be accepted of him. For we must all appear before the judgment seat of Christ; that every one may receive the things done in his body, according to that he hath done, whether it be good or bad" (2 Cor. 5:9–10). We cannot expect to be rewarded by the Lord if we have stolen time and money that should have been spent for Him.

In contrast to stealing, Paul said, "But rather let him labour, working with his hands the thing which is good, that he may have to give to him that needeth" (Eph. 4:28). Notice that there is a purpose for the work, and that purpose is that the believer might be able to help others. The Christian is one who should genuinely care about others; and the more he cares, the more he wants to give to help them in their need.

Thou shalt not steal (Ex. 20:15).

LEARNING TO LOVE
EPHESIANS 5:1–5

Does the standard of God's love seem too high to attain? Having received Jesus Christ as Saviour, we have been born of the Holy Spirit and have become members of God's family. We have become partakers in, or sharers of, the divine nature (2 Pet. 1:4), and the essence of the divine nature is love. It is the kind of love that loves even when there is no response, always seeking the highest good for the other person. That God loved us when there was no response is evident from Romans 5:8: "But God commendeth his love toward us, in that, while we were yet sinners, Christ died for us." But it can be said that because of our having received Jesus Christ as Saviour, "the love of God is [now] shed abroad in our hearts by the Holy Ghost which is given unto us" (v. 5). Since it is His love that is in our hearts, we are able to attain God's standard of love by letting Christ live His life in us as He desires. The expression of this love in us is one of the strongest proofs that we really are the children of God (1 John 4:7–16).

When Paul urged believers to "walk in love" (Eph. 5:2), he was emphasizing that our life is lived one step at a time. As we rely on the Lord for the step we are now taking, we need not worry about the steps that are ahead. Of course, Paul was referring to a person's way of life. First John 3:18 says, "My little children, let us not love in word, neither in tongue; but in deed and in truth." It is easy to talk, but it is costly to walk.

A new commandment I give unto you, That ye love one another; as I have loved you, that ye also love one another (John 13:34).

KEEP YOUR EYES OPEN!
EPHESIANS 5:7–17

Because of the subtle works of darkness and the importance of being a witness for the Lord, Paul said, "See then that ye walk circumspectly, not as fools, but as wise" (Eph. 5:15).

The word translated "see" means "to look, to consider, to take heed." It was as if Paul was waving a sign before them that said, "Stop, look and listen." Paul wanted believers to make a thorough check of the way they were living to be sure they were walking as they should be. Paul wanted them to make sure they were walking "circumspectly," which means "looking around" or "being cautious." The Greek word Paul used means "accurately" or "exactly." One of the reasons believers should live carefully is that unbelievers are observing them. To live carefully, believers must have an intelligent purpose in living. If we do not have such a purpose, our lives will not be as effective as the Lord desires.

Paul's purpose in living is seen in 1 Corinthians 2:2: "For I determined not to know any thing among you, save Jesus Christ, and him crucified." To the Philippians, he wrote: "According to my earnest expectation and my hope, that in nothing I shall be ashamed, but that with all boldness, as always, so now also Christ shall be magnified in my body, whether it be by life, or by death. For to me to live is Christ, and to die is gain" (1:20–21).

Ponder the path of thy feet, and let all thy ways be established (Prov. 4:26).

TOGETHERNESS
EPHESIANS 5:25–33

No believer lives a spiritually isolated life. Together, we are members of Christ's Body (Eph. 5:30) and have responsibilities to each other. Ephesians 4:25 says, "We are members one of another." Therefore, Spirit-filled believers treat fellow Christians as they would treat themselves. We are not to be domineering, but recognizing that Christ is the Lord of all, we are to have a submissive spirit.

As we mutually desire to do the will of God, the Holy Spirit will give us a harmonious relationship with each other. We are to submit ourselves to others "in the fear of God," which is a reverential fear lest we displease or dishonor God. Because of all that Christ has done for us, our desire should be to please Him in everything we do. As we submit ourselves to Him and to others, the devil is given no opportunity in our lives. Ephesians 4:27 tells believers, "Neither give place to the devil."

God gives the grace that is needed to resist the temptation to disrupt the harmony of believers: "But he giveth more grace. Wherefore he saith, God resisteth the proud, but giveth grace unto the humble. Submit yourselves therefore to God. Resist the devil, and he will flee from you" (James 4:6–7). When we maintain this kind of relationship with Christ, through the Holy Spirit, we have the proper basis for the various relationships in life, some of which are mentioned in Ephesians 5.

Now ye are the body of Christ, and members in particular (1 Cor. 12:27).

KEEP THE ARMOR ON!
EPHESIANS 6:10–18

The armor is not to be put on and taken off periodically but to be put on and left on. The armor is actually an attitude of faith; therefore, it is something that is put on by an act of the will and left on. As we mature in the Christian life, we will discover areas in our lives where our faith is not as strong as it should be; that is, the armor is weak in a certain place. At such a time, our responsibility is to go to the Word of God to study His promises concerning our area of weakness so that our faith will be strengthened.

Notice the parallel between Ephesians 6:11, "Put on the whole armour of God," and Romans 13:14, "Put ye on the Lord Jesus Christ." God's provision for victory is in the Person of the Lord Jesus Christ and through the Word of God.

In putting on the Lord Jesus Christ, we need to remember that the living Word (Jesus Christ) is revealed through the written Word (the Bible). In His prayer for His own, Jesus prayed, "Sanctify them through thy truth: thy word is truth" (John 17:17). We put on the Lord Jesus Christ as we study the Word of God and obey what it says.

The believer's armor, then, is not physical protective equipment but is Jesus Christ Himself. Putting on Christ is similar to what we are told in Ephesians 4:24: "Put on the new man." This new man is Christ formed in the believer. Paul was greatly concerned that this be true of every believer, and he told the Galatians: "I travail in birth again until Christ be formed in you" (4:19).

And that ye put on the new man, which after God is created in righteousness and true holiness (Eph. 4:24).

308

SEEING GOD IN YOUR CIRCUMSTANCES

PHILIPPIANS 1:12–21

The life of the indwelling Christ enabled Paul to be free from worry and self-care during his imprisonment, which could have led to death. Paul was bold and unashamed and was concerned only that Christ would be magnified in his body regardless of what awaited him—life or death. There was no wavering on his part.

We tend to think that these tremendous qualities were true only of the great men of God, such as the apostle Paul, but that it is impossible for us to attain them. Somehow Satan blinds our eyes to the fact that we can have the same determination to glorify Christ in our lives that Paul had in his. The same Christ indwells us, not only to give us the desire to glorify Him but also to enable us to have the boldness to carry out that desire.

Having told of his desire to please Christ in everything, whether through life or through death, Paul said, "For to me to live is Christ, and to die is gain" (Phil. 1:21). This was the basis for Paul's being able to live victoriously in Christ. He was not concerned about drawing attention to himself; rather, he wanted to glorify Jesus Christ in everything. All of Paul's life was focused on Jesus Christ.

It is good for each of us to weigh his or her activities and ask, *Are the things I am doing all done to further my own interests, or are they really glorifying Christ?*

I have been crucified with Christ; and it is no longer I who live, but Christ lives in me; and the life which I now live in the flesh I live by faith in the Son of God, who loved me, and gave Himself up for me (Gal. 2:20, NASB).

UNITY, NOT UNIFORMITY
PHILIPPIANS 2:1–5; PSALM 133

The Christian life is not a stereotyped life composed of rules and regulations. It may involve rules and regulations, but the Christian life is essentially the presence of Christ in the believer. This is why Paul said, "Therefore as you have received Christ Jesus the Lord, so walk in Him, having been firmly rooted and now being built up in Him and established in your faith, just as you were instructed, and overflowing with gratitude. See to it that no one takes you captive through philosophy and empty deception, according to the tradition of men, according to the elementary principles of the world, rather than according to Christ. For in Him all the fulness of Deity dwells in bodily form, and in Him you have been made complete, and He is the head over all rule and authority" (Col. 2:6–10, NASB).

It should also be remembered that the minds of different believers are not to be pressed into a single mold of thinking—this is not what is meant by being "likeminded" (Phil. 2:2). Rather, God imparts to us the matchless mastermind of Christ, so each believer will be a distinct person in himself. Believers will be likeminded inasmuch as they will seek to reach similar goals, but they will not each seek the same way, and they may not always agree as to how a particular goal can best be reached.

Let us therefore follow after the things which make for peace, and things wherewith one may edify another (Rom. 14:19).

CHRIST, THE GREAT EXAMPLE
PHILIPPIANS 2:5–11

It is apparent that there was some element of Jesus' equality with God that He was willing to set aside during His earthly ministry. One cannot give up the qualities of his inner nature, but he can relinquish the right, in some respects, to outwardly express his inner nature. Even though Christ was God Himself and had the right to display His attributes, He willingly gave up this right in order to come to earth to be the Saviour of the world. He did not cease being in the form of God as to His inner nature, but He gave up being equal with God as far as the expression of some of His attributes was concerned.

Remember that the Father did not humble Jesus Christ; He humbled Himself. There is a vast difference between being humiliated and willingly humbling oneself. Jesus Christ voluntarily took a lower position because of His love for us. And this is the same kind of attitude that should characterize those of us who know Jesus Christ as Saviour.

The Bible has much to say about both pride and humility. James 4, verses 6 and 10 says, "But He gives a greater grace. Therefore it says, 'GOD IS OPPOSED TO THE PROUD, BUT GIVES GRACE TO THE HUMBLE.'... Humble yourselves in the presence of the Lord, and He will exalt you" (NASB). First Peter 5:6 says, "Humble yourselves, therefore, under the mighty hand of God, that He may exalt you at the proper time" (NASB). Matthew 23:12 says, "Whoever exalts himself shall be humbled; and whoever humbles himself shall be exalted" (NASB).

Let nothing be done through strife or vainglory; but in lowliness of mind let each esteem other better than themselves (Phil. 2:3).

BALANCED AND BLESSED!
PHILIPPIANS 2:12–14; JEREMIAH 6:9–15

Every Christian needs to work out his salvation with a tender conscience and a watchfulness against temptations, trials or testings, shrinking from whatever might offend God or discredit His name.

Each of us needs to seriously consider whether or not there is something in our lives that is discrediting the name and Person of Christ. When we realize what He has done for us, we ought to tremble as we stand in the presence of a holy, righteous, almighty God. Not only do we stand in His presence now, but we will also stand in His presence when we give account at the Judgment Seat of Christ. When others view our lives today, what do they see? What do they talk about? We should be constantly apprehensive of the deceitfulness of the flesh. Jeremiah 17:9–10 says, "The heart is more deceitful than all else and is desperately sick; who can understand it? I, the LORD, search the heart, I test the mind, even to give to each man according to his ways, according to the results of his deeds" (NASB). We need to develop a watchfulness in regard to the power in our corruption.

In all of this a perfect balance is kept—God gives the divine enablement; we provide the human responsibility. We are not to be totally passive, for after God works in us, we are to work it out through our lives.

And herein do I exercise myself, to have always a conscience void of offence toward God, and toward men (Acts 24:16).

THE WORD IS CENTRAL
PHILIPPIANS 2:15–16; PSALM 119:9–16

Never forget the centrality of the Word of God to the believer's witness. The Christian is to study the Word, apply it to himself and then translate it into daily living before a crooked and perverse world. And every believer may be assured that as God's Word is held forth it will have an effect on those who hear it. Hebrews 4:12 says, "For the word of God is living and active and sharper than any two-edged sword, and piercing as far as the division of soul and spirit, of both joints and marrow, and able to judge the thoughts and intentions of the heart" (NASB).

There is no substitute for holding forth God's Word, for if people are to come into right relationship with Jesus Christ, they must know what God's Word says. Romans 10:17 says, "Faith comes from hearing, and hearing by the word of Christ" (NASB). So if those we witness to are to be able to have faith in Christ, they must have the Word of God presented to them.

We must first benefit from the Word ourselves before we become concerned about passing it on to others. We cannot do the work of God or have the right attitudes (as urged in the previous verses) unless God's Word is doing its work within us. The Word of God goes to the deepest parts of our nature. It exposes, sifts, analyzes and judges even our thoughts (see Heb. 4:12).

The law of the LORD is perfect, converting the soul: the testimony of the LORD is sure, making wise the simple (Ps. 19:7).

 **OCTOBER 19**

ZEAL WITHOUT KNOWLEDGE
PHILIPPIANS 3:1–11

Paul said about himself, "Concerning zeal, persecuting the church" (Phil. 3:6). This reveals the pride of personal devotion to his religious choices. In a sense, it was Paul's pride of reputation. He was more devoted than any of his contemporaries. He was not only a Pharisee, but he was also a very zealous one. He was a conscientious and relentless persecutor of all who were considered heretics outside of his pharisaic Judaism. In Paul's unsaved state in Judaism, he actually thought he was doing the will of God by persecuting the believers in Jesus Christ. He measured his religion by his hatred for Christians.

It is regrettable that even today some believers measure their Christian zeal by what they are against. Some have so much bitterness against modernists—those with liberal theology; others contend zealously over the issue of the Holy Spirit or over a particular translation of the Bible. Some have bitterness toward sinners, not distinguishing the sin from the sinner. But remember, a reputation of zeal against anything is not a proof of salvation in itself. I believe that when we are rightly related to Jesus Christ, we will have much zeal against those things that dishonor Him, but it is possible for people to be zealous against some things without having a right relationship with Christ.

Who gave himself for us, that he might redeem us from all iniquity, and purify unto himself a peculiar people, zealous of good works (Titus 2:14).

DEALING WITH YOUR PAST
PHILIPPIANS 3:12–14; 1 TIMOTHY 1:12–17

We can do nothing about the past except make necessary confession. And when confession is made, the Bible promises: "If we confess our sins, he is faithful and just to forgive us our sins, and to cleanse us from all unrighteousness" (1 John 1:9). By confession, sin is placed under the cleansing blood of the Lord Jesus Christ, and when it is under the blood, it does not condemn any longer. Unless the past is dealt with, one is not prepared to live in the present nor to go on into the future. Unless the past is dealt with, it becomes a haunting memory that saps the strength of the believer so he is unable to honor Christ in his daily life.

What God does with sin when it is confessed is explained in various passages. Isaiah 44:22 says, "I have wiped out your transgressions like a thick cloud and your sins like a heavy mist. Return to Me, for I have redeemed you" (NASB). Hebrews 8:12 says, "FOR I WILL BE MERCIFUL TO THEIR INIQUITIES, AND I WILL REMEMBER THEIR SINS NO MORE" (NASB).

Someone has said, "The present must forget the past by correction, or else the past will become a moral and spiritual liability for the future."

Consider some items that need to be forgotten: failures—they keep our faith from advancing; successes—they create pride (see Prov. 16:18); losses—they drag us down so we cannot serve the Lord the way we should; grievances—they produce false attitudes (see 1 Cor. 13:6); sorrows—God can heal all heartaches; discouragements—we need to remember Christ, not disappointments, thwarted hopes and plans.

And their sins and iniquities will I remember no more (Heb. 10:17).

CITIZENS OF HEAVEN!
PHILIPPIANS 3:17–21

All of us who have believed in Christ, like the patriarchs, are "looking for the city which has foundations, whose architect and builder is God" (Heb. 11: 10, NASB). Believers of old were "seeking a country of their own" (v. 14, NASB), and we, too, are seeking a heavenly country. Even though we reside on earth, our legal residence is in heaven.

Therefore, our minds should be on that which originates in heaven rather than on that which originates on earth. Paul told of those whose minds were on earthly things. He referred to them as "enemies of the cross of Christ, whose end is destruction, whose god is their appetite, and whose glory is in their shame, who set their minds on earthly things" (Phil. 3:18–19, NASB). In contrast to this kind of people, the believer is to follow the injunctions of Colossians 3:1–3: "If you have been raised up with Christ, keep seeking the things above, where Christ is, seated at the right hand of God. Set your mind on the things above, not on the things that are on earth. For you have died and your life is hidden with Christ in God" (NASB).

Jesus Himself prayed, "Thy will be done in earth, as it is in heaven" (Matt. 6:10). Jesus was concerned about God's will being carried out, not just in the end times but also now in the believer. So whereas the pattern of our life is heavenly, the practice is here on earth.

And now, little children, abide in him; that, when he shall appear, we may have confidence, and not be ashamed before him at his coming (1 John 2:28).

CONSIDERATE CHRISTIANS
PHILIPPIANS 3:12–14; 1 TIMOTHY 1:12–7

The word "moderation" (Phil. 4:5) emphasizes pliability and agreeableness. It is a special consideration given to other people, and it is to be the additive that causes a believer to patiently forbear under injury without desiring revenge. It is a spirit that is ready to forgive, and it possesses a gentleness of temper. It is also temperate in physical desires and demonstrates equity; that is, justice and impartiality in business.

Having moderation means a person will avoid extremes and will not be explosive. The peace of God is obviously not in a person's life if he has an explosive temper. Nor can there be peace in a stubborn heart that refuses to yield to reason or to God. Nor is there the peace of God for the one living in physical excess; this only breeds greed and discontent.

It cannot be overemphasized that the "moderation" of which Paul spoke in Philippians 4:5 is related to the indwelling Holy Spirit and the fruit that is produced by Him in our lives. That is why Paul used the word "let" in saying, "Let your moderation be known" (v. 5). We cannot self-produce moderation any more than we can self-produce the mind of Christ. Since Christ indwells us, we are to "let this mind be in [us], which was also in Christ Jesus" (2:5). So also, since the Holy Spirit indwells us, we are to let Him do His work in our lives to produce His fruit through us. And we are enabled to do this because "the Lord is at hand" (4:5).

But the fruit of the Spirit is love, joy, peace, longsuffering, gentleness, goodness, faith, meekness, temperance: against such there is no law (Gal. 5:22–23)

DO YOU HAVE "PET CARES"?
PHILIPPIANS 4:6–7; MATTHEW 6:24–34

There are at least three characteristics, or marks, that indicate we have excessive care. The first is being more concerned about things than about God's will for us. We will never have peace by acquiring things; peace comes only by being in God's will, with or without the possessions we think we so greatly need. Ours in the western world is a credit card society, and we are able to obtain about anything we want almost instantly. Then the anxiety comes in struggling to pay for all that was bought on impulse! Whether anxiety comes from wanting possessions or from concern over how to pay for them, it must be underscored that anxiety chokes the life of faith and strangles the peace of God.

A second mark of excessive care is that in our hurried state we allow ourselves to be pressured into hasty decisions and actions. Life provides many illustrations of times when we feel we must make a decision immediately, and then later we realize it was not that urgent after all. When we are in league with God, we can afford to wait for His perfect time.

A third characteristic of excessive care is that we are constantly agitated because of unrest in our souls. Faith—not worry—brings answers to prayers.

Some people have what I call "pet cares." They like to keep these cares to talk about, and one gets the feeling they do not really want to get rid of them. But God says we are to bring all of our cares to Him. Usually one discovers he is either casting all of his cares upon God, or he is keeping all of his cares for himself.

But seek ye first the kingdom of God, and his righteousness; and all these things shall be added unto you (Matt. 6:33).

THE RENEWED MIND
PHILIPPIANS 4:8–9; 2 PETER 1:1–9

A good exercise is to analyze the kind of thoughts you have been thinking. Some will be spiritual thoughts that make a positive contribution to life, others will be thoughts about things that are not necessarily good or bad, and there will be thoughts that are definitely bad—and you realize this without anyone's telling you so. The quickest way to deteriorate or to degenerate is to allow your mind to be occupied with unworthy thoughts. We soon become what we think. Thinking good thoughts contributes to building character; thinking bad thoughts leads downward.

Jesus explained that the mouth really reveals what is in the heart: "The good man out of the good treasure of his heart brings forth what is good; and the evil man out of the evil treasure brings forth what is evil; for his mouth speaks from that which fills his heart" (Luke 6:45, NASB). What the conscious mind thinks on gradually sinks into the subconscious mind and becomes the building blocks, or material, for one's character. "For as he thinks within himself, so he is" (Prov. 23:7, NASB).

We can make a positive contribution to our subconscious mind by controlling the thoughts of our conscious mind. But when we think selfishly, covetously, jealously and lustfully, these characteristics will become evident in our character.

And be not conformed to this world: but be ye transformed by the renewing of your mind, that ye may prove what is that good, and acceptable, and perfect, will of God (Rom. 12:2).

CONTENTMENT, NOT COMPLACENCY
PHILIPPIANS 4:10–13; 1 TIMOTHY 6:6–11

Nowhere does the Bible suggest that we should be content with unsatisfactory conditions. But because of our personal relationship with Christ we can be content in them. As different situations arise and we learn our lessons one after another, we will also find it possible to be content in every situation.

Contentment is one of those concepts that is easier to define than to experience. This is probably because the tendency is to seek contentment in possessions rather than in a person. We assume that contentment comes from having things, but it is possible to have deep contentment without things. So often we think contentment would be ours if we were promoted to the next highest position or if we were able to buy that object we think we need so much or if we could be accepted in a certain circle of friends. But as we advance in these areas, we discover that contentment is elusive because we are seeking it in the wrong places and in the wrong way.

Contentment does not depend on what we have; it depends on who we are. It is a spiritual attainment, not something that results from purchasing power. As someone has said, "Contentment is a state of heart rather than a statement of account."

Godliness with contentment is great gain (1 Tim. 6:6).

CAN YOU CLAIM THIS PROMISE?
PHILIPPIANS 4:17–20

Philippians 4:19 cannot be understood apart from the preceding verses. Some Christians have claimed verse 19 but have not met the conditions of the preceding verses; therefore, they are unwarranted in expecting God to keep His promise of verse 19. And when they see that God has not fulfilled what they consider to be a promise, it can make their lives a shipwreck. Thus, it is very important to understand the context of verse 19.

We will never realize the tremendous provision of verse 19 until we have met its spiritual and circumstantial requirements. Almost every promise in the Bible has one or more conditions that must be met before God's promise is fulfilled.

Philippians 4:19 says, "God shall supply all your need." We see, then, that there must be a need before God will supply. We must not presume on this promise and run ahead of God with plans of our own. Neither should we presume on God for all our wants or be careless in spending God's money. God does not promise to supply all of our wants, only our needs. The slothful, the spendthrift or the selfish person cannot claim the promise of Philippians 4:19. There must be a legitimate need. Those who are slothful and unwilling to work or who are overly ambitious to gain things need not expect to have this verse fulfilled in their lives.

It should also be understood that God meets our need for a purpose—not to relieve us of our responsibility but because He has given us responsibility. When God gives us a responsibility to fulfill, we can count on His supplying all of the resources that are necessary to accomplish it.

The Lord is my shepherd, I shall not want (Ps. 23:1).

WHAT DO YOU BELIEVE IN?
COLOSSIANS 1:1–8

Almost everyone talks about faith because almost everyone has faith in something. But faith is only as good as its object. It is important to recognize that we are not saved from condemnation by having faith in faith. Paul commended the Colossians for their "faith in Christ Jesus" (Col. 1:4).

So it is not sufficient to tell a person, "Just believe." The question is, Believe what? The message of the Gospel is not to believe in yourself, in church or in doctrine but in the Lord Jesus Christ. This implies believing in all that Christ did for us when He died on the cross in our place. It recognizes that we are sinful human beings who deserve condemnation, or else it would never have been necessary for Christ to die. It means we recognize that Christ is our only hope because if we could have been saved by some other means, Christ would not have had to die (see Gal. 2:21). Having faith in Jesus Christ implies we have placed our confidence entirely in His finished work on the cross, recognizing that He forgives our sins and gives us eternal life. One can summarize saving faith as a commitment to Jesus Christ who is our life and Lord. Faith in Jesus Christ as our Lord is also necessary for growth in our Christian walk.

And they said, Believe on the Lord Jesus Christ, and thou shalt be saved, and thy house (Acts 16:31).

LIVING TO PLEASE GOD
COLOSSIANS 1:9–12

As Paul prayed for the Colossians and their walk, or way of life, he did not pray that it might be pleasing to man but to God. In his letter to the Galatians, Paul said of himself, "For do I now persuade men, or God? or do I seek to please men? for if I yet pleased men, I should not be the servant of Christ" (1:10). Of course, when we live in a way that pleases God, many people will also be pleased by the way we live. But our focus of attention should be on pleasing God rather than people.

Living in a way that pleases God cannot be done in one's own strength. It is only by means of the indwelling Christ that the believer can exhibit the fruit of the Spirit and have a walk that pleases the Lord.

Although the believer seeks primarily to please God, not people, we must keep these truths in balance. We will not be successful in reaching others with the Gospel if we constantly displease them by our attitudes and actions. But above all, we must be true to God Himself in all that we do. As Paul sought to evangelize the lost, he was very careful not to unnecessarily offend those he was endeavoring to reach. Paul summed up this aspect of his life in this way: "Even as I please all men in all things, not seeking mine own profit, but the profit of many, that they may be saved" (1 Cor. 10:33).

For I do always those things that please him (John 8:29).

CHRIST ETERNAL!
COLOSSIANS 1:13–19

Christ existed prior to all creation. He is "the firstborn of every creature" (Col. 1:15). From the original language of the New Testament, this phrase is literally "firstborn of all creation." The Greek word translated "firstborn" does not mean that He was the first one born; rather, it emphasizes priority and sovereignty. He existed before anything was ever created. This truth is obvious from verse 16: "For by him were all things created." He had to exist before all created things in order to create them. And because He is the Creator of all things, this implies sovereignty.

John 1: 1-3 states, "In the beginning was the Word, and the Word was with God, and the Word was God. The same was in the beginning with God. All things were made by him; and without him was not any thing made that was made." Notice especially verse 3: "All things were made by him; and without him was not any thing made that was made." This directly connects with the truth presented in Colossians 1:15. The emphasis, then, of "firstborn" is one of rank and is not related to birth as we commonly think of it. Psalm 89:27 uses the word "firstborn" in referring to David's son, but it looks ahead to Christ: "I will make him my firstborn, higher than the kings of the earth."

Since Colossians 1:17 indicates that the Lord Jesus Christ existed before all created things, He Himself is uncreated, thus eternal. This verse says, "He is before all things, and by him all things consist." He is the eternal God; therefore, He is the Supreme Being.

Jesus Christ the same yesterday, and to day and for ever (Heb. 13:8).

"CHRIST IN YOU"
COLOSSIANS 1:21–29

On the surface, the emphasis of "Christ in you" (Col. 1:27) may not seem so important. But when we grasp the significance of this great truth, our thinking about Christ and ourselves will be changed and even our prayer life will be changed. I well remember when I was a young preacher and my father had grasped the glorious truth of "Christ in you." Those were good words to me, but I did not see the importance in them that my father did. But one of the red-letter days of my life was when God opened my inner eyes and ears to understand what it really is to be in Christ and to have Him in me. I then experienced a change in my outlook on life in general and on my prayer life in particular. I experienced a new insight and a new understanding of what it means to be able to say, "I live; yet not I, but Christ liveth in me" (Gal. 2:20).

The Lord Jesus Christ, who walked on this earth and who is now at the Father's right hand, must not only be a leader or teacher to us. It is not enough that He came, lived, died and rose again; He must be personally received as Saviour, at which time He will take up personal residence in our heart. And as we study the Scriptures to learn more about Him and apply the truths to our life, He will be formed in us.

An intellectual acceptance of the facts of Christ's person and work is not sufficient for what we need and want. We certainly need to know those facts, but we must go beyond those facts to place our faith in Him as Saviour and to daily experience His living power in us. This is the thrust of the Book of Colossians, and that is why I think it is so important.

At that day ye shall know that I am in my Father, and ye in me, and I in you (John 14:20).

YOU GROW THE WAY YOU WERE BORN

COLOSSIANS 2:1–7

Paul spoke here of the necessity of the Colossians to continue as they had begun. In other words, he was telling them, "Get settled in Christ; see that Christ is everything in your life." Paul wanted the Colossians to recognize that if someone taught differently, then that teaching was in error.

We are to walk in Christ the same way as we originally received Him as our Saviour. We received Him by faith; so we are to walk in Him by faith. The way of salvation is made crystal clear in Ephesians 2:8: "For by grace are ye saved through faith; and that not of yourselves: it is the gift of God." Hebrews 11:6 says, "Without faith it is impossible to please him."

Notice that Paul used the full title for the Lord: "Christ Jesus the Lord" (Col. 2:6). "Christ" means "anointed one" or "Messiah." That is Jesus' heavenly name. "Jesus" means "one who saves" and refers to the historical Person who became flesh and lived among mankind. "Lord" means "master" and refers to His supreme control of everything.

With this threefold emphasis, Paul was reminding the Colossians whom they had become rightly related to when they received salvation. He is the Anointed One of God; He is the Saviour of mankind; He is the Supreme Lord. Paul urged the Colossians to remember that they had started with Christ by faith and that now they must continue to walk with Him by faith.

But speaking the truth in love, may grow up into him in all things, which is the head, even Christ (Eph. 4:15).

NOVEMBER

Colossians, James and 1 John are the bases on which spiritual foundational truths are built for the month of November.

Colossians sets forth Christ's provision for our salvation and daily walk. The book enables us to identify with Christ in what He feels, thinks, sees, hears and speaks.

The Book of James speaks to our everyday concerns as it presents teaching about wisdom, faith, trials, temptations, patience, good works, the tongue, worldliness, God's will, humility and relationships with other Christians.

The Epistle of 1 John is a special book to many believers. It provides tests that evidence whether or not an individual has trusted Jesus Christ as his personal Saviour.

The readings for November are excerpted from *The All-Sufficient Christ: Studies in Colossians; James: The Epistle of Applied Christianity;* and *Tests of Life: Studies in the General Epistles of John.*

NOT "OUGHT" BUT "ARE"
COLOSSIANS 2:10–15

Realizing that all of the fullness of the Godhead dwells in bodily form in the Lord Jesus Christ, it is then awesome to consider that we "are complete in him" (Col. 2:10). We are filled with His fullness. Notice it does not say we ought to be complete in Him; it says we are complete in Him. Of course, believers are to constantly grow in the knowledge of Him as they progress from babes in Christ to those who are spiritually mature. But the completeness exists from the moment of salvation. This is why it can be said in 2 Peter 1:3 that Christ "hath given unto us all things that pertain unto life and godliness."

Even in our day, it is common for people to tell believers, "It is wonderful that you know Christ as Saviour and that you are endeavoring to live the Christian life the best you can, but you need something special in order to really have all that God wants you to have." They may not say it in quite these words, but this sort of teaching is causing mass confusion among Christians today. But what we need to understand is that, having trusted Jesus Christ as Saviour, we are complete in Him and need nothing else. There is no special ordinance or any special experience that needs to be tacked on to the Person and work of Christ. What can be added that the believer does not already possess in Jesus Christ? Our need is simply to appropriate what we have in Christ and thus, by faith, live accordingly.

Blessed be the God and Father of our Lord Jesus Christ, who hath blessed us with all spiritual blessings in heavenly places in Christ (Eph. 1:3).

PRACTICING YOUR POSITION
COLOSSIANS 3:1–4

It is wonderful to realize that, as believers, we live by the power of Christ's resurrection life. As we do this, we are letting Christ live again in the sense that He is living out His life through us. This is what Paul desired for the Ephesian believers, for he prayed that they might know "what is the exceeding greatness of his power to us-ward who believe, according to the working of his mighty power, which he wrought in Christ, when he raised him from the dead, and set him at his own right hand in the heavenly places" (Eph. 1:19–20). This ties in beautifully with Paul's statement in Colossians 1:27: "Christ in you, the hope of glory."

It must be remembered that we are not robots, operated by push buttons. We are beings with the power of choice, and we must decide to apply these truths to ourselves. God wants us to surrender to Him as an act of faith. When we do this, God works on our behalf. This is not necessarily only a New Testament truth. The psalmist wrote: "Commit thy way unto the LORD; trust also in him; and he shall bring it to pass" (Ps. 37:5). Philippians 2:12 and Galatians 5:16 also indicate that we are to work out the salvation that has been worked within us and that we are to live by means of the Spirit.

Paul stressed to the believers in Colossae—and to us—that, as a result of their standing in Christ, they had a great responsibility to "seek those things which are above, where Christ sitteth on the right hand of God" (Col. 3:1).

For we walk by faith, not by sight (2 Cor. 5:7).

THE LIFE THAT IS NEW
COLOSSIANS 3:5–11

In Colossians 3:10–11 Paul revealed three truths about those who have put on the new man. First, they have a divine nature. Each person who trusts Christ as Saviour has "put on the new man, which is renewed in knowledge after the image of him that created him" (v. 10). It is not just that a person wants a new nature—he has a new nature. We translate our position into daily living as we say yes to Christ and no to sin.

Second, those who have trusted Christ as Saviour also have a new unity: "Where there is neither Greek nor Jew, circumcision nor uncircumcision, Barbarian, Scythian, bond nor free" (v. 11). The new unity transcends all races, social positions, cultural differences— even economic and political status. Such distinctions belong to the old man, not to the new man. And because God makes no distinctions between the categories mentioned in verse 11, neither should we who know Jesus Christ as Saviour.

Third, those who have trusted Jesus Christ have a new relationship: "Christ is all, and in all" (v. 11). This is a new relationship where Christ is in absolute control. Is Christ in control of your life? Not just in control of something, but is He in control of all things? Is He truly "all, and in all"?

And the glory which thou gavest me I have given them; that they may be one, even as we are one (John 17:22).

GOD'S KINDNESS
COLOSSIANS 3:12; TITUS 3:1–7

The believer is to put on "kindness" (Col. 3:12). This refers to a gentle, gracious disposition. When I think of this quality, a particular godly leader comes to mind. Years ago another leader in the area did him much harm and sought to ruin his reputation. In a board meeting with this godly leader, some of us expressed concern about what this other person was doing to him. This godly leader then made a statement I shall never forget: "I have determined in my heart to show love and kindness toward this Christian leader with all that I have." And he did. This is what kindness is all about.

A biblical illustration of showing kindness is seen from the life of David. The former king, Saul, had despised David and sought to kill him several times. But David never took advantage of Saul; in fact, Saul's son Jonathan became his closest friend. After the deaths of Saul and Jonathan, David asked, "Is there yet any that is left of the house of Saul, that I may shew him kindness for Jonathan's sake?" (2 Sam. 9:1). It was then brought to David's attention that Jonathan had a crippled son, Mephibosheth (v. 3). David sent for Mephibosheth, and 2 Samuel 9 concludes by saying, "So Mephibosheth dwelt in Jerusalem: for he did eat continually at the king's table; and was lame on both his feet" (v. 13). In addition to providing for Mephibosheth continually, David also restored to him the land that had been confiscated from Saul. This was true kindness in action.

And be ye kind one to another, tenderhearted, forgiving one another, even as God for Christ's sake hath forgiven you (Eph. 4:32).

BEWARE OF FALSE PEACE!
COLOSSIANS 3:13–17

We must beware of false peace. Some who do wrong may have a peace about it, but it does not come from God. As someone has said, "Peace of heart alone is not always the peace of God."

A significant test to apply to determine the origin of the peace is this: If I have peace in my heart about a matter, do I also have peace with others in the Body of Christ concerning it? Understandably, not everyone will agree on any single issue, but if only the person himself thinks he is right, he has reason to question his decision. If we are out of the will of God, we will bring discord and disharmony to the Body of true believers. I realize the difficulty in assessing who is a true believer, especially in a group situation. Sometimes those who are part of the group do not evidence salvation themselves. Other times, some may clearly evidence salvation but give little evidence of mature judgment in things related to the Christian life.

One of the best safeguards against a false peace is simply making sure that you have the desire to please Jesus Christ in all that you do. If it is your concern "that in all things he might have the preeminence" (Col. 1:18), you can trust Him to bring conviction and a lack of peace when your life is not honoring to Him.

Great peace have they which love thy law: and nothing shall offend them (Ps. 119:165).

GETTING "ON TOP" BY "GETTING UNDER"

JAMES 1:1–8

The more often faith is tried, the easier it becomes to endure trials because they produce patience. And through trials, the believer becomes more steadfast in his faith.

Endurance is the ability to withstand hardship or stress. Patience is the ability to bear pain without complaint, evidencing self-control. In a sense, both of these ideas are involved in the statement of James that "faith worketh patience" (James 1:3).

The Greek word translated "patience" is made up of two words that literally mean "to remain under." When a person remains under a testing, he endures that testing, and the testing itself produces patience as the believer remains under the burden. Self-control, which is so closely related to patience, is part of the fruit of the Spirit mentioned in Galatians 5:22–23. Thus, if we wish to acquire more patience and self-control, it means we will have to endure more testings.

Even though the testings are severe, the Christian who has total confidence in Christ can have joy in the midst of the testings. And the patience we develop will enable us to wait until the Lord fulfills His promises to us. Hebrews 10:36 says, "Ye have need of patience, that, after ye have done the will of God, ye might receive the promise." Galatians 6:9 says, "Let us not be weary in well doing: for in due season we shall reap, if we faint not."

Rejoicing in hope; patient in tribulation; continuing instant in prayer (Rom. 12:12).

GOD IS NOT IMPRESSED
JAMES 1:9–11

When James wrote concerning a brother of "low degree" (James 1:9), we must remember that he was writing from a human viewpoint. Only humans characterize one person as being of low degree and another as being of high degree, because God is not a respecter of persons. James was writing about a "brother"; that is, one who has trusted Jesus Christ as Saviour. Within the family of God everyone is equal in God's eyes. The low are exalted, the high are brought low. God calls for lowliness of heart as seen in the Person of Jesus Christ.

The reason we should not be overly impressed by whether a person is of low estate or high estate is that his earthly possessions have nothing to do with his relationship before God. Jesus pointed out this truth by telling a parable about a rich man, who said, "I will say to my soul, Soul, thou hast much goods laid up for many years; take thine ease, eat, drink, and be merry. But God said unto him, Thou fool, this night thy soul shall be required of thee: then whose shall those things be, which thou hast provided?" (Luke 12:19–20).

Riches do not make a person better than anyone else, nor do riches prevent sickness or death.

Since Christ is meek and lowly in heart, those who know Him as Saviour and who allow Him to live out His life through them will exhibit the same characteristics.

The LORD maketh poor, and maketh rich: he bringeth low, and lifteth up (1 Sam. 2:7).

THE BIRTH THAT BRINGS DEATH
JAMES 1:12–15

When temptations to do evil come into our lives, let us never think that they have come from God; instead, God is doing what He can to prevent us from falling into sin. However, our flesh is so weak that we disregard Him occasionally and follow evil.

James said, "Every man is tempted, when he is drawn away of his own lust, and enticed" (James 1:14). Notice especially the words "and enticed." Lust comes from the enemy within—the old nature; enticement comes from the enemy without—the devil.

James 1:15 not only tells us more about the source of sin but also its final result: "When lust hath conceived, it bringeth forth sin: and sin, when it is finished, bringeth forth death." James personified lust and sin here and spoke of conception, birth and death.

Lust is personified as a harlot who conceives and then bears a child called "sin," whose father is the devil. Then sin also conceives and brings forth a grandchild, who is known as "death."

When a sinful desire enters the mind, it will grow in the mind until the deed is executed if it is not checked at once. As a rule, the mind eventually acts out what it dwells on.

Be not overcome of evil, but overcome evil with good (Rom. 12:21).

GOD ENJOYS GIVING!
JAMES 1:16–18

James left no doubt about the fact that God is the giver of all that is good. James cautioned, "Do not err" (James 1:16). The Greek word translated "err" means "to go astray" or "to go off course." It was used to describe a ship that had been driven from its course and was in severe danger. So James was not referring to making a minor mistake but to making a serious error in judgment that could have awesome and terrible results.

Notice that James did not say "every great gift" but "every good gift" (v. 17). It does not matter whether the gift is large or small, anything and everything that God gives is good. Sometimes the one under severe trial might question whether everything that comes from the hand of God is good, but James assured such a person that he never needs to question this. Keep in mind that James was referring to gifts—things that are not obtained by merit but purely by God's grace.

James stressed that the kind of gift of which he was speaking "is from above" (v. 17). Here James contrasted the things of heaven with the things of earth. We are so easily entangled in earthly affairs and so easily consumed with the desire for those things that do not last. We will not live on this earth forever, so even our trials should be viewed in the light of eternity.

According as his divine power hath given unto us all things that pertain unto life and godliness, through the knowledge of him that hath called us to glory and virtue (2 Pet. 1:3).

OPEN EARS—CLOSED MOUTH
JAMES 1:19–21

James wanted all believers to be alert to comprehend the Word of God. This is very important since "faith cometh by hearing, and hearing by the word of God" (Rom. 10:17). The Word of God gives us faith to believe, and when we believe, God creates new life within us.

Many people hear the Word of God, but to some of them it is only words; they do not accept it as the Word of God. What a paradox it is that all creation obeys His Word except we who are made in the image of God and have the ability to choose. Many people have an extensive knowledge of the Word of God, but they do not really believe what it says, so they do not respond to it as His Word.

We should not be quick to retort when someone has spoken against us. To be quick with an answer can sometimes get us into much trouble. Consider what the Word of God has to say about these matters. Proverbs 29:20 says, "Seest thou a man that is hasty in his words? there is more hope of a fool than of him." Proverbs 10:19 says, "In the multitude of words there wanteth not sin: but he that refraineth his lips is wise."

A rule that should govern our lives is stated in Proverbs 15:1: "A soft answer turneth away wrath: but grievous words stir up anger."

The soul of the transgressors shall eat violence. He that keepth his mouth keepeth his life (Prov. 13:2–3).

HAVE YOU LOOKED IN THE MIRROR?

JAMES 1:22–25

Whereas James 1:22–24 view the person who does not act upon the basis of the Word, verse 25 looks at the person who does act on the basis of the Word of God. He is like one who does something about what he sees in the mirror. His positive attitude is beautiful, as was David's when he said, "Search me, O God, and know my heart: try me, and know my thoughts: and see if there be any wicked way in me, and lead me in the way everlasting" (Ps. 139:23–24). David was asking God to x-ray his heart. The obvious implication of David's words is that no matter what God discovered, David was willing to correct. On another occasion, David told the Lord, "Examine me, O LORD, and prove me; try my reins and my heart" (26:2).

As James spoke of looking into the divine mirror, he referred to it as "the perfect law of liberty" (James 1:25). The word "law" generally connotes meanings of bondage, such as in the Old Testament Law. However, this is not the case when referring to the "law of Christ." Galatians 6:2 refers to this law: "Bear ye one another's burdens, and so fulfil the law of Christ." The law of Christ is the "perfect law of liberty" spoken of in James 1:25.

We must never forget that freedom to sin is not liberty, because "the wages of sin is death" (Rom. 6:23). This is true of sin committed during any age, or dispensation. James was not referring to a license to sin when he spoke of the "perfect law of liberty" (James 1:25).

If ye know these things, happy are ye if ye do them (John 13:17).

THE RELIGION GOD WANTS
JAMES 1:26–27

When Jesus Christ is really indwelling a person, it will result in true religion. The word "religion" as used in James 1:26–27 is not synonymous with the word "salvation." James used it in the sense of an outward expression of that which is inward. The inner faith in Jesus Christ as one's personal Saviour results in salvation; expressing that faith outwardly is one's religion, according to the way James used the word. When one has faith in Jesus Christ, it is only normal and natural for this faith to express itself outwardly. There will be a new motivating power within, and that new desire is an evidence that you are a child of God. The manifestation of Christ's life through an individual is proof that that person is rightly related to Jesus Christ by faith. In other words, faith in Christ will result in love for others, and this is what James referred to as "pure religion."

The Lord Jesus Christ showered His love on those who could not help themselves and who could not, or would not, return His love at that time. When we know Him as personal Saviour, we will have this same kind of love. We will love those who are helpless and unable to return our expressions of love. It is relatively easy to be friends with those who are friends in return or to give to those who give in return. However, our Christianity is woefully deficient if we give in order to receive or if we give and expect an even larger gift in return. This is not pure religion. So when a person is rightly related to Jesus Christ—when he has pure and undefiled religion—he will express the love of Christ to those who are in dire circumstances and unable to return similar expressions of love.

My little children, let us not love in word, neither in tongue; but in deed and in truth (1 John 3:18).

GOD'S ROYAL LAW

JAMES 2:1–13

James summed up man's responsibility to his neighbor by urging him to fulfill the "royal law" (James 2:8). He who fulfills this law of Christ will love all men alike and will look with contempt on none. Because he will be concerned about the value of a human soul, he will see no distinction between the rich and the poor.

Observe how serious it is to show respect of persons: "But if ye have respect to persons, ye commit sin, and are convinced of the law as transgressors" (v. 9). To respect one person above another is to violate the letter and the spirit of the law of Christ; thus, it is sin. To look with disdain on someone else is to oppose the indwelling Christ and the concern He has for everyone.

The poor become so very rich in Christ, whereas the rich (as the world considers them) have to humble themselves to realize that their riches offer them nothing of eternal value. It is necessary for the rich to come empty-handed and receive salvation as a gift. The poor must come in the same way, but it seems exceedingly difficult for many rich people to humble themselves to this extent.

He that oppresseth the poor reproacheth his Maker: but he that honoureth him hath mercy on the poor (Prov. 14:31).

NOT WORDS BUT WORKS
JAMES 2:14–26

A cold, austere, intellectual faith that does not manifest itself by action is nothing more than a mental assent to the existence of God. James taught that this kind of faith is really no faith at all—it is a dead faith. It is not enough just to believe that God exists or even to believe that He died on the cross for the sins of the world. An individual must realize he will be eternally condemned apart from what Jesus Christ did for him personally on the cross, and he must place his faith in Jesus Christ as his personal Saviour. Such a person who recognizes all that Jesus Christ has delivered him from will have an active, vibrant faith, evidenced by a change of behavior.

James was particularly concerned with the display of works before one's fellowman in order to be justified before others. The works proved that the act of salvation really had taken place. The context of James 2 indicates that James was talking about being justified before men.

James was concerned about looking beyond a person's words to see whether or not his life supported what he said. In James 2:14 James did not say that the person had faith but that the person only said he had faith. James was really asking, "What use is the kind of faith that only talks and does not act?" This is the same question raised in verse 16 where the person who claims to have faith does not demonstrate it by doing something for the needy. And James made the point in verse 20 that faith without works is useless, it "is dead."

Not every one that saith unto me, Lord, Lord, shall enter into the kingdom of heaven; but he that doeth the will of my Father which is in heaven (Matt. 7:21).

A MATTER OF LIFE AND DEATH!
JAMES 3:1–6

Consider four parallels that a fire has with words spoken by the tongue: It hurts, it spreads, it consumes, but it can have a good use under control.

It only takes one false or bitter word to hurt deeply. In fact, the hurt may be so deep that recovery is impossible.

Just as fire spreads, so do spoken words. Some people are always willing to listen to destructive words about others, and they spread the words further so the damage becomes even more extensive.

Just as fire consumes, so do words spoken by a tongue that is out of control. Fire will destroy anything combustible that lies within its path. Words, too, have been known to destroy careers and lives. This is especially seen in the news media when political viewpoints are at stake.

We who know Jesus Christ as Saviour need to think solemnly about this matter so our tongues are not used to the disadvantage of others. Proverbs 18:21 says, "Death and life are in the power of the tongue, and those who love it will eat its fruit" (NASB).

Think of it! The power of death and life reside in the tongue. And the last phrase of this verse especially applies to those who spread gossip: "Those who love it will eat its fruit."

Whoso keepeth his mouth and his tongue keepeth his soul from troubles (Prov. 21:23).

THE SECRET OF A CONTROLLED TONGUE

JAMES 3:7–12

Is it not strange that the tongue can be praising God one moment and be slandering some person the next moment often right in the church where the tongue had been used to praise God? We may even hear the preacher talk about not slandering others, but before we leave we will say things concerning others that amount to slander. Such inconsistencies are not found in nature, but out of the human being can come both bitter and sweet words.

Remember that the tongue speaks only what is in the heart. Godly words can come only from a godly heart. To have a godly heart, we must follow the instructions found in Romans 6. We must know what our position is in Christ; we must reckon, or count, upon it as being true because it is true; and we must yield ourselves completely to Christ (see vv. 6–7,11–13). This involves our intellect, emotions and will.

Words come from our thoughts, and thoughts come from the mind; therefore, it is possible to control our words by controlling our minds. We who know Jesus Christ as Saviour can have our minds controlled by "bringing into captivity every thought to the obedience of Christ" (2 Cor. 10:5). He alone is worthy and is able to give us victory.

Set a watch, O Lord, before my mouth; keep the door of my lips (Ps. 141:3).

WISDOM FROM HEAVEN
JAMES 3:13–18

It is significant that the characteristics James first listed for godly wisdom are purity and peaceableness. These two have an important relationship. An individual is made pure through faith in Jesus Christ, and this establishes peace between God and himself. Romans 5:1 says, "Therefore being justified by faith, we have peace with God through our Lord Jesus Christ."

Once this peace has been established through a vertical relationship between the believer and God, the believer will then have a basis on which to establish peaceful horizontal relationships with his fellowmen.

James also said that the wisdom that is from above is "gentle" (James 3:17), so each believer should reflect this gentleness in his life. Paul told Timothy—and all believers "The servant of the Lord must not strive; but be gentle unto all men" (2 Tim. 2:24). Titus 3:2 sounds a similar note: "To speak evil of no man, to be no brawlers, but gentle, shewing all meekness unto all men."

A wise person is tender and full of mercy and sympathy. Such a person shows compassion, or pity, for the less fortunate. This was emphasized by James when he said, "Pure religion and undefiled before God and the Father is this, To visit the fatherless and widows in their affliction" (James 1:27).

The fear of the LORD is the beginning of wisdom: a good understanding have all they that do his commandments: his praise endureth for ever (Ps. 111:10).

THE WAR WITHIN
JAMES 4:1–3

James was well aware of the fact that conflict among believers comes from the personal war that goes on within each person. This conflict within the believer is also referred to in Romans 7:23: "But I see another law in my members, warring against the law of my mind, and bringing me into captivity to the law of sin which is in my members." Also, Peter warned, "Dearly beloved, I beseech you as strangers and pilgrims, abstain from fleshly lusts, which war against the soul" (1 Pet. 2:11).

James's reference to killing was not necessarily referring to taking a person's life but to destroying someone's character. Previously, James dealt with the viciousness of the tongue. When the tongue is out of control, it can be a lethal weapon used for character assassination.

These are sobering words from the Bible, and today more than ever we need to carefully examine our lives. Much bitterness is displayed not only among the unbelieving world but also among those who call themselves Christians. Sometimes, in the name of Christ and in a desire to be separate from sin, Christians commit sin by bitterly attacking fellow believers. We are to take a stand against sin, but we must guard our hearts so that the old nature does not take over, allowing the bitterness of hatred to grip us. Even though we may totally disagree with what another person is doing, we are still commanded as believers to seek that person's highest good.

He that hideth hatred with lying lips, and he that uttereth a slander, is a fool (Prov. 10:18).

DON'T COURT THE WORLD
JAMES 4:4–7

Consider the accusation of James concerning the illicit love affair with the world as stated in the following paraphrase: "You are like an unfaithful wife who loves her husband's enemies. Don't you realize that making friends with God's enemies—the evil pleasures of this world—makes you an enemy of God? I say it again, that if your aim is to enjoy the evil pleasure of the unsaved world, you cannot also be a friend of God" (James 4:4, Living Bible).

Being a friend of the world indicates that the person agrees with the values of the world system. The Old Testament prophet Amos asked, "Can two walk together, except they be agreed?" (Amos 3:3). The believer who is able to be in agreement with this evil world system is woefully out of fellowship with Almighty God, who saved him from the penalty and power of sin.

If a person has a consistently worldly lifestyle, it is a clear signal that he has never trusted Jesus Christ as his personal Saviour. On the other hand, there are believers who are out of fellowship with the Lord and who are worldly for a time. Perhaps this is because many want Christ as Saviour but not as Lord. They want the assurance and peace of knowing that they are saved from eternal condemnation, but they also want to live to please themselves rather than letting Christ be the Master of their lives.

Love not the world, neither the things that are in the world. If any man love the world, the love of the Father is not in him (1 John 2:15).

YOU GET NEARER
BY GETTING LOWER
JAMES 4:8–12

Concerning James's command to "draw nigh to God" (James 4:8), we must remember that it takes time to be holy. Although our position in Christ at the moment of salvation provides an absolute holiness, as we live the Christian life from day to day, it takes time to apply the principles that result in holy living. But as we move toward God, we can count on God's moving toward us. However, we must remember that our moving is the result of His indwelling power (see Phil. 2:12–13).

James said, "Draw nigh to God, and he will draw nigh to you" (James 4:8). He added, "Cleanse your hands, ye sinners; and purify your hearts, ye double minded" (v. 8). This injunction to cleanse oneself is most likely a reference to believers who have fallen into worldliness. God will not work through dirty hands that are contaminated by the value system and sins of the world. Hebrews 10:22 tells us, "Let us draw near with a true heart in full assurance of faith, having our hearts sprinkled from an evil conscience, and our bodies washed with pure water."

The lesson for each believer is to humble himself, not to wait for the Lord to humble him. True humility is to comprehend our own utter unworthiness apart from Christ. Of course, seeing ourselves as we really are is also impossible apart from the grace of God. As we appropriate all the grace that God has bestowed upon us, we will become humble before Him.

By humility and the fear of the LORD are riches, and honour, and life (Prov. 22:4).

GOD WILL GUIDE YOU
JAMES 4:13–17

We do not need to be in a state of unrest about the future. Some worry needlessly and wonder, *Why doesn't God let me know what He has in mind for me in the future?* Some young people may be thinking about the mission field and wondering what God's will is for them five or ten years from now. It is important, however, that we recognize that God knows everything about the future, even if we do not, so the important thing is to trust Him today with our lives and leave the future to Him. If God is calling you today into some particular ministry, then obey Him, even though you do not know what the future holds.

As we are sensitive to God, we can expect Him to guide us. Psalm 32:8 says, "I will instruct thee and teach thee in the way which thou shalt go: I will guide thee with mine eye." I'm so glad He guides us with His eye because He can see far beyond anything we can see. Because God knows the future completely, He will never be too late in telling us exactly what we need to know. Some things we need to plan for in the distant future, but most things are achieved simply by walking by faith today. As we trust God to give us wisdom for today's decisions, He will lead us a step at a time into what He wants us to be doing in the future.

The meek will he guide in judgment: and the meek will he teach his way (Ps. 25:9).

PRICES—OR VALUES?
JAMES 5:1–6

Christians can become so addicted to money and to achieving a higher level of living that they lose all perspective and forget what they are really here on earth to accomplish. Those who live only for the pleasures of the moment stand under the condemnation of Paul's words of 1 Timothy 5:6: "She that liveth in pleasure is dead while she liveth." Many Christians have had the vitality taken from their spiritual life because of their great concern for the things of the world. They are saved, but their lives do not reflect the glorious difference that Christ can make when a believer focuses his attention on eternal values instead of temporal ones.

An important question that every family needs to face is, How much money do we need in order to live in the comfort we prescribe for ourselves? We also need to ask, Have we set our standard of comfort too high? Regrettably, many people have set their standard so high that they have to spend so much time obtaining an income for that level of life that they really have no time to live. How sad to spend so much time earning a living that you do not have time to enjoy the living. I am not referring to those who must work long hours just to keep the family fed and clothed. I am referring to those who have become so addicted to the luxuries of life that they think the luxuries are essential. Such an attitude greatly affects our spiritual priorities—spiritual things are bound to suffer and to take second place to the things of the world. It is important then that we do some clear thinking about our attitude toward what this world has to offer. Although some have the attitude that money is the answer to everything, James 5:1–6 reveals that this belief is certainly not true.

The blessing of the LORD, it maketh rich, and he addeth no sorrow with it (Prov. 10:22).

HE IS AT THE DOOR!

JAMES 5:7–12

To "grudge not" is to "complain not." We are not to groan or grumble against each other. In this life, where there is the tendency to be partial to others who have more than we do, James reminded us not to be grumbling and complaining about others. We are not to develop an attitude of thinking the other person always has it better than we do. We must remember that the Lord can come back at any time to judge us for such attitudes. James said, "The judge standeth before the door" (James 5:9); in other words, He is ready to enter the door. Having this concept of the soon return of Christ keeps us from being so critical of each other. Always remember, Christ is about to enter the door, so the words you speak should be wholesome rather than negative or hurtful.

So realizing that the Lord may soon return will have a significant effect on our attitudes toward others. We will not be so quick to criticize others when we realize the Lord is about to return to judge us for what we have said. The Lord is fully able to judge the motives of our hearts (see 1 Cor. 4:5), but we must never take that prerogative upon ourselves. The Lord will judge not only the good and bad things we have done but also our good and bad attitudes. If you have been mistreated and have borne up under it in a way that glorifies the Lord, you may be assured of a reward. If you have been neglected by friends and by the world, the Lord will take care of that also. Let us trust Him completely to reward as He sees best because He is absolutely just and loving.

And every man shall receive his own reward according to his own labour (1 Cor. 3:8).

SICKNESS AND SIN
JAMES 5:13–16

The reason for calling the elders was apparently because the sickness referred to by James was a sickness that resulted from sin. The elders were the spiritual leaders of the assembly of believers, and because of the type of problem involved, they—not a physician—were to be called. It was the responsibility of the spiritual leaders to deal with, and pray for, those who had gone astray and as a result had been stricken by a sickness.

James did not use the word that is associated with ceremonial anointing but the word that is associated with the treatment of wounds. The word James used is often found in secular medical treatises of New Testament times. The oil was, in itself, a healing ointment. So we see that James was referring to the best-known medical treatment of the time—that is, rubbing with oil.

The rubbing with oil was to be accompanied by prayer. This was apparently to be done first because the original language indicates that the elders were to pray over the sick person, having anointed him with oil (see James 5:14).

From this passage some derive the teaching of divine healing apart from medicine, but such a view is not supported by the text. The oil was an accepted medical treatment of the day, so this passage actually encourages the use of known medical practices in addition to prayer for healing. Of course, the confidence of the elders was to be in God's ability to heal, not in the medical treatment itself.

For if we would judge ourselves, we should not be judged (1 Cor. 11:31).

PRAYER THAT WORKS
JAMES 5:17–20; 1 KINGS 18:36–39

Because this was such a crucial prayer, it is worth noting the specific things for which Elijah prayed. He had four specific requests of God. First, "Let it be known this day that thou art God in Israel" (1 Kings 18:36). The burden of Elijah's heart was that others would know the true God and that they would realize that He alone is God.

Second, "That I am thy servant" (v. 36). This revealed Elijah's humble attitude—he wanted to be known only as a servant of the true God.

Third, he asked God to show "that I have done all these things at thy word" (v. 36). Elijah not only wanted to be known as the servant of God but also as an obedient servant. He especially did not want the prophets of Baal to think that he had dreamed up all of this on his own. He wanted them to be clearly convinced that God had directed him. This is also an indication that God is a personal God. Baal could not direct anyone; even those who worshiped him could not expect personal guidance.

Fourth, Elijah prayed, "Hear me, O Lord, hear me, that this people may know that thou art the Lord God, and that thou hast turned their heart back again" (v. 37). Elijah wanted his prayer to be heard by God, and he wanted the people to return to God.

Then the fire fell! It consumed the sacrifice, the wood, the stones, the dust and the water that had been poured in the trenches. "When all the people saw it, they fell on their faces: and they said, The Lord, he is the God; the Lord, he is the God" (v. 39).

And whatsoever we ask, we receive of him, because we keep his commandments, and do those things that are pleasing in his sight (1 John 3:22).

352

LIFE, LIGHT, LOVE
1 JOHN 1:1–4

There are three key words in the epistle of 1 John. They are "life," "light" and "love." These words are used many times in this epistle.

That God has given us eternal life is clearly stated in 1 John 5:11–13, which are key verses to the study of this epistle. God has given us eternal life, and that life is in His Son. If we have the Son, we have eternal life; if we do not have the Son, we do not have eternal life.

Eternal life is a special quality of life that makes it possible for us to fellowship with God. More than eternal duration of life is meant.

The other two words, "light" and "love," provide the test whereby we may know whether or not that life is within us. We are told that God, as to His nature, is light and that there is no darkness in Him. And if we walk in the light as He is in the light, we have fellowship one with the other. Light reveals righteousness, and it also reveals sin. By virtue of the light, we can know whether or not we have eternal life.

The love spoken of is a God-given love, and it becomes both the outward expression of the inward life and another test whereby we may know that we have such life. The love of God has been shed abroad in our hearts by the Holy Spirit (Rom. 5:5) so that the man who is born of God loves others. This is the very essence of Christianity.

Eye hath not seen, nor ear heard, neither have entered into the heart of man, the things which God hath prepared for them that love him (1 Cor. 2:9).

CAN YOU SEE WHERE YOU ARE GOING?

1 JOHN 1:5–10

For a person to walk in the light requires that he first receive Christ as personal Saviour. The light of God's Word must first have enlightened that person's heart and convicted him of his sin. That same light reveals to us the holiness of God and brings us to a reverential fear of Him, something foreign to the natural man (see Rom. 3:18).

That same light reveals to us how Christ came to reconcile us to God. To us is offered "the righteousness of God which is by faith of Jesus Christ unto all and upon all them that believe: for there is no difference" (v. 22).

Christians who walk in the light become increasingly conscious of the holiness of God and of the sinfulness of sin. They are not deluded into denying that they have a sinful nature. They realize that they still have sinful tendencies that are expressed in fleshly impulses, nonspiritual inclinations and standards of living that are patterned after the world rather than after God. These are all sinful in the sight of God, and to call them righteous rather than sinful is to walk in darkness. Should we even so much as waver in our trust in God, we sin, for the Word says, "Whatsoever is not of faith is sin" (Rom. 14:23).

I am the light of the world: he that followeth me shall not walk in darkness, but shall have the light of life (John 8:12).

HIS UNFINISHED WORK
1 JOHN 2:1–6

First John 2:1 could be translated: "These things write I unto you that ye do not commit a single act of sin." John was not dealing with habitual sin but with single acts of sin. This is a high standard, and you may wonder if it is possible for a child of God to successfully live this way. We need to realize what Christ has actually done for us.

In the light of our experience, however, this may well cause us to despair, for we realize that we do commit acts of sin. The next phrase in 1 John 2:1 says, "And if any man sin, we have an advocate with the Father, Jesus Christ the righteous." When we do commit an act of sin and Satan would accuse us before the Father, there is no way he can reach us because we stand before God in the righteousness of Christ, "even the righteousness of God which is by faith of Jesus Christ unto all and upon all them that believe: for there is no difference" (Rom. 3:22). So Jesus has become our righteousness, and He stands in the presence of God on our behalf.

Who is he that condemneth? It is Christ that died, yea rather, that is risen again, who is even at the right hand of God, who also maketh intercession for us (Rom. 8:34).

OLD YET EVER NEW
1 JOHN 2:7–11

The statements concerning the old and the new commandment sound paradoxical. They can be readily reconciled, however. The apostle John wrote here, as 1 John 2:9–11 shows, about our love for one another. In a sense this is not a new commandment; it is an old one that goes back to the time when God made man in His own image. Since man was made in the image of God, love was part of the expression of his life. It is old also in the sense that the Old Testament Law was summarized in the commands to love God and love our neighbor.

From all of this one might conclude that there is nothing new about this commandment at all, and yet there is an aspect that is new. We are given the clue to this in the expression, "The darkness is past, and the true light now shineth" (v. 8). Here again the present tense was used, and the translation could read: "The darkness is passing, and the true light is now shining." Under the Old Testament Law, people were commanded to love, but the Law did not provide them with the ability to obey. Only as the Holy Spirit could get control of individual hearts was this possible.

This is my commandment, That ye love one another, as I have loved you (John 15:12).

WATCH OUT FOR WORLDLINESS!
1 JOHN 2:12–17

Ask yourself these questions: What is the purpose of my life? What am I going after? What are my pleasures? What are my practices? What kind of places do I frequent? Could I invite God to look with approval on all that I do and seek for?

Worldliness in its final analysis is an attitude of heart toward things and persons. It is the old-nature attitude and can affect every phase of our lives.

The word "lust" does not necessarily mean something evil. The context helps to determine whether it is used in a good sense or a bad one. The word itself means a passionate desire or a craving after something. In this passage it is used in a bad sense, and we are warned first of all to not have a passionate craving for, or a reaching after, things of the flesh, which is the old nature.

The eyes must be carefully guarded. We are warned con¬cerning the lust of the eyes, or the strong, passionate desires that arise because of what the eyes see. A great deal of our present-day advertising is built on eye appeal and is designed to stimulate our baser passions.

The pride of life incorporates the idea of one who claims credit and glory for something that is not really his. We can see it very clearly in the person who constantly brags about his own resources and possessions.

Who gave himself for our sins, that he might deliver us from this present evil world, according to the will of God and our Father (Gal. 1:4).

DECEMBER

The daily readings for December are based on 1 John and Revelation, along with selected material from Theodore H. Epp's book on the Holy Spirit, *The Other Comforter.*

The Epistle of 1 John emphasizes the need to walk in fellowship with Jesus Christ, to avoid friendship with the world, to test the spirits to see if they are of God and assures us that we can know for sure—even now—that we have eternal life.

Mr. Epp's book *The Other Comforter* covers a vast amount of biblical information about the Holy Spirit. It relates that information in a practical way to the Christian's daily experience.

Revelation tells of the apostle John's vision of Jesus Christ in chapter 1. It records Christ's messages to the seven churches in chapters 2 and 3. Material based on these chapters reveals what a great God we serve and the importance of being faithful to Him in every area of life.

The readings for December are excerpted from *Test of Life: Studies in the General Epistles of John; The Other Comforter: Practical Studies on the Holy Spirit;* and *Practical Studies in Revelation, Vol. I.*

WITH US—NOT OF US
1 JOHN 2:18–9

We are able to detect who the antichrists are: "They went out from us, but they were not of us" (1 John 2:19). This does not mean that they left a particular denomination or church. They left the fundamental doctrine of Jesus Christ. The Word says they were never born again. Verse 19 makes that abundantly clear. The words "no doubt" are in italics in some translations, indicating that they were added by the translators. Consequently, the verse actually says, "They went out from us, but they were not of us; for if they had been of us, they would no doubt have continued with us."

True Christians are recipients of eternal life, and therefore "they shall never perish, neither shall any man pluck them out of my hand," the Saviour said. "My Father, which gave them me, is greater than all; and no man is able to pluck them out of my Father's hand. I and my Father are one" (John 10:28–30). The person who has eternal life cannot be taken away from God.

A true child of God will not accept any doctrine that denies that Jesus was and is the eternal God. A person who says that Jesus is not God is not a child of God and cannot go to heaven.

For many deceivers are entered into the world, who confess not that Jesus Christ is come in the flesh. This is a deceiver and an antichrist (2 John 1:7).

IT JUST DOES NOT BELONG!
1 JOHN 3:1–10

To live under the dominion of sin without any evidence of righteousness demonstrates that the person has not been born again. The reasons for this are clearly pointed out in some of these verses. First John 3:4, for example, says that sin is contrary to the law of God. Verse 5 says that sin is contrary to the mission, or the work, of the Lord Jesus Christ. Christ not only came to take away the guilt of sin, but He broke sin's power so that the believer need not live under its dominion. When we do commit an act of sin and then confess it, God is faithful and just to forgive our sins, and our Advocate with the Father maintains our standing of righteousness before Him.

Some have used these verses to teach that a person reaches a certain place in his Christian life after which he no longer commits any sin. These verses do not give any license to sin, but they contrast the state, or behavior, of the children of God with the state, or behavior, of the children of the world.

A continual practice of sin in the life shows that the person is a child of the devil rather than a child of God. "The devil sinneth from the beginning" (v. 8), and his children continue to live in sin, for that is in keeping with the character of their heredity.

Know ye not, that to whom ye yield yourselves servants to obey, his servants ye are to whom ye obey; whether of sin unto death, or of obedience unto righteousness? (Rom. 6:16).

LOVE MUST SERVE
1 JOHN 3:11–24

The word for love in 1 John 3:11 does not refer to a sentimental love but is a strong word that describes God Himself It is the kind of love that recognizes a need and responds to that need.

An illustration of this contrast is seen in the case of Cain, who was of the Wicked One and killed his brother (v. 12). He killed Abel because his own works were evil and his brother's were righteous. Cain did not have love in his heart because he was not a child of God. He had hatred, and for that reason he murdered Abel.

First John 3:16 shows that true love is climaxed by our being willing to lay down our lives for fellow believers. This is the very opposite of being willing to slander and spread evil reports concerning God's children. This kind of love is very practical, for John said, "But whoso hath this world's good, and seeth his brother have need, and shutteth up his bowels of compassion from him, how dwelleth the love of God in him?" (v. 17). God expects us to share the temporal and spiritual provisions that He makes for us. How can anyone, looking on this lost world, say that he loves the Lord and yet not seek to make known to the unsaved the unsearchable riches of Christ?

Because the Scriptures say that no murderer has eternal life abiding in him, we need not conclude that a murderer cannot be saved. He can be if he will come to Christ and receive Him as Saviour.

By this shall all men know that ye are my disciples, if ye have love one to another (John 13:35).

TRUTH, NOT POPULARITY
1 JOHN 4:1–6

It is sad, but many who talk about our Saviour and use His name do not believe that He is the eternal God, the Creator of all things, and that He came to die for the sins of mankind.

In the verses previous to this, the apostle discussed false teachers who talk about Jesus but fail to acknowledge that He truly is the Son of God. Such people are representatives of Satan, not messengers of God. They speak the type of message that the world loves to hear. Often based on human philosophy, it caters to the pride of intellect so prized by most people. Such teachers and those who delight in their teaching are unbelievers. Where, then, do you stand with reference to this matter? If you agree with them, then you, too, need to be born again.

On the other hand, how do I know that I am of God? I believe His Word. I believe that Jesus Christ is the eternal God, that He dwells in a glorified human body and that I shall be like Him, for one day I shall see Him as He is. I have no doubt about it. The people who are of God will accept this message, but those who are of the world will reject it. Classify yourself according to your attitude. It will let you know whether or not you are saved.

Ye are of God, little children, and have overcome them: because greater is he that is in you, than he that is in the world (1 John 4:4).

 **DECEMBER 5**

THE POWER TO LOVE
1 JOHN 4:7–21

The apostle did not say, "Try to create and produce love." He said, "Let us love." In other words, we are to release that love.

Some may protest and say they cannot love certain people. That is true from the natural standpoint, but we are not dealing with natural love. It is divine love, the love with which God loved us when we were unlovable and our sins had separated us from Him.

God, as to His nature, is love. And this love is shared with the believer. It has been shed abroad in the heart of each one (see Rom. 5:5). This love of God will grow within us and flow through us in an unbroken stream if we will let it. The Christian life, which is the power of the Holy Spirit within, is a life of love.

This love of God matures the Christian. I have seen many of God's people grow older in the Lord and grow more Christlike as they walked with Him from day to day. They took more time to be with the Lord and had their hearts filled with Him. Through this, their love was perfected toward others. This mature love expressed through God's people demonstrates to others that Christ lives in us.

The LORD hath appeared of old unto me, saying, Yea, I have loved thee with an everlasting love: therefore with lovingkindness have I drawn thee (Jer. 31:3).

A SIN UNTO DEATH
1 JOHN 5:14–21

We do not always know whether a Christian's sin is unto death; for that reason my own suggestion is that we should be sure to pray for such a person if we are in doubt. If we see that God is not going to answer, it could be that the person prayed for has committed a sin unto death. But I will continue to pray for such a person until the Spirit in some way makes it plain just what has happened in his life.

I believe that the sin unto death is a deliberate sin of a believer against better knowledge. When John wrote about committing this sin, he used the tense so often employed throughout his first epistle, the tense that signifies continuation of action. In my opinion the sin unto death is a deliberately planned and willful persistence in some evil course with the guilty person presuming on God's grace or mercy.

The death that results from this sin, as far as I can determine from Scripture, is physical death, not spiritual death. There is a vast difference between the two.

There may be those who have said, "Since I am eternally saved, I can live just as I please." They willfully and deliberately ignore the new life within them and its urging to godly living. I believe such a person stands in danger of committing the sin unto death.

Keep back thy servant also from presumptuous sins; let them not have dominion over me (Ps. 19:13).

THE SPIRIT ALSO LOVES YOU!
ROMANS 15:30–33

The Holy Spirit is a Person because He has emotions. He has the ability to love. Romans 15:30 says, "Now I beseech you, brethren, for the Lord Jesus Christ's sake, and for the love of the Spirit, that ye strive together with me in your prayers to God for me." This teaches us that the Holy Spirit has the capacity to love. He not only influences us to love, but He also loves us.

John 3:16 reveals that God the Father loves us. Philippians 2:5–8 describes how the Lord Jesus Christ loved us personally by making Himself of no reputation, taking the form of a servant and becoming obedient to death on the cross. There is no question about His love for us.

Neither is there any question about the Holy Spirit's love for us. He patiently seeks us when we are in sin and away from God, and when we trust Christ as Saviour, He regenerates us and begins to transform us into the image of God's Son.

If the Father had not loved the world, if the Son had not loved us and died for us, if the Holy Spirit had not loved us, convicted us and transformed us, where would we be spiritually today? Our salvation depends as much on the love of the Spirit as it does on the love of the Father and of the Son.

But the fruit of the Spirit is love (Gal. 5:22).

CONTROLLED TO CONVICT

JOHN 16:5–14

The indwelling Holy Spirit helps us to share Christ with others. The Lord promised this in John 15:26–27: "When the Comforter is come, whom I will send unto you from the Father, even the Spirit of truth, which proceedeth from the Father, he shall testify of me: and ye also shall bear witness, because ye have been with me from the beginning." The Holy Spirit confirms to us what is true about Christ, and we, in turn, share those truths with others.

If the Spirit of God is responsible to convict the world of sin, He must first of all convict us of sin because we are the ones He indwells—we are the tools He will use. He not only makes the life of Christ real to us, but He also causes us to understand our own sinfulness. We can do little to impress others with the awfulness of sin if we ourselves are not acutely aware of our own sinfulness.

This is possibly one basic reason why the world is not convicted of sin yet is bound for hell at an accelerating speed. We are the key to the world's conviction and conversion. This is why we need to be controlled by the Holy Spirit. Only as we are completely surrendered to Him can He use us to convict people around us of sin, righteousness and judgment. It is necessary for us to surrender completely, not for personal enjoyment but so the Father's work in the world might be done in and through us.

Blessed is the man unto whom the LORD imputeth not iniquity, and in whose spirit there is no guile (Ps. 32:2).

SEALED AND SURE!
2 CORINTHIANS 1:18–22

A key verse related to the sealing of the Holy Spirit is Ephesians 1:13: "In whom ye also trusted, after that ye heard the word of truth, the gospel of your salvation: in whom also after that ye believed, ye were sealed with that holy Spirit of promise." This truth is also stated in 2 Corinthians 1:22: "Who hath also sealed us, and given the earnest of the Spirit in our hearts."

God the Father has anointed us and sealed us, according to 2 Corinthians 1:21. The seal, however, is the Holy Spirit Himself. The persons sealed are those who have trusted in Christ. This is clear from the Scripture verses already quoted. The basis for this sealing is belief in the Gospel of Christ. When a person trusts Christ, the Holy Spirit indwells the believer and God seals the believer by the Spirit. The Holy Spirit is given to us as the earnest, or down payment, of our further inheritance.

The Word of God does not say that the Spirit is given only to the spiritual Christian. Believers can, and sometimes do, become carnal; nevertheless, they are sealed by the Spirit of God. Paul told the Corinthians that he could not write to them as spiritual believers but had to treat them as "carnal, even as ... babes in Christ" (1 Cor. 3:1). Yet to this same group he wrote: "Now he which stablisheth us with you in Christ, and hath anointed us, is God; who hath also sealed us, and given the earnest of the Spirit in our hearts" (2 Cor. 1:21–22).

Now if any man have not the Spirit of Christ, he is none of his (Rom. 8:9).

THE WORD CLEANSES YOUR WALK
JOHN 17:13–19

The Bible speaks of our being sanctified by the Word of God as well as by the blood of Christ and by the Holy Spirit.

Just as Christ is not of the world, so the believer is not of the world. God uses His Word, under the power and work of the Holy Spirit, to bring about the changes He wants in our conduct. Concerning this our Saviour prayed in John 17:16–19, "They are not of the world, even as I am not of the world. Sanctify them through thy truth: thy word is truth. As thou hast sent me into the world, even so have I also sent them into the world. And for their sakes I sanctify myself, that they also might be sanctified through the truth."

This sanctification by the Word of God is a continuous process; it goes on from day to day. Obviously, in order to be set apart by the Word of God, we must learn to know the Word of God. Some people are not separated from the old life of sin as they should be, even though they have made a profession of faith in Christ. The reason is not necessarily that they are not born again but that the Word of God does not have the place in their lives it should. The Holy Spirit indwells them, but because they have not studied the Word of God and allowed the Spirit to apply it to their lives, they have not experienced the purification and cleansing that follows.

Now ye are clean through the word which I have spoken unto you (John 15:3).

FULLNESS BEGINS WITH THIRST
JOHN 7:37–39

Along with obeying we must desire to be filled and then appropriate the filling. Our Lord said in John 7:37, "If any man thirst, let him come unto me, and drink."

Here are two prerequisites for the filling of the Holy Spirit—thirst and trust. Thirst suggests desire, and drinking suggests obedience and trust.

Included in this desire to be filled with the Holy Spirit must be our wanting God to judge and put away sin in our lives. We must desire to be separated unto the Lord from the world and its evil system. We must reckon ourselves dead to sin and alive to God. This is true positionally, but it can be made true in our spiritual life only as we yield to the Holy Spirit's control.

We must also desire the fruit of the Spirit in our lives. Do we want love, joy, peace and these other evidences of the Spirit's life in us? Do we long to enthrone Christ as Lord?

Thirst should cause us to drink, and desire should cause us to trust. In the words of our Saviour, out of our innermost beings "shall flow rivers of living water" (v. 38). We not only trust Christ to save us from sin, but we also trust Him to fill us with the Spirit. This particular phase of believing, or trusting, in Christ should be a continuous attitude of trusting, of committing ourselves to the Lord in order to be controlled by the Holy Spirit.

And be not drunk with wine, wherein is excess; but be filled with the Spirit (Eph. 5:18).

370

HOW TO MIND YOUR MIND
2 CORINTHIANS 10:1–6

We must depend on the Spirit's power to control our thoughts. Here is what the Scriptures have to say on that point: "The weapons of our warfare are not carnal, but mighty through God [the indwelling Holy Spirit].... bringing into captivity every thought to the obedience of Christ" (2 Cor. 10:4–5). Only the Spirit of God can make this possible in our lives, and He does it only when we are under His complete control.

When an evil thought comes to our mind, what are we to do? We should turn it over to the Spirit and ask Him to take charge. I have personally done this for years. It is the only method that works for me. I cannot help it when a thought comes, whether it is good or bad. I do not, however, have to dwell on that thought. So the moment a wrong thought comes, I ask the Holy Spirit to take over, for that is His responsibility. When I give Him control, He gives me victory. I have experienced this thousands of times.

Thoughts that come to our mind can also be the Holy Spirit's reminder to pray. In 1 Thessalonians 5:17 we are told to pray without ceasing. Can we possibly do that? Only by letting the Holy Spirit control us. As He dwells in us and we continue to give Him control so that no sin hinders His working in our hearts, He reminds us of the things He wants us to pray about.

And be renewed in the spirit of your mind (Eph. 4:23).

THE LAW OF LIBERTY
GALATIANS 5:1–7

The law of Christ is a law of liberty, a law of freedom made operative through the Spirit of God within us.

Nothing in our sin nature could produce a godly life. Indeed, it is opposed to righteousness. It is void of all power to do what pleases God. Though we may know what the right standard of righteousness is because we have God's Law, we do not have in ourselves the ability to meet the Law's righteous demands. All the Law can do under such circumstances is to demand death as a penalty. But since Jesus Christ paid the death penalty the Law required and has provided life and liberty, we are free to let Christ live His life in us. This is done through the working of the Holy Spirit.

Paul wrote in Romans 8:2: "For the law of the Spirit of life in Christ Jesus hath made me free from the law of sin and death." The word "law" does not refer to Old Testament Law but to a principle, a new method God has provided whereby the Holy Spirit produces the life of Christ in us. This is referred to in the Bible as the law of Christ (Gal. 6:2; 1 Cor. 9:21).

The Mosaic Law did not provide freedom from sin for us, nor could it produce righteousness in us because we were spiritually incapable of obeying it. God, however, sent His own Son "in the likeness of sinful flesh, and for sin, condemned sin in the flesh" (Rom. 8:3). Christ judged, or dethroned, the power of sin and set us free so that it is possible for us to please God with lives of righteousness.

For the law of the Spirit of life in Christ Jesus hath made me free from the law of sin and death (Rom. 8:2).

372

SPIRITUALITY DEMANDS HONESTY
ISAIAH 6:1–8

The Bible has a great deal to say about the conscience. Much is said to believers with regard to the conscience. For example, Paul wrote in Romans 9:1, "Say the truth in Christ, I lie not, my conscience also bearing me witness in the Holy Ghost." The apostle connected his conscience and the Holy Spirit in such a way as to show that the Holy Spirit works with the believer's conscience to keep it clear, to keep it functioning as it should.

One of God's attributes is His holiness. He hates—and will eventually destroy—evil, but He loves good. A person's conscience reflects God's attitude in this. It condemns sin and approves what is right.

God created people with a conscience to hate sin and to love right. The conscience condemns sin and approves of what pleases God. So through the conscience God still works in people.

The believer who wants to be filled, or controlled, by the Holy Spirit must allow God to instruct and control his conscience. Therefore, since God the Holy Spirit works through the conscience, it must be trained by the Word of God to be sensitive to the Spirit's dealing. A clear conscience will characterize a spiritual person. We need an alert conscience, as Paul said, "My conscience also bearing me witness in the Holy Ghost" (Rom. 9:1).

Thy word have I hid in mine heart, that I might not sin against thee (Ps. 119:11).

PRAYER AND THE TRINITY
JOHN 14:12–17

Each member of the Trinity has a distinct role in prayer. The Father waits at the throne of grace to hear the prayers of us who trust His Son. The Lord Jesus Christ is our Advocate in the presence of God the Father. The Holy Spirit, on the other hand, is the Advocate in our hearts, teaching us to pray.

We can view it from another position. The Holy Spirit in us prepares the case we need to make. Christ pleads that case before the Judge. God the Father, as the Judge, hears the case. So we pray to the Father through the Son in the power of the Holy Spirit.

Prayer is not something natural. Prayer to God is not the same as communion with our family or friends. It is on a spiritual level and goes beyond the natural and the physical.

The Son receives from the Father and reveals for our benefit what God wants us to know. But the Holy Spirit within us acts as an interpreter of spiritual truths.

Christ's unceasing intercession for us is indispensable. We need this in order to receive that which the Father has planned for us. But just as essential is the intercession of the Spirit within us, praying for these things in our behalf and accepting from the Son what the Father desires to provide us with.

If ye abide in me, and my words abide in you, ye shall ask what ye will, and it shall be done unto you (John 15:7).

LEARNING HOW TO PRAY
1 JOHN 5:1–13

We need the Holy Spirit to help us pray. Our own prayers tend to be selfish. It is natural for us to concentrate our prayers only on our own desires and needs. A large part of our praying is concerned with our families or our own personal needs.

On the other hand, the Holy Spirit teaches us to pray for God's work and for others. The so-called Lord's Prayer in Matthew 6 instructs us how to pray beyond our own desires. It begins, "Our Father which art in heaven, Hallowed be thy name. Thy kingdom come, Thy will be done in earth, as it is in heaven" (vv. 9–10). The first three requests of this prayer center around God Himself. What motivates our usual praying? Do we seek the glory of God only? This is where the Spirit of God must help us.

We find also that our prayers often lack insight. We just do not know how to pray in the will of God. John told us in his first letter: "And this is the confidence that we have in him, that, if we ask any thing according to his will, he heareth us" (5:14). We need to learn what God's will is. But sometimes we do not know what we should pray for. And if we know what we should pray for, we do not always know how we should pray for it. This is why we need the help of the Spirit. Our infirmities would make true prayer impossible were it not for the Spirit's enabling.

Let us therefore come boldly unto the throne of grace, that we may obtain mercy, and find grace to help in time of need (Heb. 4:16).

FIRE ON THE PRAYER ALTAR
COLOSSIANS 4:12–13

We often pray out of a sense of duty, paying a sort of lip service to what we believe. The average prayer meeting today is a sad event for this very reason. Sometimes we who are there scold those who are absent, and we look down on them. Sometimes those who attend the prayer meeting feel themselves to be better than those who do not. This attitude hinders real prayer.

We are inclined to say the same things over and over again without really ever getting down to the real business of praying. Prayer is one of our weapons against sin. But if we remain indifferent to the seriousness of sin, our prayers will lack fervor, and we will not care about those who are lost or the interests of God. We just do not know how to pray.

Paul told us in Romans 15:30: "Now I beseech you, brethren, for the Lord Jesus Christ's sake, and for the love of the Spirit, that ye strive together with me in your prayers to God for me." Paul encouraged his readers to pray fervently and to strive in prayer. This involved agonizing and wrestling in prayer. Ephesians 6:12 says, "We wrestle not against flesh and blood, but against principalities, against powers, against the rulers of the darkness of this world, against spiritual wickedness in high places." When these things confront us, we need to know how to pray fervently. That is why Paul said in Ephesians 6:18, "Praying always with all prayer and supplication in the Spirit, and watching thereunto with all perseverance and supplication for all saints."

Praying always with all prayer and supplication in the Spirit (Eph. 6:18).

376

POWER IN PRAYER
ROMANS 8:22–28

Our difficulties in prayer also show up in our lack of power and faith. Of course, if our prayers are selfish, inconsistent and lacking in spiritual understanding, they cannot be powerful. But more than that, they are empty because they are not supported by faith. Without faith we know it is impossible to please God (Heb. 11:6). James told us that the person who prays must "ask in faith, nothing wavering. For he that wavereth is like a wave of the sea driven with the wind and tossed. For let not that man think that he shall receive any thing of the Lord. A double minded man is unstable in all his ways" (James 1:6–8).

Do we have faith to ask God for the big things He wants to give us? Only the Spirit of God can provide us with that faith. We must pray, "Lord, teach us to pray." Our prayers must be in harmony with God's will, and then we can expect things to happen as God wants them to happen. We will see answers and victories.

We often think that if we have a burden to pray about something, God is bound to answer us if we get someone else to pray with us. Such unity in prayer is merely man-made. True unity must come from the Holy Spirit. He must lay the burden on our heart and on the heart of someone else. We may not even know who that other person is, but we can be praying together.

Therefore I say unto you, What things soever ye desire, when ye pray, believe that ye receive them, and ye shall have them (Mark 11:24).

VICTORY ON THE MOUNT
EXODUS 17:8–16

The Christian's war with the flesh is seen in the Israelites' desert experiences as outlined in the Old Testament. This age-old battle is seen in Amalek's attempt to keep Israel out of the land of promise. The simple statement is made in Exodus 17:8: "Then came Amalek, and fought with Israel in Rephidim." This historical battle furnishes us with a good illustration of the internal warfare every believer in Christ experiences.

Amalek is a type of the flesh. He did not want the Israelites to claim their inheritance in Canaan. Amalek was strong and had high aspirations. He did not like the idea of being subdued but wanted rather to be in control. So it is with our fleshly nature.

Joshua was the leader of the Israelites in this battle. Though he was an able general and fought well, Israel's subsequent victory was not attributed to him or his army but to the Lord.

Moses also fought in the battle—on a mountaintop by prayer and faith. He interceded, using the rod of God as his authority. As long as he kept his arms and the rod raised, the Israelites were winning. When his arms dropped, then Amalek began to win. Aaron and Hur finally came to his aid and held up his arms as he interceded for Israel. This brought the final victory.

Believers have two members of the Trinity interceding for them—the Holy Spirit and Christ. This assures us of victory. We do not need to fear defeat if we will allow the Spirit of God to have control.

Wherefore he is able also to save them to the uttermost that come unto God by him, seeing he ever liveth to make intercession for them (Heb. 7:25).

POWER FOR WITNESS IS YOURS
JOHN 15:17–27

Through the power of the Holy Spirit we are able to bear witness of the Saviour. This promise was made by our Lord to His disciples before His ascension: "And that repentance and remission of sins should be preached in his name among all nations, beginning at Jerusalem. And ye are witnesses of these things. And, behold, I send the promise of my Father upon you: but tarry ye in the city of Jerusalem, until ye be endued with power from on high" (Luke 24:47–49). These words were fulfilled when the Holy Spirit was given on the Day of Pentecost. He began a work then that He now continues—indwelling believers and empowering them to witness as they give Him complete control of their lives.

This is confirmed by Acts 1:8: "But ye shall receive power, after that the Holy Ghost is come upon you: and ye shall be witnesses unto me both in Jerusalem, and in all Judaea, and in Samaria, and unto the uttermost part of the earth."

The disciples no longer hesitated to witness after the Day of Pentecost. We read in Acts 5:32: "And we are his witnesses of these things; and so is also the Holy Ghost, whom God hath given to them that obey him."

And, behold, I send the promise of my Father upon you: but tarry ye in the city of Jerusalem, until ye be endued with power from on high (Luke 24:49).

A WITNESS THAT COUNTS

ACTS 4:8–14

A witness is one who has personal knowledge of some person or event. We who are born again have personal knowledge of Christ. If we do not know Him, we are not born again. The person who has experienced the new birth is a new creation in Christ Jesus. This is not something that could take place in our hearts without our knowledge. We may not know the exact time or day or place where this transaction took place, but we do know that God has done something for us. Most people who are born again know some of these details, but not all do. If the new birth has taken place in our hearts at all, however, we have witnessed the working of the Holy Spirit in our life. This puts us in a position to testify concerning this truth.

A witness in court is there to give evidence. He tells what he has seen and heard. It is our responsibility to tell of Jesus Christ who has saved us. This witnessing is to take place in Jerusalem, Judaea, Samaria and the uttermost part of the earth. We are to begin testifying of Christ where we are, and then we are to seek, by every means possible, to spread the Gospel to the ends of the earth. Since the Holy Spirit has come, we have no excuse for avoiding or excusing ourselves from witnessing.

But ye shall receive power, after that the Holy Ghost is come upon you: and ye shall be witnesses unto me (Acts 1:8).

PRACTICING GOD'S PRINCIPLES
PROVERBS 3:1–8

God has given us some basic principles to guide us in any situation. One of these is 1 Corinthians 10:31: "Do all to the glory of God." We cannot sin to the glory of God. Let us be sure that whatever we do is for His glory.

Another principle is Ephesians 5:20: "Giving thanks always for all things." If we cannot thank the Lord while we are doing a certain thing, then we should not do it. At the same time, let us be thankful Christians for all God does for us.

A third principle is Colossians 3:17: "Do all in the name of the Lord Jesus." Suppose you wonder, *Should I go to this place?* Could you go there in the name of the Lord Jesus Christ?

A fourth principle is Philippians 4:6–7: "In every thing by prayer and supplication with thanksgiving let your requests be made known unto God." We are to pray about everything.

If we cannot do what we plan to do for the glory of God, if we cannot give thanks for it, if we cannot do it in His name, if we would not feel right in praying about it, then we should not do it. This means we must be saturated with the Word of God so that the Holy Spirit can bring the Word to our remembrance to guide us through every phase of life.

Whether therefore ye eat, or drink, or whatsoever ye do, do all to the glory of God (1 Cor. 10:31).

THE BOOK WITH A BLESSING
REVELATION 1:1–8

A blessing is promised, first of all, to those who read the Book of the Revelation. Some may have bypassed this book because they find it full of figures and symbols they do not understand, and what they do understand makes them afraid. The promise of God is that we will be blessed if we read it. This is an age that emphasizes happiness, but true happiness to the Christian lies in following the directions of the Lord.

And this is also a promise to those who hear the words of this book. This would have reference to listening to others reading it or us making it our own. This would include studying it and remembering what we find in it.

The third aspect of this beatitude has to do with those who "keep those things which are written therein" (Rev. 1:3). God does not ask us to read the Book of the Revelation so that we might speculate concerning future events. It does not mean reading it in order to satisfy our curiosity concerning God's future program. If we read it with the purpose of discovering the principles of life that God has revealed in it and determine by His grace to conform to these principles, then we will indeed be blessed.

There is an urgency expressed in this verse also with regard to such obedience. We are told here that the time of the fulfillment of these events is close at hand. This is in line with Peter's admonition in 2 Peter 3:11–12: "Seeing then that all these things shall be dissolved, what manner of persons ought ye to be in all holy conversation and godliness, looking for and hasting unto the coming of the day of God."

Heaven and earth shall pass away: but my words shall not pass away (Mark 13:31).

382

THE GLORIFIED CHRIST
REVELATION 1:9–20

In this glorious picture of Christ, He is represented as being completely clothed down to the foot. This was the opposite of Adam who, when he sinned, found himself to be naked. Our Lord was stripped of His clothing when He died for us on Calvary, but now He has been appointed High Priest and Judge and as such He is fully clothed with the authority of deity upon Him.

He also has the girdle of authority that was given Him because in His coming to this earth He emptied Himself of His heavenly glory and took on the form of a servant. He was made in the likeness of man and was obedient unto death, even the death of the cross. Now God has highly exalted Him and given Him a name that is above every name. So it is as the One with absolute authority in the universe that He examines and warns and comforts the churches.

His examination of the churches is not confined to just congregations as such. The individual is very much included. The churches are made up of persons, and each person is closely examined by the Saviour.

He also stands among the churches as the rightful Judge. He was judged on the cross because of our sins, but now as the resurrected Christ all judgment has been committed into His hand. What He commands cannot be successfully defied. All will have to listen whether they want to or not. Even those in the graves will, at the right time, hear His voice and come forth. His word is final.

Unto him be glory in the church by Christ Jesus throughout all ages, world without end (Eph. 3:21).

383

FELLOWSHIP FIRST, THEN LABOR
REVELATION 2:1–7

Christ said to Ephesus that there was some love for Him, but the first love was gone. He appreciated their labors and the fact that they had kept their house doctrinally clean. He commended them for their good works, but He could not in faithfulness to them overlook their neglect.

It is possible for us to labor for our Lord to the place where we have no time for fellowship with Him. And the charge He made to His people in Ephesus was not that they had lost their first love but that they had "left" it. We can sometimes lose something we don't want to lose, but to leave something could mean a deliberate choice to leave it. We might say that these early Christians had abandoned their first love because they had become so occupied with service.

What is this first love that is sometimes called the "foremost" love? It is complete devotion to Christ, not merely religious duty. It is heart devotion that has no thought for self.

How much time do we spend with Him in the morning? Fifteen minutes? Is that the measure of our love for Him? We must ever remember that Christian activity alone robs us of our personal fellowship with Christ, robs us of spiritual usefulness. If we really love Christ, we will keep His commandments. It will not be a matter of we "ought" to keep His commandments, but we "will" keep them. Fellowship with Him produces the right kind of spiritual activity.

And to know the love of Christ, which passeth knowledge (Eph. 3:19).

WINNING A CROWN
REVELATION 2:8–11

The word "tribulation" in this passage is very strong. This is not speaking of the time of the Tribulation (Rev. 6–19) but of a particular kind of suffering. They were under the pressure of persecution. It was a very severe test, and some of them may have thought they were being tried beyond their ability.

The tribulation spoken of in this passage could be likened to grain being crushed in a stone mill. Or it might be likened to a winepress with the juice forced out of the grapes under great pressure.

The crown of life does not refer to eternal life, for these Christians already had eternal life. The crown believers receive is a victor's crown, and as a result, we will reign with Christ. If we suffer with Him, we shall reign with Him, and if we deny Him in the time of suffering, He will deny us the privilege of reigning. We are told in Revelation 3:21 that if we are overcomers, we will sit with Him on His throne. So the crown given will be a victor's crown, but it will also be a royal crown in the sense that we will reign with Him.

Christ's crown of thorns will be replaced with God's crown of life for us. We shall be victorious, yes, more than conquerors. All of this reflects back to Him who was dead and is now alive. We have nothing to fear when we trust in Him.

Let us go forth therefore unto him without the camp, bearing his reproach (Heb. 13:13).

ONLY GOD SEES EVERYTHING
REVELATION 2:12–17

The Lord knows all about our living conditions, the temptations to which we are exposed and the motives that govern our conduct. He can judge us correctly. This is a factor we must bear in mind with regard to our evaluating another person's actions. We need to know how much the other person has to face and resist before we can be even reasonably accurate in our approving or disapproving of the other person's conduct.

Are we sure that if we would face the same problems in the same environment as the person we tend to criticize that we would do any better than he did? Or it may be that in our case it is easy to run the race because there are few obstacles to hinder us.

Do we realize how easy it is to murder character by simply not knowing the facts about the other person? Our judgment may be harsh whereas our Saviour, knowing the circumstances, would render an entirely different judgment than ours. For lack of adequate knowledge, we might even commend a person when there is nothing to commend.

We must always keep in mind that there are hidden recesses of the heart that only God can know. Few of us know the burdens others may be carrying. There is a great Judgment Day coming when the Lord Himself will evaluate what we have done in this life for Him. In that judgment (known as the Judgment Seat of Christ, 2 Cor. 5:10), we will not be judged as to whether we will get to heaven or not. That is not what is in view here. There is no doubt that our Lord, who will be Judge at that time, will reverse many of our quick and unfair judgments.

Therefore judge nothing before the time, until the Lord come (1 Cor. 4:5).

THANK GOD FOR THE GODLY!
REVELATION 2:18–29

There were some good people in the Church of Thyatira. The Lord knew their works, all the hard work they were doing and the love that was the basis for it and their faithfulness to Him. He saw all they did even to their giving of a cup of cold water. Some people are quick to spread a great banquet, but they are slow to give just a cup of cold water. The smallest deed of kindness done in our Lord's name will not go unrewarded. There is too much today of the big showy things. Let us remember that God does not overlook the ministry of the little things.

The Lord commended some in Thyatira because they were hard working and the things they did increased in value. The last things they did were better than the first things.

We might well ask ourselves if we are growing in our spiritual lives. Were the works done after our conversion the greatest works for the Lord? Have we left our first love? Or are we progressing in our Christian lives to where we are more effective in what we do for the Lord as the days go by? Apparently some in Thyatira. had come back to their first love and were growing in grace and in the knowledge of Christ.

For God is not unrighteous to forget your work and labour of love, which ye have shewed toward his name, in that ye have ministered to the saints, and do minister (Heb. 6:10).

SERIOUS CHRISTIANITY
REVELATION 3:1–6

So the warning is to be watchful, a warning that is as much for us today as it was for Sardis in John's day. The things that remain and are ready to die must be strengthened. We must wake up to reality, examine the conditions and seek to remedy them in the wisdom and power of the Lord. This is not only a message for the church as a whole but for each individual in the church.

God will not accept an imitation. If our Christianity is not in demonstration of the Spirit and of power, His power will be removed. The Lord knows we cannot demonstrate true Christianity in our own strength. Nevertheless, many are trying to do so and, of course, are missing it.

The Lord Jesus Christ has given Himself to us, and the Holy Spirit is working out the life of Christ in us. But when we turn from this, the only alternative God has is to remove His power from us.

There is too much playing church today. The Lord will allow this playing to continue, but He will remove effective power from such groups. Some are building great buildings that produce a show of power. God may leave us with the outward show but minus the inward power. This is what Christ's warning of coming as a thief is all about.

For our gospel came not unto you in word only, but also in power, and in the Holy Ghost, and in much assurance (1 Thess. 1:5).

THE MASTER'S MINORITY
REVELATION 3:7–13

First of all, He says, "Thou hast a little strength" (Rev. 3:8). He speaks then to a minority group, not to a majority group. The world usually measures strength by numbers, but this is not the Lord's method. The Lord deals here with the remnant. It is through remnants among His people that God has done some of His greatest works. We read in Isaiah 1:9 that the Lord would have destroyed Israel like Sodom and Gomorrah had it not been for a remnant, a minority group that stayed true to Him. The Lord started the Church with 12, then there were 120, then on another occasion there were 500. The Day of Pentecost saw 3,000 added to the Church, but this was still a small number compared to the world at large. In the early foreign ministry of the Church we find Paul and a few associates canvassing the world with the Gospel. God apparently has always worked through a minority group.

Now what is the message that the Lord has for this minority group who believes the authority and inspiration of the Scriptures and who gladly bows to Christ's personal lordship? The message for these is "Behold, I have set before thee an open door, and no man can shut it" (Rev. 3:8). We hear so much today, almost too much, about closed doors. We must not overlook the open doors that are before us. We must honor Christ, recognizing that He has absolute control of all history and that He has been given a name that is above every name. Final authority lies with Him, and full and complete power to accomplish His aims resides in Him. So when He promises that an open door is before us and no one can close it, we should obey Him and enter.

What shall we then say to these things? If God be for us, who can be against us? (Rom. 8:31).

THE CHURCH OF THE BLIND
REVELATION 3:14–22

To be "wretched" means to be "oppressed" with a problem or burden. Who does not have such oppressions or burdens? Yet here was a church boasting of its wealth and its place in the world, but so spiritually helpless that it was not lifting those with burdens but was hindering and degrading them. Their wealth was actually a burden to them, but they did not know it.

The Lord says that this was a "blind" church. They saw nothing clearly. They were nearsighted in the sense that they saw only earthly things. They had no heavenly vision. They had no grasp of what there is beyond this life. They perhaps hoped, as people are hoping today, that everything would be all right on the other side of death, but they did not know.

They lacked real spiritual vision because they lacked spiritual life. Furthermore, they had no real sense of spiritual distance. Many people are so broadminded today that they cannot see to do anything except what is confined within their own narrow limits of knowledge and prejudice. They do not accept the broadmindedness of Jesus Christ where He makes Himself available to everyone. "Blind leaders of the blind" is the way the Lord described them, and sad to say, many church leaders fit this category.

Being blind, they lacked discernment. They could not evaluate things properly in the light of heaven and eternity. Heaven has to do with spiritual values, while the riches that men go after here are only material and cannot gain one thing for heaven so far as salvation is concerned.

But he that lacketh these things is blind, and cannot see afar off (2 Pet. 1:9).